TWO AT A TIME

Two at a Time

by

David Nickson
Lord Nickson KBE

The Memoir Club

© David Nickson 2005

First published in 2005 by
The Memoir Club
Stanhope Old Hall
Stanhope
Weardale
County Durham

British Library Cataloguing in
Publication Data.
A catalogue record for this book
is available from the
British Library

ISBN: 1 84104 122 X

Typeset by TW Typesetting, Plymouth, Devon
Printed by CPI Bath

General Sir Hugh Stockwell was Commandant of the Royal Military Academy Sandhurst when I was a cadet. His advice to us was:

'Always, always, all your life, run up the stairs two at a time.'

I have attempted to follow it.

DEDICATION

I dedicate this book to Louise, to our three wonderful daughters,
Felicity, Lucy and Rosie, and their husbands,
and to our nine grandchildren.

Contents

Foreword

by **The Right Honourable The Lord Kingsdown KG**
Governor of the Bank of England 1983–1993

These memoirs are above all very entertaining, but they also constitute an important commentary on life in this country in the second half of the last century.

David Nickson seems to have been in continuous demand to take the chair of one official body after another alongside the boards of breweries, banks and commercial companies. The intriguing challenge for the reader is to discover why, because the writer is attractively modest in his own analysis, except for an occasional gem of profound wisdom and common sense, especially on the art of chairmanship and how to get there.

At the heart of all this are a family man's values and pleasures. Boyhood in the Welsh countryside in the company of his father who was an Eton housemaster of fascinating brilliance led on to a life-long devotion to country sports, which are beautifully and accurately described, evidently from a wealth of material in his game books. One suspects that this recreation, probably never far from his mind, gives the secret for his success in dealing with the problems of official life (and he experienced them in company with those at the very top in politics of his day) or corporate governance.

Work or sport – they are both dealt with here in profusion in this very readable autobiography, and the author leaves you to decide which comes first in life. Dare one venture to say that he would be hard put to it to answer his own question? But he has no hesitation in saying where his family comes. There is a lot to be learned from the life and career of David Nickson.

Introduction

Yesterday the funeral of Queen Elizabeth, the Queen Mother took place in Westminster Abbey. For ten days the whole nation has been glued to its television sets to witness scenes of mourning, pomp and pageantry. For days press and television have been full of tributes to this wonderful lady. The universal sense of grief, sympathy and respect for the Royal Family has surprised many, in an age when political correctness and cynicism seem to have superseded older, more traditional values. At least one million people turned out to witness the funeral procession in London. Many people were interviewed while waiting in the queue to file past the coffin in Westminster Hall. Most commented that they were there out of admiration and affection for the Queen Mother, but many also said that this was history and they wished to be part of it. She had lived throughout the whole of the twentieth century and was born when Queen Victoria was still on the throne in 1900.

For us, as we watched on television, it was particularly poignant to see the coffin arrive at Windsor Castle and disappear through Henry VIII gateway and the Horseshoe Cloisters. For Windsor Castle was Louise's home. We were married in St George's Chapel in 1952, and earlier that year, half a century ago, had witnessed together the funeral of King George VI from the garden at 8 Lower Ward. I was in uniform at the time as a young officer in the Coldstream Guards. Later that afternoon, once the crowds had dispersed, Jane, my mother-in-law, asked me if I would take a cousin of hers, Cicely Jelf, into St George's to see the Chapel. I took her round through the Horseshoe Cloisters and in at the north door of the Chapel by which the Military Knights' families sometimes entered. The doors were unlocked. There were no police or stewards in evidence. So we walked in, finding, to my consternation, that the vault in the middle of the aisle was still open and within it lay the coffin of the King with a single wreath on top with the inscription 'with love from Lilibet'. We backed out, acutely embarrassed to have accidentally intruded in this way. Yesterday after fifty years of widow-hood Queen Elizabeth, the Queen Mother joined her husband in King George VI Memorial Chapel; and with them both lie the ashes of their younger daughter Princess Margaret who had died only two months earlier. How inconceivable today it would be for the monarch's coffin to remain unguarded in an unlocked church without police or security officers to protect it.

Two years earlier aged twenty I had been on guard at Windsor Castle on Good Friday 1950. I had received an invitation commanding me to present myself for dinner with the King and Queen that evening. I was exceedingly nervous but Patrick Plunket, the Equerry, was charming and put me at my ease. So far as I can remember only members of the Household were present; there were no other guests. We sat down perhaps ten for dinner. I was on the Queen's left. She immediately started to chat to me in the most natural and friendly way asking about Eton where my father was a housemaster. No doubt she soon had me talking too much, a fault that has remained with me all my life! When the ladies retired I was told to move to sit on the King's right over the port. I would have loved to hear him talk about shooting but so far as I can recall the talk was all about politics and current affairs. Two remarks I do remember verbatim. The Labour Government of Attlee had been in power for five years. Taxation was at penal levels and austerity post-war Britain had a long way to go before the swinging sixties. Hugh Dalton, the Chancellor of the Exchequer, had just resigned over his infamous budget leak. 'Damn it all,' said the King, 'that fellow Dalton ought to know better. He was raised under the shadow of Windsor Castle.' (Dalton's father, I think, had been a Canon at St George's.) A moment later he said, 'People talk about the idle rich. I don't know what they mean. They are no longer rich and they are certainly not idle.' After dinner I sat on a sofa with Princess Margaret. She must have found me incredibly dull and unsophisticated. I can only remember that she was pretty and I was tongue-tied.

Two months later the King presented new colours to the 3rd Battalion Coldstream Guards on Horse Guards Parade. My role was to carry the old Regimental colour off the parade ground before the full parade started. Dick Gubbins was carrying the King's colour. We marched off under the Horse Guards arch and were then allowed to go upstairs to watch the rest of the parade from one of the windows. Once the ceremony was over and the Battalion had marched off, back to Wellington barracks, we clattered down the stone steps with our bearskins under our arms. To our horror we saw a lot of very senior officers in scarlet tunics and bearskins, plastered in medals and gold braid, standing chatting under the arch. One of them was the Monarch! We retreated as unostentatiously as we could back up the stairs. When subsequently we arrived in the officers' mess anteroom at Wellington barracks the Commanding Officer, George Burns, greeted us with his typical chortle and asked in no uncertain terms what we thought we were doing interrupting all those senior members of the Household Brigade while they were talking to their Sovereign. The King had asked, 'What are those two officers doing?' To which George Burns had replied, 'Well, Sir, they took off the old colours before you came onto parade.' 'Humph,' said the King, 'they have had a damn idle day!'

Fifteen years earlier in May 1935 Britain had celebrated the Silver Jubilee of King George V and Queen Mary. My sister Mary, whose poetry and novels delight so many, has a far better memory for detail. She writes:

> We were up at Cefn so I suppose Eton must have had a special holiday. [Our father was then an assistant master at Eton and Cefn was our grandparents' second home in North Wales.] David and I had flags to wave and red, white and blue paper hats. Hugh Hughes, the gardener, put up a tall flagpole at the end of the lawn, Katie Jones, the cook, came out from the kitchen with ginger-haired Bertha, the housemaid of the time, and as the Union Jack was hoisted, Hugh, my father and the uncles fired a salute – one shot for each year of the King's reign. David, armed with a toy gun which fired 'caps', stood proudly to attention, revelling in the occasion but – oh the shame of it – I had to be ignominiously removed, screaming, the moment the bangs started.
>
>   The following year the King died and we wore black crepe armbands stitched onto the sleeves of our green tweed coats. I loved this sign of mourning and made a fuss when we were deemed to have demonstrated our loyalty for long enough and my mother removed them. The day after the funeral in St George's Chapel we were taken up to the Castle to see the flowers. In particular I remember a cushion of white flower heads against a yellow background depicting the King's favourite grey pony Jock. This made a great impression on me. Always a sucker for animal sob stories I thought the pony's loss of his master infinitely sadder than the nation's loss of a King.

Two days ago our eldest daughter Felicity and Jamie, with Emily, Sophie and Harriet, took their place in the long queue across Lambeth Bridge to file past the Queen Mother's coffin, as she lay in state. They will remember this for the rest of their lives. Perhaps they will wonder what points of history touched previous generations of their family and regret, as we do, that there is no written record to which they can refer.

Louise's father, Beetle Cockcraft, was born in 1880 and died in 1963, thirty-two years before Beetle II, Alexander Nickson Campbell, was born. He too, in time, may wonder about his great-grandfather and wish that he knew more about a soldier who served as a young man in the Boer War, was awarded the DSO and mentioned four times in dispatches in the 1914-18 war and was still serving in the Royal Artillery until the early years of the 1939-45 war when he became a Military Knight at Windsor.

Beetle the First left some fragile and somewhat sketchy records of the Cockcraft family tree. But he was a fascinating storyteller and Louise often suggests that what he could not remember he made up! It is now a matter of great regret to me that I did not listen more carefully to his stories, question him more intelligently and above all have the ability to recollect the many things he did tell me. I would love to be able to write these down for succeeding generations but now it is too late.

My mother's father, William Henry Dobie, did indeed do this for the Dobie family when he was in his seventies. I have a copy of the Dobie Book which I value highly as a record of my Scottish roots near Lockerbie and as an account of a distinguished medical family, graduating from Edinburgh University, but practising for the main part in Chester. There my grandfather looked after W. E. Gladstone, the Prime Minister, at Hawarden and indeed signed his death certificate. He was also doctor to the Grosvenor family at Eaton.

So now, spurred on by the events of the last few days, I'm going to start on a project I have long had in mind; to attempt to set down for our children and grandchildren, and such other readers who might conceivably be interested, an account of my own immensely lucky and happy life, and as an appendix (for I cannot believe they will have much interest for the non-family reader) such records as we have about our various ancestors. This I hope may be a more interesting and perhaps a more durable way to record our family history than a series of indecipherable and indigestible genealogical trees.

10 April 2002   The River House
                                                               Doune
                                                           Perthshire

CHAPTER 1

Parents and parents-in-law

MY FATHER, the middle of three brothers, was a very special man both as a father and a schoolmaster. He had a unique sense of humour, a brilliant gift for poking fun at himself and, in the kindest of ways, at others, particularly those who, in his view, took themselves too seriously – 'a lovely, upright, funny, special man' as my sister recalls. He had a fine intellect and was a considerable scholar both of the Classics and of English literature. He was an outstanding if unorthodox teacher. He loved to draw cartoons modelled mainly on the work of H.E. Bateman. These adorned his school reports as well as his schoolroom blackboard, and frequently to our great delight he drew for my sister and myself. But his greatest gift as a schoolmaster was his ability to give his boys confidence in themselves. He created virtue by imputing it. Time and again in the letters written to my mother or myself on his death in 1983 Old Etonians repeated the theme that he had been responsible for making them believe in themselves and had helped them to perform beyond their natural ability.

This he did for me all my life. He was a marvellous companion. He taught me, and we shared, a great love of sport, fishing and shooting in particular. As a small boy he was my constant guide and mentor with rod or gun. School holidays were one long pursuit of small trout in the streams and lakes of North Wales in the spring and summer, and of rabbits and woodpigeons with, if we were lucky, the occasional woodcock or duck on the Welsh hillsides and marshes in the winter. At Eton we fished for chub with cherries in the stream that runs between Fellow's Eyot and Luxmoore's garden. We continued to fish and shoot in each other's company until his death. Today I often use a rod which I gave him for his eightieth birthday, on which he caught the last few salmon of his life. At heart and by upbringing he was a trout fisherman rather than a salmon fisher and tied, with his neat fingers and innate tidiness, the most exquisite tiny trout flies for fishing the South Country chalkstreams. I still have boxes of them. When I was abroad in the army, and after we came to live in Scotland, he used to write to me at least once a week in his small meticulously neat handwriting regular 'bulletins'

1

describing in great detail all his sporting exploits. Our relationship, or so it seems to me, was far more like that of two very close brothers than that of father and son. I am sure this is not unique but talking to various friends about their own fathers I suspect that it must be fairly rare.

As well as debunking those he felt were pompous or grand or over affluent he was a great hero worshipper of those he admired, particularly his elder brother. He was a modest man himself and had no great ambitions in his chosen career as a schoolmaster beyond that of being a housemaster at Eton. He was educated first at Moorland House, a preparatory school belonging to an uncle of my mother's, hence the eventual linkup with the Dobie family, and then at Shrewsbury. Here his friend and contemporary was my own housemaster, Jack Peterson, later to become Headmaster. Cyril Allington, author of so many good Anglican hymns and father-in-law to the future Prime Minister Alec Douglas-Home, was also the Headmaster at Shrewsbury during the 1914–18 war. When he went on to be Headmaster of Eton one of his first steps was to appoint two of his star pupils from Shrewsbury both of whom had achieved firsts, Jack Peterson at Oxford, plus blues for cricket and football, and my father from Pembroke College, Cambridge. They remained firm friends all their lives. I was lucky to be in Peterson's. It makes a great difference at Eton if you are in a good house with a good housemaster, and certainly we felt we were quite the best. We had some exceptionally nice people many of whom have remained my lifelong friends and we were outstandingly successful at games.

My father took on his house in 1939 right at the start of the war. In those pre-war days it was an accepted fact that, though an assistant master's pay left one near the breadline, once one had a house it was the normal expectation to make a decent income out of boarding fees. Some masters were comfortably off but neither my father nor my mother had any independent means at that time. They borrowed against the day that they would have a Boys' House. The war put an end to any chance of paying off this loan. Consequently our parents were fairly hard up right through our childhood though they never let us become aware of this. Certainly I would never have gone to Eton if my father had not, as a master, been exempt from paying tuition fees. When the moment came for him to retire after holding his house for the fixed term of fifteen years in 1955 he was fortunate that one of the two family houses in Wales was vacant and my uncle, his elder brother who was Chairman of the family business, offered him a seat on the board. He jumped at the chance to retire to his beloved North Wales and enjoy the leisure that had come to mean more to him than his career. But I suspect that there was another reason. I had recently resigned from the Regular Army to take up a job in Scotland. I had not gone into the family business. My uncle was disappointed in me for leaving the army, but I was his only likely male heir and it had always been assumed that one day I would inherit his shares in the family business and the Welsh houses and land. He was a somewhat lonely, and by then somewhat peppery bachelor. My father had always hero-worshipped him and was well aware that by moving to live near him he could not only provide companionship but also, I suspect, help to keep things warm for me. Thus my parents spent twenty-five happy years in retirement in Wales.

My uncle Jack was probably as big an influence on me as my father. He seemed to me as a boy, glamorous, good-looking and indeed in the modern jargon a role model. He had gone straight from Shrewsbury in 1918 into the Royal Welsh Fusiliers in the final months of the war, was sent out to the trenches in France, was wounded but survived (just) and returned a hero with an MC and bar still aged eighteen. He was offered a regular commission and it was a matter of lifelong regret to him that he was unable to take this up owing to his father's insistence that he should go into the family business. This he did, while remaining a Territorial officer. He lived a fairly carefree life for the next twenty years based either at his parents' home at Neston or in North Wales. He was well enough off, had fast cars, played polo and generally for the next two decades lived the bachelor's life typical of those who had been fortunate to survive the war. But it was shooting and fishing that dominated his recreation.

He ran a celebrated North Welsh pheasant shoot in the thirties belonging to the Mostyn family at Gloddeath near Llanduno. He became a noted high pheasant shot himself. He was a tenant of one of the Williams Wynn moors near Corwen called Henfaes along with our great family friends the Glazebrooks, and fished for salmon on the Welsh Dee. Most summers in the thirties he sailed across the Atlantic to fish a famous and prolific salmon river on the north shore of the gulf of St Lawrence in Quebec called the Romaine. This invitation came through a regimental connection with the Dobell family and led to a lifelong friendship with a nephew of Willy Dobell, Dominick Browne. After the 1945 war they took a fifteen year lease on the best grouse moor in North Wales called Ruabon, which had been burnt out by the incendiary bombing raids on Liverpool as it was ignited as a decoy to divert the German bombers. The keeper's house had been hit and the keeper killed. I can remember him starting to negotiate this lease with the owner,

Owen Wynn, over a glass of champagne at the Anglesey Hunt Ball in 1949 when I was on leave from Sandhurst. I had some wonderful days there and on 12 September 1966 my uncle, my father, Dominick and his son, Peter Browne and I, with three other guns, shot 150 brace of grouse. This will probably remain forever the record bag in Wales post 1940. (Huge bags had been shot on Ruabon in the early 1900s.) He had imported an experienced if autocratic head keeper from Yorkshire called Thompson who had achieved wonders. There was a tourist road across the moor to Llangollen. Thompson nailed an adders skin to a notice saying: 'Beware! These large snakes are numerous and dangerous.' Not so many people got out of their cars after that.

My uncle liked to think big, but he was not a dedicated man of business saying, as I remember, 'The whole point of having a family business is to pay other people to do the work for you so that you can enjoy yourself,' tongue in cheek perhaps, but not, I suspect, too far from his outlook! Almost all the sport my father was able to enjoy throughout his life as an impecunious schoolmaster was as a guest of his brother. They were great companions from boyhood onwards, until near the end of his life illness, loneliness and alcohol made my uncle increasingly irritable and intolerant.

He had two great sadnesses. Despite his continued involvement with his regiment he never lost his regret that he had not become a regular soldier and, after his brilliant start, gone on to become a General. He had the command, the decisiveness and the ability to get on with people in all walks of life to have gone this far. This is why he was so keen for me, as the son he never had, to make the most of the chance he had missed; and why he was so upset for a while, that I too, though for different reasons, gave up a promising start to a military career to go into business. But I have been lucky enough to have had the opportunity to realise my ambitions in other walks of life, a fulfilment that has given me an insight into how my uncle must have felt privately when he saw his friends and contemporaries go on to a public recognition that he might have hoped for himself. He became a full Colonel after being recalled and commanding battalions in the 1939–45 war but he was too old to fight again. He was always known to my father and us children affectionately as 'Col'. He was involved in many activities in Caernarvonshire, becoming Vice-Lieutenant of the county and of course was Chairman of G and J Nickson until his death in 1969.

His other great sadness was an affair of the heart. He fell in love with a beautiful red haired Canadian girl in the early twenties. They were engaged. Maybe she found her prospective mother-in-law too dauntingly possessive, maybe she fell in love with someone else, for the fact is that she broke it off and married Ronnie Cumming, later chairman of United Distillers. Uncle Jack never married. Nor, so far as I am aware, did he ever afterwards show much interest in so doing. My father found an unanswered letter on my uncle's desk, after he had died, from Mary Cumming (née Hendry) wondering how life had fared for him more than forty years on. The remarkable twist to this story is that a few years later my niece Belinda, Mary's elder daughter, married Charlie Cox, Mary Cumming's grandson.

In Appendix II on the Nickson family I have thought it worth recording verbatim some of his brief but glorious three weeks in the trenches in September 1918.

My Dobie grandparents had three children. Uncle John, who continued the medical tradition in Chester, was a boyhood school friend of the Nickson boys and fished with them in North Wales and Canada, a great catcher of big fish, and a tremendous chuckling teaser of small nephews. Aunt Ruth was a dear, sweet natured, self deprecating person who married a parson on the first day of the 1939 war so could not wear her white wedding dress. She was my Godmother, never forgot my birthday, caught her first and only two salmon with us on the Conon aged seventy and was able to come to my introduction to the House of Lords when she was eighty-five.

My mother was the middle child and by far the strongest character of the three. Older than Ruth by six years she was not always particularly kind to her and an affectionate but wary relationship continued into their old age. She was head girl at her school in Yorkshire, Queen Ethelberger's, and then used to drive my grandfather on his doctor's rounds in a wide variety of 1920s cars. She remained an enthusiastic if somewhat idiosyncratic motorist into her nineties. She married my father in Chester Cathedral in 1927, where in 1930, I was later christened. Then followed the life of a schoolmaster's wife, first in Baldwin's End Cottage, then as the war started in Common Lane House. The five years of the war must have been a very tough time for her trying to bring up two children without much help and running the administrative and domestic side of an Eton Boys' House. She was fiercely loyal to her family and would, I have absolutely no doubt, have sacrificed her life for us if circumstances had demanded it. In a sense she did just that for her whole being resolved round the lives and doings of her husband and her children. She had few interests and not many close friends independent

of my father. In her eyes I could do no wrong, which was probably very
bad for me and certainly pretty hard on my sister, who would say that
our mother kept her on a very tight and repressive rein right up to the
time she married aged twenty-two. Holidays were always at my
grandparents' homes in Cheshire or North Wales. My mother adored
Cefn. It was a sanctuary for her from Eton, the War and possibly the
strong presence of her mother-in-law at Hinderton Lodge. Life there was
totally dedicated to pursuit of sport, fishing or shooting, sometimes on
my own but always with my father if he was there. There was no
corresponding interest or recreation for my sister. She is now extremely
funny at my expense as to the subordinate and frequently intensely
boring role she had to play following rod, gun or cricket ball. I doubt if
I thought about it at the time but looking back on it now my mother
was at times quite rough with my father. He was the gentler, meeker
character. But it certainly did not slow him down in his single minded
recreational activities of fishing and shooting! In short my mother was a
remarkable homemaker and if there is one theme that runs through
everything it is the strong adhesive ties of family life. This applied to
Dobies as well as Nicksons and it is the greatest joy to see the tradition
carried on by all our daughter's families and all my sister's children's
families. My mother was the archetypal matriarch to whom the credit for
much of this should go. All our children adored her and she was
absolutely brilliant with small children. She died in her nineties, an
indomitable and hugely adored old lady. On her desk when she died was
an application form for a railcard. Opposite the line marked 'hobbies
. . .?' she had written the one word 'Living', not a bad motto at ninety
two.

   The Dobie book gives a fine insight into her family characteristics and
as I read it again I increasingly realise that many of my own traits and
attitudes to life, not least a strong constitution, perennial cheerfulness and
continued optimism in almost all circumstances, are owed at least as
much to the Dobies as the Nicksons.

   My father-in-law, William Louis La Trobe Cockroft, 'Beetle' to all
who knew him, was over seventy by the time Louise and I became
engaged. He was a man of slight build and medium height, but every
inch was that of a retired soldier. He must, I think, have taken after his
mother. We only have one photograph of her as a slim dark girl, whereas
the photographs of his father and grandfather show somewhat stout and
portly figures in military uniform. He clearly inspired great affection and
respect from all who served and worked with him, but no doubt he could

have seemed somewhat formidable at times to junior officers and on occasion to his only daughter, of whom he was immensely proud and to whom he was utterly devoted. He was always kindness itself to me.

He was commissioned into the Royal Field Artillery from Woolwich in 1899 and by 1900 he was in South Africa in the Boer War. How I wish we could remember more of the stories he told us of his experiences. On one occasion his Battery ran out of ammunition for their field guns, but on discovering that the standard issue jam tins fitted the bore, they fired those instead. His charger 'Jenny' was killed under him in action. Her hoof is preserved among the ornaments in the drawing room here today. He served on Lord Milner's intelligence staff and was mentioned in despatches on 10 September 1901. After the war he was seconded to the Colonial office as an Administrator in the Orange River Colony. We have an invitation in the name of Lieut L. Cockcraft RFA to attend the Coronation of King Edward VII and in 1904 he was back at Woolwich in the 87th Battery where he was described as being full of energy with many bright ideas, driving the battery horses in the Brigade brake and tandems. For three years from 1906 he was seconded to the West Africa Frontier Force surviving the dangers of tropical diseases and, so the story goes, playing his violin at the request of a West African potentate, King Prempi of the Ashantis.

At some stage he lost all his belongings in a fire and was shipwrecked on his first leave home in the SS *Jebba* on the Bolt Tail off the coast of Devon in the middle of the night. The passengers were all rescued by being pulled up the cliff by breeches buoy. He was taken in by a local family called Morris and subsequently married the daughter, Valerie. They had one son, Louise's half-brother Peter Cockcraft (the last Cockcraft to bear the name), who also in due course became a soldier and died in 1988. But the marriage was unhappy and ended in divorce. Beetle was a Staff Captain in Western Command for the three years leading up to the 1914 war and, in some capacity, was on duty at the installation of the Prince of Wales in Caernarvon Castle in 1911.

In the 1914–18 war Beetle served with distinction in Egypt, Cape Helles, Gallipoli and from 1916 to the end of the war in France, where he was three times mentioned in despatches and received the Belgian Croix de Guerre. He was awarded the DSO in the 1916 Birthday Honours List for his services in Gallipoli. At one moment he was buried alive in France by the explosion from a huge German shell. But this did not account for the rather prominent hole on top of his bald head. This happened playing polo after the war when he had a crashing fall and was so badly injured that they had to erect a tent over his body so that the doctors could attend to him before he could be moved. In 1925 he finally got command and was promoted to Lieutenant Colonel. His final command, before retirement on half pay in 1929 at the age of fifty, was 19th Field Brigade Royal Artillery in the British Army on the Rhine at Wiesbaden.

Here he had taken his young bride, Sylvia Mather (Granny Jane to all our children) after they were married in 1923. Beetle had met the Mather family when he was stationed in Staffordshire. A dashing horseman, much decorated though recently divorced and aged forty-three, his increasingly frequent presence at Huntley Hall near Cheadle where the Mathers lived can have left little doubt that he was interested in their daughters. Margie the eldest thought she had caught his eye, but it was the tall, slim, delightful younger daughter who attracted him. They must have had a difficult courtship for divorce was not lightly regarded in conventional county families and Beetle was twenty years her senior. However they overcame any difficulties and were married in the Chapel of the Savoy in London.

Beetle and Jane must have made a dashing couple and Beetle, with his glamorous young bride, must have been the envy of all his junior officers! But he had only six more years in the army until he reached the age of fifty. Retirement probably came as a disappointment to him because two of his confidential reports indicated that he was destined for higher rank. 'A capable and clear headed officer . . . of distinct personality, self-reliant, with the knack, I should say of getting things done. I recommend him for promotion' – this from a report following his attendance at a senior officers' course in the early twenties – and again from Lt.-General Sir W. Thwaites on his retirement – 'He has served me well and is an officer considerably above the average – he has produced good results with a number of young and inexperienced officers, which many another man would not have been able to do. He has a very determined personality and a very quick brain and is able to appreciate a situation rapidly on sound lines. He is an admirable organiser, a first rate horseman and a keen sportsman. Although a hard taskmaster he is immensely popular with all ranks. I consider him an officer of outstanding merit and am prepared to say that from my experience of him his retirement will be a loss to the service. I should be glad if you could bring these points to the notice of the selection board.'

The *Wiesbaden Times* reported:

On the day of Colonel Cockcraft's departure he was taken from his home at Blesbrich to the main station on a limbered wagon, drawn by a six-horse team, the riders being officers of the Brigade. Ahead of the limbered wagon rode four trumpeters and alongside it were six mounted Pennant bearers of senior rank. Behind came all the NCOs of the Brigade, mounted.

The cavalcade swung into Kaiser Frederich Ring at the gallop and swept along towards the main station entrance in great style. Pedestrians stared in amazement, the happening providing them with a novel sight and one rarely witnessed out here.

Lt.-Col Cockcraft entered the train in the presence of a great number of members of his command and a large number of friends. The usual parting salutes were given and as the train steamed out tumultuous cheers were sent up for this popular officer.

Retirement could hardly have come at a worse moment, coinciding with the great depression and the general strike. Employment for a retired officer aged fifty was difficult. Beetle turned his hand to many things including a laundry round and operating speedboats at Hove in Sussex, where he and Jane first settled and where Louise was born on 7 August 1930. Two or three years later they moved to Ashtead in Surrey, where they remained until Beetle was recalled to the colours at the outbreak of war in 1939. They had become experts in making sweets for a private clientele, hence Jane's delectable fudge which she continued to make for the delight of her family into her nineties. Beetle commanded the 50th Anti-tank Training Regiment for two years, first at Aldershot and then at Church Stretton in Shropshire. Here it was that he met my Great Uncle George Nickson who had retired there after he had been Bishop of Bristol. When Beetle was appointed as a Military Knight of Windsor in 1941 Uncle George gave him an introduction to my father who was a Housemaster at Eton. Thus was the connection first made between the Cockcraft and Nickson families.

The Military Knights of Windsor proudly claim to be the oldest military establishment in the Army list. Formed in1348 by King Edward III shortly after the battle of Crecy, the foundation consisted of knights who, having taken their private armies to France to fight for the King, had been taken prisoner by the French who had demanded heavy ransoms in return for their release. In most cases, these unfortunate warriors were reduced to absolute poverty and were forced to beg for alms. Known as Alms Knights and nicknamed 'Poor Knights' they formed part of the College of St George that was created to support the

establishment of the Most Noble Order of the Garter. In 1559, Queen
Elizabeth I, acting on the will of her father Henry VIII, signed a statute
reducing the original number of Knights from 26 to13. New accommodation was built for them in the Lower Ward, and from then on they
were allowed to be married. King William IV, in 1833, changed the
designation to that of the Military Knights of Windsor and granted them
permission to wear the uniform of officers on the unattached list. This is
still worn today and consists of a scarlet tail-coat, sword, cocked hat with
plume and a white cross belt bearing the badge of St George. There is a
good photograph of Beetle in this uniform in front of the lovely
Elizabethan fireplace in the Royal Library.

For the next twenty years Beetle and Jane became two of the best
known and best loved figures in the Windsor Castle community. Their
home at No. 8 Lower Ward became open house for countless friends.
When they first arrived the Home Guard (Dad's Army!) was already a
year old. The Castle Battalion (9th Berks Regiment), was short of
officers. Beetle would have been other than himself had he not at once
accepted the post of 2nd-in-command and thrown himself with vigour
into the work of administration and training. Upon this he superimposed
a leading role in the Castle organisation for Air Raid Precautions. These
were no mean responsibilities at a time when the Royal Family were in
continuous residence in addition to the Castle's normal population of
several hundred residents – as well as untold quantities of Crown
treasures. During the V I (the infamous 'doodlebugs') and V II bombing
raids in 1944 he had to tell the King that he could not go onto the roof
of the Castle with the Princesses to watch! His untiring services were
recognised by the award of the MVO. On his death in 1963 Sir Michael
Adeane, the Queen's Private Secretary, wrote to Jane: 'The Queen was
so very sorry to learn of Colonel Cockcraft's death in hospital this
morning. Her Majesty knows how much he will be missed here – both
in the Castle and in Windsor and she and the Duke of Edinburgh join
in sending you and your daughter their heartfelt sympathy.'

He was involved in organising the first Garter Service after the war
and persuaded them to put down the blue carpet as he did not think
the Knights would enjoy walking on the stones! He and Jane were
regular and stalwart members of the normal Sunday congregation of St
George's Chapel and indeed it was their parish church, where Louise
was confirmed by the retired Archbishop of Canterbury, Cosmo Lang,
and where later on we were married by the Dean, Bishop Eric
Hamilton.

The war over, he took on the thankless task of initiating the Civil Defence organisation, bringing to it the restless driving force that was his distinguishing quality. He was also active in many local activities, including the Berkshire County Council and the Windsor Borough Council (on which he was chairman of the housing committee and would have been Mayor of Windsor in 1952 had he not felt unable to carry the financial obligation in the same year as his daughter's wedding!). He also played a leading part in the County Boys' School, the Victoria League, the Conservative Association, the Forces' Help Society and the Royal National Lifeboat Institution. In all these activities Jane played a full and essential supporting role.

Late in life, under the influence of one of the Canons of St George's, Beetle became an enthusiastic Mason, and set off to meetings in London with all the paraphernalia, much to the amusement of his family.

Beetle was a keen and aggressive bridge player, putting his wife and daughter off for life. He was the original DIY enthusiast though his improvisations were of the distinctly Heath Robinson variety. Every year after we were married he used to come to stay with us in Scotland for two to three weeks to do all the odd jobs of which I was, and still am, incapable.

This then was the environment in which Louise grew up. She joined the Morshead family in Garden House, the home of the King's Librarian Sir Owen, for lessons from his remarkable wife Paquita. Their two daughters Mary and Phoebe, Anne and Carola Verney, Joan Parker and my sister Mary became lifelong friends. They were enrolled in the Castle Company of the Girl Guides and later as Sea Rangers joined SRS *Duke of York* with Princess Elizabeth and Princess Margaret where they were drilled by a Grenadier Company Sergeant Major and largely treated as friends and companions on the many camps and activities. They camped at Frogmore where they were visited by the King and Queen who took part in the camp fire sing-songs and ate their camp food. The annual Christmas pantomime for the Household was a particularly memorable occasion organised for the members of Madame Vacani's dancing class in which the two Princesses took lead roles. There is a good photograph of Louise as a courtier in tights. The pantomime took place in the Waterloo Chamber and, as the famous Lawrence portraits had been removed for safe keeping, the walls were decorated with pantomime posters. When the great Windsor fire burnt the roof off in the 1990s these posters were once again exposed for all the world to see. Louise has many memories of her Windsor days as a girl, including roller-skating round the Round

Tower with the Morshead children, until warned off for making too much noise by the Governor Lord Wigram. After the war the Sea Rangers all went on an MTB at Dartmouth and attended the end of term dance there in their first long dresses. They all attended the Queen's wedding in 1947 in the forecourt of Buckingham palace. King George VI saw them and said, 'You all look very cold and hungry. You had better come inside and have something to eat.' An invitation that was accepted with alacrity!

The Queen must have looked back on those days with nostalgia for every ten years or so she organised a Sea Ranger reunion at Windsor to which Louise and her gang went regularly. The last of these took place on 31 May 1997 at Frogmore when husbands were also invited. Unfortunately I was taken violently short with some form of gastric bug; I am pretty sure the Royal security officer regarded me with the greatest suspicion as I kept on leaving the Queen's personally conducted tour to visit the splendid Victorian loo off the hall. In between these dashes for safety I was standing out in the garden at one stage with HM and Louise and others. I heard overhead what I thought was a familiar bird cry from Australia and blurted out in my impulsive way, 'Good heavens, Ma'am, I'm sure I heard a parakeet.' 'Oh yes,' she replied, 'they come over from the safari park and are a perfect nuisance.'

These, then, are the records and recollections which have been passed down to us for Louise's side of our family; they take us up to her girlhood at Windsor in the years just following the 1939–45 war.

CHAPTER 2

Early years

I THINK I MUST HAVE BEEN a rather wet little boy. Certainly when I first went away to school at Sunningdale, at the age of eight in September 1938, I wept copiously; and continued to do so for two or three years as each holidays neared an end. It was not that I remember being particularly unhappy at school. I just loved home. My sister Mary and I had a happy and protected childhood. In the term time this was at Eton where my father was an assistant classics master. Holidays meant our Nickson grandparents' houses at Neston in the Wirral for Christmas, and in the Conwy valley in North Wales for Easter and the summer. We usually paid a briefer visit to my mother's parents in Chester where the Dobies were doctors for four generations.

I only remember one variation to this routine. In 1936 my father had a sabbatical and unsurprisingly elected to accompany his elder brother, my Uncle Jack, on one of his regular salmon fishing trips to Canada in June and July. I doubt if this was too popular domestically; certainly there was no way that my mother was prepared to take her children on her own to stay with my grandparents where her mother-in-law exercised such a dominant influence. So we went to Scotland for the first time to stay with my Godmother Grizel Hartley at her house at St Catherine's on Loch Fyne. Hubert and Grizel were a legendary Eton Couple, enormously generous to generations of Etonians; not themselves blessed with children, they compensated by great kindness to other people's. Hubert was a housemaster at Baldwin's Bec near my parents' house at Baldwin's End Cottage. He was a Coldstreamer in the War and later gave me his uniform. I wear his Coldstream sword to this day when in uniform as Vice-Lieutenant.

My sister would say that Grizel had a greater influence on her as a girl than anyone else, opening new doors on the adult world of culture and sophistication, and giving her the confidence, freedom and determination to break out from my mother's narrow and perhaps over-protective stockade. Grizel had a wide and catholic collection of friends, and in Peter Lawrence's book after her death she was credited with forty-seven

13

Godchildren. She and my mother could hardly have been more different but they were close friends.

In these days of the disastrous European Common Fisheries policy it is perhaps worth recording that my abiding memory of my first visit to Scotland was of the glut of herrings in Loch Fyne. They were given away free by the bucket load on the pier at Inverary. Gannets dived and dived all day, plummeting into the water with a most satisfactory splash for an excited little seven-year-old boy. Towards the end of the holidays my father returned and we went fishing for trout with a worm in the burns running into the loch. My first trout had been caught on a fly at the age of four or five in North Wales. I can see it now as it came whizzing out as a result of a violent strike to hit my father on the ankle. It might have been all of five inches long. For years I cultivated this instantaneous reaction as small trout rose. It was so satisfying to see them flying over one's head and very effective provided the gut stood the strain. But one day a whopper of about eight inches shed the fly in mid-air to fall ten yards behind me into a standing oat field. I crawled about looking for it unsuccessfully for ages with tears streaming down my cheeks.

At Eton our house was next door to Fellow's Eyot, a field separated from Luxmoor's garden by a small tributary of the Thames. In this stream lurked leviathans: roach, dace and chub. Here my father took me to fish in the early mornings when he had no early school, plodding through the wet grass in gumboots, armed with a bag of cherries from the School Stores. For chub love cherries. The stone is carefully extracted from the fruit and a hook inserted in the cavity. The cherry is allowed to bob down the run with a small boy and his rod hidden behind a bush; and Oh the excitement when the cherry is swallowed and battle commences.

Sunningdale School was owned by the Headmaster, George Fox. It had a well-deserved reputation for winning scholarships to Eton. There was never any danger that I was likely to trouble the College examiners. Whether this was a disappointment to my father with his outstanding classical brain I do not know. If so he never let me be aware of it. I did pass into Eton in the summer of 1943 into 'Remove', the highest form available to 'oppidans', Eton's term for the thousand or so boys who were not as clever as the seventy select 'collegers'. But this may have had more to do with Sunningdale's experience in preparing boys for the Common Entrance exam than to my intellect, for I certainly struggled to hold my position during my first year.

After the war Charlie Sheepshanks bought Sunningdale Shool from the Fox family and became Headmaster. The Sheepshanks were family friends and in 1953 he married my sister. In 1938 he was an assistant master before leaving to join the Grenadiers and fight the War. There his greatest friend was Brian Johnston, the renowned and much loved BBC cricket commentator. So I must be one of the few people who can claim to have been taught mathematics by my future brother-in-law. Charlie was a very special man and like my father a wonderful schoolmaster; marvellous at getting the best out of small boys, funny, idiosyncratic, a brilliant and very competitive ball games player, a good grouse shot, a knowledgeable and passionate gardener, he was loved by generations of Sunningdale boys and their parents. After he and Mary made their home at the school it became a second home to us and to our children for nearly twenty years whenever we were south from Scotland. After they inherited Arthington Hall, the family home near Harrogate, and retired there, they continued to provide open house to us in the most generous way.

At Sunningdale I enjoyed all games except for boxing where I was far too frightened of getting a bloody nose. Football and rugger were fun but I was neither fast enough nor heavy enough to excel at either. I learnt to play Eton Fives and this was the only game at which I subsequently represented Eton. Cricket became a lifelong passion. I made some runs for the first eleven. There was one memorable occasion when we bowled out the whole of the Earlywood second XI for two runs. I took five for one. The other run was a wide. But after that I varied my action every week in attempted imitation of whatever bowler was top of the first class averages. As a result I never did decide whether to become a fast or a slow bowler, and quite soon stopped being a bowler of any description, at least one to whom any captain ever wished to entrust the ball. Much later on in the army I took to keeping wicket with much enjoyment. Ludgrove were our traditional rivals. They usually beat us on the games field but seldom academically. In 1938, the last summer before the War, my father took me to the Oval to see the fifth Test Match against the West Indies. England won and both Hutton and Hammond made centuries.

The war came. It made remarkably little difference to an eight-year-old's routine. I can remember the sandbags being built round the Eton houses and my father joining the local Dad's Army. He never could take himself very seriously in uniform. Air raids and later flying bombs were more an excitement than a terror. The sirens wailed most nights. The searchlight beams traversed the sky. Barrage balloons were ubiquitous. The irregular drone of the German planes seemed different from ours. The high-pitched whine of high explosive bombs followed by the crump always seemed to just be far enough away; though Eton was hit and the house of Dr Ley, the College Chapel organist, destroyed. Flying bombs in 1944 meant night after night in the air-raid shelters. If the sirens went in the daytime everyone was supposed to kneel down with their hands over their heads under the nearest suitable cover until the all-clear, a rule more honoured in the breach than the observance by most masters as time went on; for it provided limitless scope for misbehaviour in class if the 'beak' chose to dive under his own desk like a dog in its kennel. On one occasion my father was walking back to his own house in Common Lane from his schoolroom in Montague James Schools, and as was his wont, called in at Keate House for a gin and tonic with his friend Denys Wilkinson. The Lower Master 'Legge' Lambart was scuttling along the garden path when the siren went. He took cover under a rhododendron bush on all fours in the approved position. On rising to his feet he was not amused to find two of his colleagues, glasses in hand, grinning down at him from the window above.

One 'doodle-bug' sticks in my memory. We were on our way back to Eton from our holidays in Wales and had changed stations from Euston to Paddington where we waited for the train to Slough. There were several hundred people on the platforms under the glass roof when the sirens sounded and the by now familiar drone of the flying bomb approached. The engine cut out. It sounded very close. The silence seemed forever. Strained faces looked all around us. My mother extended her arms to enfold us. The crash when it came no doubt had tragic consequences somewhere close by, but it missed the station.

The train journeys at the start and end of each holidays seemed endless. There was no heating. Soldiers crowded the corridors sitting on their kitbags. Sometimes we had a seat, sometimes not. The arrival at Llandudno Junction in the clear cold air of the Conwy valley, after the Thames valley fogs, must have seemed a blessed sanctuary to my mother, and it did to us children too. Cefn and all that went with it sank into our souls as a symbol of peace and happiness in contrast to the war-torn South-East and the return journey that meant 'back to school' at the holiday's end. Austen Williams, an ancient man in an even more ancient car, or so it seemed to us, met us at the station before driving gloomily at about ten miles an hour the whole way home. But there we got a wonderful welcome from Mrs Jones, the cook-housekeeper, a tiny Welshwoman with a very large heart.

Eton played such a major part in the first twenty years of my life. How many times must I have filled in forms with the questions: 'Place of birth'. . . *Eton*. 'Educated'? . . . *Eton*. It was both home and school. It was all very familiar to me when I arrived at Mr Peterson's House for the Summer half of 1943. I was often asked what difference it made having my father as a master. Eton is a big place and many days I never even passed him in the street. He was popular and well respected. I never remember being teased about him in an unkind way and, as I was a pretty law abiding citizen, I don't think that I was an embarrassment to him too often either. The worst punishment I had from Jack Peterson, 'M'Tutor' (as one's housemaster was called), was a 'Georgic', five hundred and thirteen lines as I recall from Virgil, to be written out in a fair hand. The crime did not seem too heinous at the time and I suspect that secretly Jack Peterson was not too displeased. I was due to play the semi-finals of the Lower Boy Fives competition with my Sunningdale partner, Colin Fox, younger son of the headmaster. Colin was a colleger so we had agreed to meet at the fives courts. But I had 'flu and was confined to bed with a temperature. If I had failed to turn up we would have been scratched. I got up, dressed, crept out of the house and played the match, which we won. I thought I had made the return trip successfully and was back in bed when I was summoned to the housemaster's study. Miss Holland, 'M'Dame' in Eton parlance and the equivalent of a matron, was a formidable small lady, not to be trifled with. She had visited my room, found the bed empty and my pyjamas hidden in my ottoman. It was a fair cop!

M'Tutor was an exceptional and perceptive man. His life was blighted during my time at school by the illness and early death of his lovely wife, Rosemary (née McNeile, another well known Eton family). He became sad and wistful thereafter, particularly when with such a joyful and happy family as ours. He had a great ability to sum up boys' strengths and weaknesses; of Roger Gibbs, who later had such a distinguished career in the City of London but who departed from Eton without much academic success, he wrote: 'Statistics would tend to show that Gibbs will not make a success of his life but on this occasion I suspect that statistics will be proved wrong.' In 1943, at the end of my first half, he wrote to my father excusing my own poor performance in 'trials', the Eton slang for exams, in the following terms: 'An almost infinite capacity for enjoyment must have severely tested his youthful stamina, for there is no sort of activity into which he does not throw himself with wholehearted abandon'; and, a year later, in referring to the episode related above: 'He got quite a long way in his Fives competition . . . – further perhaps than he should have done! I am glad he has been naughty really: the devil must have an innings sometime.'

He was my father's closest friend at Eton. He left to become Headmaster of Shrewsbury in 1952. But I suspect he was too kind and gentle a man to have been rated a very successful Headmaster there.

I visited my parents' 'private side' as distinct from the 'boy's side' most Sundays for tea when other boys would be going out with their parents anyway. Otherwise we developed an unspoken arrangement that we would keep our lives apart during the week. When I became more senior in my last year or so I just came and went much as I pleased when time or circumstance permitted.

Peterson's was a successful and happy house. This made a big difference. In a school with over a thousand boys it mattered more in many ways than the school itself. I had a wonderful five years. If there were unhappy moments I cannot now recall them. There were certainly few idle moments. I made some lifelong friends and am still in fairly regular touch with a dozen or so. After a tough first year I was able to cope adequately with the work. School Certificate at sixteen fixed one's final position before the last two years as a specialist. I ended up at number eleven thus just missing the Upper Sixth, the top ten boys who used to progress into Chapel as the 'Ram', a slow march on the way in and an almost unseemly quick march to get out. In due course I made my house 'library', the equivalent of a house prefect, and was Captain of the house in my last half. Peterson's always had two or three members of 'Pop', the self-elected club known as The Eton Society. This was to some extent self perpetuating because you were more likely to be proposed and supported by friends in your own house. I was very lucky to have the whole of my last year as a member of Pop, the most coveted position in the school and the equivalent then of a school prefect.

At the school concert at the end of each term the four most senior boys sang the 'Vale' just before the whole school let fly at the top of their voices for the Eton Boating Song. The 'Vale' was one of the great Eton songs and very emotional if you were leaving after five happy years. Music has never been one of my strong points. I enjoy singing familiar hymns in church but my family tell me that I spoil the service for at least five pews in front of me. So the fact that I had to sing a solo caused hilarity among my friends. The third verse is the most challenging:

> Old Eton places, old Eton faces
> Though we be parted far away,
> Seen ever clearly, loved ever dearly,
> Shall then be with us as today;

My parents at Cefn Isaf about 1960

My father-in-law   *My mother-in-law*

My Uncle Jack

My sister and brother-in-law, Charlie Sheepshanks, with the Arthington tapestry

My sister and my father on the River Conon in 1980

My first trout aged four

My first grouse aged twelve

*My first two salmon aged fifteen
from the Welsh Dee*

*My two largest salmon aged twenty –
25½ and 24½ lbs from the River Wye*

Louise as a courtier in the Windsor Castle pantomime

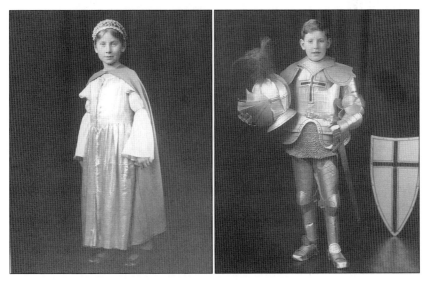

*My sister as Una and myself as St George in costumes
made by my grandmother about 1936*

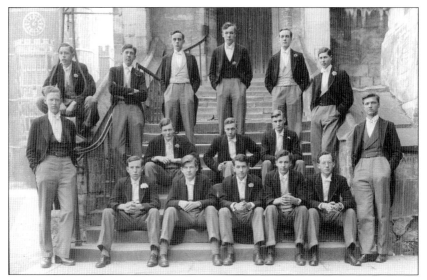

Eton − The Pop photograph − March 1948
<u>*Seated, front row L to R:*</u> *Self, Raef Payne, Tony Lloyd (now Lord Lloyd of Berwick),*
David Sandeman, Simon Sainsbury
<u>*2nd row:*</u> *Douglas Hurd (now Lord Hurd of Westwell), Tom Hare (my best man),*
Antony Acland
<u>*Standing:*</u> *Ewen Macpherson, Tom Stacey, George Nissen, Miles Jebb*
(now Lord Gladwyn), Anthony Butterwick, Ralph Assheton (now Lord Clitheroe),
Cecil West, David Callender

My leaving photograph   *'M' Tutor' − Jack Peterson*

Louise aged twenty

Our wedding in St George's Chapel, Windsor Castle 18 October 1952

Top left: Felicity and Jamie's wedding at St Mary's Aberfoyle, 24 May 1980

Bottom left: Lucy and Melfort at his Investiture with the OBE at Holyrood Palace in July 2003

Bottom right: Rosie and Alastair's wedding at St Mary's Cathedral Edinburgh, 28 November 1992

Each house familiar, each smooth meadow,
Each bend of river, each old tree –
Hearts growing older, love never colder,
Never forgotten shalt thou be!

Fortunately my fellow soloists were more accomplished; Tony Lloyd, Captain of the School and now a distinguished Law Lord, Antony Acland, Captain of the Oppidans, later head of the Foreign Office and our Ambassador in Washington, later to be Provost of Eton and a Knight of the Garter, both still friends of mine, and Raef Payne, who became an Eton housemaster but is sadly now dead.

I left Eton with much sadness and look back with nothing but happiness and gratitude. The only setback I had had was to fail to get into the cricket eleven during my last summer half. So my ambition one day to bat at Lord's was never fulfilled. The only regret is that since we came to live in Scotland after I left the army I have had so few opportunities to visit Eton and have rather lost touch. It seems very unlikely that any of our grandsons will go there. A few years ago the splendid tradition was started of having reunion dinners for all who left in a particular year. My year, 1948, came up quite early in the cycle and I greatly enjoyed it. I sat next to the Provost, Antony Acland. I cannot now recall whether it was on that occasion or slightly later that the idea came to me that we should organise a Pop dinner on the fiftieth anniversary of our leaving. Tony Lloyd had been President, following Jan Collins. I had a word with Tony in the House of Lords and he was enthusiastic. Antony kindly suggested we held it in Election Chamber, a holy of holies to which as a mere oppidan I had never entered, and even more generously had us and another contemporary, Douglas Hurd, to stay in Provost's Lodge. We had about twenty people at the dinner in 1998. It was a great success. We were all nearly seventy and inevitably there were some sad gaps: Raef Payne for one, Tom Hare another, who had been my partner in the Eton Fives pair and later the Best Man at my wedding. He had died of cancer a few years earlier.

On leaving Eton we must have been far more sheltered and immature than today's young. Certainly I know I was. I suppose it was partly that as a result of the war opportunities for parties and other excitements were far fewer, partly because we spent all our holidays in a fairly remote part of the country. Anyway girls had not come into my life at all and I was exceedingly nervous and tongue-tied whenever I came across one. It was suggested that we should have a Pop party when we left before we all went into the army, for National Service was compulsory for everyone then. It was decided that this should take the form of a theatre party followed by a dance at the Savoy. I thought this was a very bad idea. I did not know any girls.

My mother came to the rescue by ringing up Jane Cockcraft in the Castle at Windsor to ask if her daughter Louise, a friend of my sister's, would come as my partner. She had been to stay with Mary in Wales in the holidays once or twice. So far as I was concerned her only claim to fame had been that she was the only one of my sister's friends who had volunteered to come ferreting with me! She and her mother had also come to the final School Concert to hear my untuneful solo. So we went up to London, saw the musical *Bless the Bride* and danced at the Savoy. We never looked back. Jan and Sally Collins were there too. The strange reflection on those times compared to today, and on my Eton friends then, is that so many of us got engaged and married within two or three years of leaving school, and so many of us have already celebrated our Golden Weddings!

In the years immediately following the war it seemed natural for me to follow many of my Eton contemporories to Sandhurst before achieving a Regular Commission. We had only missed fighting by a couple of years. Although I did have the qualifications and the opening for my father's old College at Cambridge, Pembroke, I had not inherited either his intellect or his scholarship as successive Eton reports made clear enough. Probably it was my Uncle Jack's influence that tipped the scales towards the army. It was Hubert Hartley who recommended me to the Coldstream Guards, a choice of regiment which my uncle heartily approved.

The transition from the rather grand existence during one's last year at school to being chased round the barrack square at the Guards Depot at Caterham by a ferocious drill sergeant was savage. No question of a gap year then! I had applied to join the Coldstream Guards, as had many boys from M'Tutor's, been accepted by the Regimental Lieutenant Colonel, Roddy Hill, at the Regimental Headquarters in Wellington Barracks, passed the Army Exam, and the Regular Commissions Board at Knepp Castle in Sussex, and duly found myself as No 407991 Recruit Nickson on the platform at Victoria Station one April morning in 1948 to enter the then equivalent of the 'boot camp' for sixteen weeks. We survived; to emerge fitter, smarter and far more worldly wise. One or two of us escaped the visit to Pirbright in midcourse because we were selected to play for the Depot in the annual Cricket Week. For two mornings we rose at leisure, visited the NAAFI and enjoyed our cricket.

On the third day an Irish Guards drill sergeant found us still in bed at 7 a.m. For the next four days we rose at five, scrubbed our barrack room floor on our knees until it was time to go to play cricket at eleven, returned to our barrack room when stumps were drawn at six, to continue to scrub the same floor until lights out at ten thirty. Our non-cricketing friends had envied us when they left for Pirbright; the boot was on the other foot when they returned to hear of our experiences!

If Wellington boys had the edge on arrival at the Depot, because they took their school Corps more seriously than did most Etonians, those of us from the Guards depot certainly got off to a flying start at Sandhurst. The Regimental Sergeant Major and most of the Company Sergeant Majors were from the Brigade. We knew how to polish our kit to their exacting standards. We knew how to be on parade always five minutes early. We knew how to lift our knees and stamp our feet. We knew how to slope and order arms to the precise millisecond of the 'one–two–three'. And they were not slow to recognise the products of their own university. The Adjutant and Assistant Adjutant were also from the Brigade of Guards. It all helped to make that vital good first impression. I was in Normandy Company in Victory College in Intake IV, i.e. about two years after Sandhurst had started up again as a peacetime Military College. We were there for three terms of six months starting in September 1948 with the hope of being commissioned in December 1949. All our National Service companions who were only in for eighteen months in total had gone to Mons or Eaton Hall to become officers a year ahead of us.

In Normandy Company I found a boy from Sedbergh who had been on the same RCB as I had, called Bob Tweedy. We had been required to give a 'lecturette' on a subject of our own choice. Unfortunately for me he had chosen exactly the same subject on which I felt I could speak without notes with some confidence, namely the life history of the Atlantic salmon. He was called immediately before me, so I had to think of an alternative subject pretty quickly! However we both passed, and became firm friends on the back of our shared enthusiasm for fishing. We bought our first car together, a 1929 Baby Austin. It had no body to speak of, the bonnet was painted scarlet and the petrol supply switched on under the bonnet like a motor mower. Bob once succeeded in driving it all the way up to his home in Edinburgh. I was less adventurous; but on one occasion had great difficulty in avoiding running into the back of the Provost's funeral procession in Eton High Street, and was politely

requested by my future father-in law to refrain from parking it outside
his house in Windsor Castle when I was calling to see Louise! She came
with me to the various Sandhurst dances and was rapidly becoming my
first and only girl friend.

At the end of my first six months I was promoted to Lance-Corporal
and after a year became the Senior Under Officer for my Company. My
two predecessors both became distinguished Riflemen and full Generals,
Roly Guy and Jimmy Glover. I met them once or twice some forty years
later. Hughie Stockwell was the Commandant of the Royal Military
Academy, an old Royal Welsh Fusilier friend of my uncle's and a great
character. He used to drive around the grounds on a Corgi scooter with
his three star badge prominently displayed. Later he commanded the
ill-fated Suez campaign in 1956. It is to him that I owe the title of this
book. 'Always, always, all your life,' he said, 'run up the stairs *Two at a
Time*.' I have tried to follow this both literally and metaphorically!

I enjoyed my time at Sandhurst, starting to discover my capacities and
limitations, playing hard and working even harder. Cricket in the 2nd
XI was fun. I once got a hundred against the Berkshire Police but as at
Eton was not good enough for the Sandhurst XI. Cross country running
was a new sport for me. I just made the Sandhurst VIII but as I was
always last in that company I seldom finished in the top dozen when we
ran against outside opposition and usually trailed around near the back of
the field. All the same that is the last time I remember revelling in the
feeling that one was as fit as one could possibly be.

Various great men visited us to talk about the War and leadership.
Field Marshal Slim took the passing out parade when the Adjutant
traditionally rides his grey horse up the steps of Old College. He gave a
memorable talk on two kinds of courage; the instantaneous gallantry
when adrenalin is running high in contrast to the cold calculating courage
of steeling oneself to proceed against known and fearsome odds. I have
a photograph of myself escorting him when he was inspecting Normandy
Company. A similar picture shows a very different occasion when King
Abdullah of Jordan, grandfather to King Hussein and great grandfather to
the present King, inspected us in full Arab robes. A few years later he
was assassinated. Montgomery and Alexander came too to deliver talks
to the Academy. But of all these great men it is Mountbatten who left
the most lasting impression on me. He looked magnificent in his uniform
as Admiral of the Fleet with row upon row of medals. He knew better
than anyone how to create a dramatic impression on a thousand young
men attempting to win a commission into a junior Service!

In December 1949 I left Sandhurst with an Officer Cadet Scholarship prize and was duly and proudly commissioned into the Coldstream Guards, joining the Third Battalion at Victoria Barracks, Windsor. Visits to 8 Lower Ward became more frequent. It was sheer luck that I was not posted to the Second Battalion in Malaya, who were fighting the terrorists in the jungle. Who can tell what different course my life might have taken? On such quirks of fate does so much depend. George Burns, the best-loved Coldstreamer since the War without a doubt, was my first Commanding officer. David Kennard was second in command and Keith Barlow the adjutant. All had been decorated and seemed awe-inspiring figures to a very junior ensign. Many other lifelong friends were in the Battalion: Mike Hicks, who had been in M'Tutor's at Eton and went on to become a General; John Vaughan who achieved one of the few 'A's at the Staff College, and would certainly have done so too, had it not been for a cruel car crash that brought his military career to an abrupt end; and Ian Jardine, a company commander with an MC won just before the crossing of the Rhine and so a few years older than us. He became my constant sporting companion on the river and in the shooting field for thirty years until his far too early death aged fifty-nine. All three asked me to be Godfather to their sons: Bill Hicks, now a distinguished QC; James Vaughan in Lloyds; and Andrew Jardine, now an estate agent at Berkely Castle in Gloucestershire.

In April we moved up to Wellington Barracks to prepare for London Duties and the Trooping of the Colour. I was the Ensign to Number Two Guard. John Vaughan, who was carrying the Colour, developed some minor illness that prevented him performing for the final dress rehearsal, known then as the Duke of Gloucester's rehearsal, since he was due to take the salute. So on that occasion I did have the honour to carry the King's Colour, unrehearsed for the role as I was. I can well recall the agony of trying to keep my right arm horizontal in the heavy tunic during the march-past with the Regimental Sergeant Major, Charlie Smy, behind me whispering his repeated exhortation to 'keep your bloody arm up, sir.' John had recovered by the day of the Trooping itself a few days later so I reverted with some relief to carrying my sword instead.

The London season was starting to get back into a swing after the war; 'deb' dances, cocktail parties, nightclubs, the Guards Boat Club at Marlow were all available to us. The fact that I had virtually no money and could not afford a car, while most of my contemporaries were much better off, did not seem to stop me enjoying myself to the full. Duties included St James's Palace Guard, which included Buckingham Palace, the Tower of London Guard with the famous Ceremony of the Keys and the Bank of England where the subaltern was provided with a whole decanter of port to himself. You were allowed to invite visitors to lunch or dinner on all guards except the Bank Picket and Louise found her way on more than one occasion. We looked pretty splendid in our scarlet tunics and bearskins, with swords and much gold braid. London was coming back to life after the War. London belonged to us. Life was sweet and we knew it.

Another friend in the Third Battalion was Richard Wraxall. We went down to stay at Tyntesfield, his magnificent Victorian house near Bristol, on a number of occasions. The most memorable was for the twenty first birthday party of his younger brother, Eustace Gibbs. Over fifty of us stayed in the house for a long weekend. A photograph was taken and we still refer to this on occasions to remind ourselves who was there. Little did we realise that we were staying in one of the grandest houses in England for which the National Trust paid over twenty million in 2002 on Richard's death. It has featured endlessly on TV in recent months in a series of programmes. We have watched in fascination the state of decay, now to be seen by the public for the first time, of rooms we knew in better shape over fifty years ago. Richard was a kind and generous man, but he took himself and his inheritance rather too seriously, sadly never married and had become very reclusive in the last twenty years of his life. Eustace was much more talented and sociable than his elder brother. He was musical and had a distinguished career in the Foreign Office before becoming Vice-Marshal of the Diplomatic Corps. He inherited the title but not the property.

By May Louise and I were unofficially engaged though we could not announce it for another eighteen months. Early marriages were not encouraged in the Regiment. They interfered with one's career. Strong pressure was later put on me to think again. It would prevent my becoming adjutant. Anyway the army did not pay marriage allowance in those days until one was twenty-five and we had little money except my pretty meagre ensign's pay. When I was accepted for the Regiment my father had been told that I would need private means of at least £150 per year. Somehow he and my mother had generously found that for me. It was barely enough as a bachelor but would certainly not support a wife!

In November the Battalion's brilliant London season was over. We were sent out to Tripoli for a three-year tour of duty. Louise and I parted not knowing when we would see each other again. What should have been an exciting new adventure for me was clouded in sadness. But this was peacetime. How much more poignant and often tragic must have been the millions of similar partings only five years earlier during the war.

We sailed from Dover to Calais on Armistice Day. Ian Jardine had obtained permission to drive out to North Africa and had asked me to accompany him. Richard Wraxall was also taking his car. So we set off in two elderly Ford estate cars to drive through France to Marseilles to catch a ship to Tunis. It poured with rain for four days. Ian's car leaked on both sides of the windscreen. We had one pair of gumboots between us, so the driver wore the right boot and the passenger the left. I was driving through Avignon when an apparently irate *gendarme* blew his whistle for me to stop. 'You've torn it now,' said Ian; whereupon the policeman leaned over to say that 'the Milord Anglais' was twenty minutes ahead of us. Richard had left a message in a lordly fashion just as if he had been dealing with an under footman at Tyntesfield. In Marseilles Ian and I went out on the town. Richard, clearly thinking we were heading for some low dive, declined to accompany us. In fact we had a hilarious evening in a fun fair on the bumping cars. Tunis was an eye-opener. I had no conception of the poverty, the cripples begging on every street corner, the flies, the dust and the heat. We ran out of petrol and had to push a handbarrow for miles to find a hotel. My cartridge magazine with my carefully husbanded supply of twelve-bore ammunition was stolen.

We drove along the North African coast, following in the steps of the First Army only seven years earlier, and so into Libya and on to Tripoli. This was a city of two halves, with the old Arab quarter full of humanity, smells, narrow streets, noise and bargaining merchants; while the Italian colonial buildings dominated the waterfront, the restaurants and the main shopping thoroughfares. In those days of course Libya was a monarchy under King Idris and favourably disposed to both British and Americans. Gadaffi's revolutionary regime was still in the future. We were stationed in Gialo barracks, later to be bombed by the Americans in the ill-fated attempt to kill him. The Battalion duly arrived by troopship to join our little advance party and we took over our duties from our own First Battalion. By this time Bill Gore-Langton was commanding us. He had lost his right arm in the Italian campaign but still contrived to shoot and fish, and more threateningly to drive his car at ferocious speed through throngs of Arab pedestrians, changing gear with his left hand while the steering wheel looked after itself. My company commander was Lewis

Dawnay from Inverkip. Later he sold me my first yellow Labrador. He survived on a diet of pink gin and ate nothing; sadly but unsurprisingly he died not too long after we returned home.

Life settled into a routine of desert exercises, the inevitable parade ground drill (we trooped the colour in the sand with the same officers in command of the escorts as had paraded on Horseguards a year earlier), parties at the yacht club or with married officers in their quarters, cricket on matting wickets, tennis and bridge. I played a lot of bridge in the army and still greatly enjoy the game today. Mike and Jean Hicks, recently married and with a small house, were extremely kind to me. We ventured out whenever opportunity permitted to chase the occasional duck or snipe on the wadis, or quail walked up through standing crops with scant regard for the owner's feelings. But the best of the shooting expeditions were far inland across the wide hard hot desert, camping for two or three nights under the endless star studded canopy of dark blue sky, to walk after *chikkor*, a sort of partridge rather like a Frenchman, or to wait at dawn for the sandgrouse to flight in to the wadis for water. They had an evocative wild bubbling cry, heard long before you saw them. It reminded me of early morning wigeon flights in Wales and I longed to be back at home. But this did not stop me shooting one hundred and twelve to my own gun one memorable morning with John Nelson who was commanding the third battalion of the Grenadiers and, as I was by then Liaison Officer at First Guards Brigade, he had kindly invited me to accompany their expedition.

At last in September 1951 I was sent home to attend two platoon commander's courses; at the small arms school at Hythe in Kent before Christmas, and on the tactics course at Warminster in January and February. Here I met a lot more friends from other regiments, two of whom have remained close friends in Scotland ever since, Bill Bewsher of the Royal Scots and Charlie Moncrieff of the Scots Guards. By this time I was becoming an ambitious and competitive soldier and managed to obtain the only 'A' grade awarded on both courses. But Louise and I had formally announced our engagement in December and parting to return to the Middle East was no easier than the time before. During my time at home Nasser had deposed King Farouk of Egypt and we had been moved down to guard the Suez Canal. So I went out by troopship to Port Said and so down to Fayed where we were to spend the next two years in a horrid, hot, sandy, tented camp behind a barbed wire perimeter. Keith Barlow became ill so I took over as temporary adjutant until Pat MacLellan was sent out to relieve me.

Our wedding was arranged for 18 October 1952 in St George's Chapel at Windsor. Louise with her parents had to make all the arrangements. I did not arrive home on leave until thirty-six hours beforehand having been held up for two days in a transit camp by a sandstorm. She had to obtain a special licence and buy her own wedding ring! It was, as it so often is, a golden St Luke's Day, for a wedding which now fifty years later has itself qualified for Gold! We honeymooned at first in Devonshire before setting out back to Tripoli where I had got permission to command the Battalion Rear Party, consisting of about a dozen soldiers and over a hundred wives, before returning to Egypt to take up a job as Staff Captain First Guards Brigade. We caught a train from Victoria to Paris for one night and then on to Venice, a city for which we formed a romantic and lifelong affection, and have visited on many occasions in recent years with friends and our family. We had run out of money by then and had to exist largely on wedding cake eaten out of a tin. Eventually we made our way to Naples via Rome by train and so onto the ship to travel across the Mediterranean. It was pretty rough and Louise was miserably seasick. Douglas and Sue Noel had lent us their flat overlooking the Royal Palace. Douglas was on the pier to meet us; otherwise we would have had not a penny to pay for a taxi. He described my responsibilities to me and left to rejoin the Regiment in Egypt.

I have always been fairly punctilious about keeping my personal finances and accounts in good order, eschewing all my life the borrowing of money. It amused me to find, as I turned out some old records for this book, that I had carefully written down the full cost of our honeymoon and our total assets and liabilities as we embarked on our married life.

We did not have much money! My army pay was as follows:

	£	s	d
Basic Daily Pay		19	6
Local Overseas Allowance		2	0
Marriage Allowance		8	0
Ration Allowance		4	0
Total per day	1	13	6
Total per week	11	14	6
Total per month	46	18	0
Total per year	562	16	0

I suppose £500 p.a. in those days would be equivalent to £12,000 p.a. or a bit more in today's money. Still we only had about £150 p.a. of private income. It was not a fortune on which to embark on married life at the age of twenty-two!

There was a large American Air Force base near Tripoli and some of our regimental wives had been on their own for over a year. There were the inevitable matrimonial problems. As I had only been married for ten days myself I hardly felt qualified to give advice! Most of the families were billeted with Italian landladies. They were insatiable in their demands for rent. When I visited them a fair percentage seemed to have had a previous existence as Neapolitan brothel keepers. It was an interesting introduction to married life. Meanwhile Louise sought a losing battle against the cockroaches in our flat and courageously ventured out on foot to obtain food, as she had no car. We visited the famous Roman sites at Homs, Sabratha and Leptis Magna and were starting to enjoy ourselves when disaster struck. I suddenly developed a violent fever and rapidly became delirious. Louise contacted the British Military Hospital and I was unceremoniously removed by ambulance. Soldiers appeared to fumigate our clothes, our bedding and everything in the flat. Nobody had the faintest idea what disease I had contracted. Poor Louise was left alone with no communications, no transport and for all she knew no husband. I was blissfully unconscious of all this for several days.

By good fortune Bob and Olive Windsor-Clive were back in Tripoli on leave from the Canal Zone and on hearing of Louise's plight took her into their home. After several false starts the doctors finally discovered that I had a form of typhus just in time to administer the fairly recently discovered antibiotic. Apparently typhus was unknown in North Africa at that time so they had not suspected it. The assumption was that a bedbug had bitten me in Naples. If so, 'See Naples and die' might have been an all too apt quotation. Louise has memories of being driven once a day to see me in hospital through a glass screen, necessitating a journey in the front seat of a three-ton truck driven by a guardsman who succeeded in running over no fewer than three cats on one trip. Telephones were not available in those days. She had sent a telegram home to my parents reporting the diagnosis; unsurprisingly they had drawn the probable gloomy conclusion after consulting a medical dictionary.

By Christmas I was better but it had been a close shave. We were given only one week's sick leave in Malta before Louise had to fly home and I to the Canal Zone. Malta was freezing. Our flight across in a small plane coincided with a violent thunderstorm and we were tossed around like thistledown. In a lifetime spent in planes of one sort or another I never remember a more fearsome experience. It was Louise's first flight. She was very brave, largely I suspect because anything was preferable to being tossed about in a rough sea. We stayed at the Xara Palace Hotel where an Admiral Hill was also staying. He took a great fancy to Louise and plied her with crème de menthe. It is the only time in my life that I have ever seen her the worse for wear! For the first time in our lives we finished *The Times* crossword together the next day. We had not had the easiest start to our married life!

The next year was pretty dull. First Guards Brigade Headquarters provided my first taste of staff work. Luckily I shared an office with George Ramsay of the Scots Guards who was DAQMG. He was great fun and very helpful in keeping me on the right lines. We were the only non Grenadiers in an HQ dominated by Brigadier Geordie Gordon Lennox and by David Fraser the Brigade Major, both of whom went on to become Generals. David Maitland, another Grenadier, was G3. He too became a firm friend in Scotland in later years. I think that by this time I was coming to the conclusion that the uncertainties of married life as a soldier with all the inevitable partings were going to be hard to take. I was also pretty bored by the Canal Zone, heat, flies and sand with little chance to go beyond the barbed wire confines of our camp. But I had formed no plans to leave the army until Jan Collins, a close friend from my house at Eton, asked me if I would be interested in joining his family publishing business in Scotland as a management trainee. At first I did not give this much thought. I was sufficiently competitive and ambitious to relish the prospect of a military career that showed, so I was led to believe, some early promise.

But then I was asked to play cricket as a wicket keeper for the British Troops in Egypt on a three-week tour of Kenya. I was thrilled and flattered. I assumed that having been selected I could automatically go. I think in a Coldstream environment permission would have been given. Little did I realise the regimental nature of the Grenadiers! I was told that I could not be spared, as we were under twenty-four hours notice to go to Cairo. I stupidly replied that we had all been longing to get to Cairo for over two years but the prospect of our getting there was nil! I was extremely disappointed; and, small though this issue now seems, that and my illness undoubtedly did affect my attitude to the army at that time. Louise and I had seen very little of each other since our marriage the previous autumn, and the uncertainties and humdrum nature of peacetime soldiering in a particularly unattractive posting had begun to pall. So that when, a few months later, Jan's invitation was renewed I decided to take up his offer to have a talk with his father as soon as I returned home to England.

I rejoined the Battalion to return home for Christmas 1953. I had been due to go to the Small Arms School at Hythe as an instructor in April but by then had 'put in my papers' to leave the army. We did not know whether this would be granted. So Louise and I found ourselves hunting for our first home in both Kent and Scotland at the same time.

CHAPTER 3

William Collins
1954–1985

THUS IT WAS that I began my career in industry in 1954 as a management trainee with William Collins, the publishers, in Glasgow.

Throughout the Fifties and Sixties inflation averaged only 3 per cent,
a level not achieved again for thirty years. Partly as a legacy from the war,
restrictive practices, lack of capital investment and Victorian working
methods in Victorian buildings characterised much of British Industry.
This was particularly true of the general printing industry, which shared
common Trades Unions with Fleet Street and working practices which
owed their origins to the imperative to bring out tomorrow's edition of
newspapers rather than any logical connection with book publishing,
printing or binding, and which in the competitive climate of the
twenty-first century beggar belief. The transition from the culture of the
Brigade, where discipline prevailed and officers' orders were instantly
obeyed, to that of a junior trainee in a Dickensian environment was stark;
as stark indeed as the transition from one's final glorious year at Eton to
scrubbing the barrack room floor at the Guards Depot! I was given no
formal management training and had no professional or technical
qualifications. In short I was, and to a large extent remained throughout
my business career, an amateur in an increasingly professional world.
Perhaps this is a typical indictment of the shortcomings of much of
British management over the last generation; but somehow I have
managed to survive on a combination of a modicum of common sense,
the gift of the gab and a lot of bluff!

Collins was one of the leading and most commercially successful
London publishers. But the firm's origins lay in the printing and
publishing of Bibles, Children's and Educational books and stationery and
diaries in Glasgow. Over 3,000 people, 75 per cent of them women and
girls, were employed in the printing and binding factories. Young girls,
from fifteen upwards, pushed vast barrows of books and paper from floor
to floor up uneven wooden ramps. They wore clogs and were shouted
at by ferocious forewomen, who had served their own time thirty years
earlier. It was not uncommon for three generations of the same family

31

to be serving in the same department. The annual outing 'doon the watter' to Rothesay and Dunoon on the Clyde was an unforgettable experience. Bottles of gin were secreted below babies in prams as the assembled throng were seen off from the Broomielaw pier in Glasgow to the strains of Harry Lauder songs. These same girls were trained to an amazing level of dexterity in handling quires of printed paper, called signatures, for folding, bundling and binding into finished books. Their pay levels were far below those of the trained journeymen whom they served. It was not until the introduction of the Equal Pay Act in the 1960s that it became more productive for many operations to make the appropriate investment in modern machinery. Indeed I was brought up on the maxim that we owed our ability to compete internationally on our unlimited supply of cheap female labour! Not a very politically correct statement for the twenty-first century. How times have changed; and how successful we have been in achieving social progress – but at the expense of exporting manufacturing jobs to the Far East by the hundreds of thousands. Satisfactory profit margins and a lack of real competition for twenty years after the war produced a dangerous level of complacency. It was not until vastly superior print quality at much cheaper prices started to flood in from the United States and especially Japan that Collins' manufacturing management and the Printing Unions had to sit up and take notice. But by then it was too late.

However Collins was a marvellous place to work and Glasgow and the West of Scotland a wonderful environment in which to bring up a young family and to enjoy oneself. I made some great friends in the business and had many excellent colleagues. Most of the managers were the salt of the earth, loyal to the Collins family, proud of their firm, and almost without exception kind and tolerant to me, whom they might so well have resented as being an upstart with an unearned silver spoon in his mouth. Perhaps some of them did, but they never showed it. It was fun, too, to work in a successful publishing company. Books by best-selling authors like Agatha Christie, Peter Cheyney and Howard Spring rubbed shoulders in the Collins catalogue with the wartime biographies of Montgomery, Brian Horrocks and Douglas Bader's blockbusting winner *Reach for the Sky*; later it was fascinating to meet those whose names, as a result of being published by Collins, became internationally known, like Joy Adamson of Elsa fame and Alastair Mclean. Fontana Books were started with the best selling religious titles of C.S. Lewis's *Screwtape Letters* and J.B. Phillips' *Letters to Young Churches*. Mark Collins, Jan's younger brother, subsequently ran Fontana Books, Collins' paperback imprint, with outstanding success for many years.

Billy Collins, Jan's father, later Sir William, was the most successful commercial publisher of his generation, a literary entrepreneur of dynamic energy, a man of great presence and charm, who started many publishing initiatives such as the New Naturalist series and the famous Collins pocket guides to wildlife, creating the style for almost all imitative field guides ever since. The new book publishing was carried out from the London offices in 14 St James's Place. Here Billy was supported by a team of distinguished editors, many of whom such as Mark Bonham-Carter, Philip Zeigler, Richard Ollard, Raleigh Trevelyan and Adrian House made their mark in other walks of life or as authors in their own right.

Though I was never part of the literary or editorial sides of the business, my roles always being more administrative or commercial, my visits to London were frequent and it was very congenial to rub shoulders with the famous. Field Marshal Montgomery was an occasional visitor to Glasgow to see his books printed. He had just been paid a huge advance, for those days, on his royalties. On one occasion I was introduced to him over lunch in the Glasgow boardroom as a recent recruit from the regular army. 'Why did you leave? You can't have been at all a keen soldier,' he barked. Humphrey Philips, a Director and incidentally a cousin of Louise's, came to my rescue by saying immediately, 'Well, Sir, perhaps you never had a good offer from a publisher.' At which the great man had the decency to laugh. Later, in 1963, he performed the opening ceremony for Collins' first modern new building on Cathedral Street in Glasgow (now the library for Strathclyde University). He spoke a good deal about himself as was his wont, but then said he had no great quarrel with us as his publishers except as publishers of Bibles and hymnbooks. He was always being asked to sing hymns that started 'Oh Paradise! Oh Paradise! How I long for thee.' 'Well,' he said, 'I don't. I don't. I would like to sing a hymn that goes –

> Oh Paradise! Oh Paradise
> I have a little shop,
> and just so long as profits last,
> here I mean to stop!'

So the myth that Montgomery had no sense of humour whatever is not wholly true.

In passing I can't resist quoting another little rhyme, at which he smiled, and which reputedly appeared in a Collins Bible catalogue of the nineteenth century:

Holy Bible, Writ Divine
Bound in leather, One and Nine
Satan trembles when he sees
Bibles sold as cheap as these.

My first proper job in Collins was to run the publicity department in Glasgow. This was very much a subordinate to the far more important operation in London where a celebrated character in the book trade called Ronald Politzer promoted all Billy Collins great best sellers with flair and imagination, while another legendary figure, Sydney Goldsack, sold them by the barrowload to the bookshops through a highly experienced team of representatives. There was a mysterious esoteric alchemy about the sale of books. A Boots buyer, responsible in those days for their important book department and library operations, and doubtless having acquired his marketing skills at Proctor and Gamble, wrote an article in the *Bookseller* saying that books could be sold like soap. He was ridiculed and ostracised!

My little operation was more concerned with the humdrum business of promoting Bibles, dictionaries, diaries and stationery products. Hardly had I got the job when the Suez crisis loomed and I received an immediate call to return to the army as a reserve officer. Everyone was very kind to me as I prepared to go off to war, only for the order to be rescinded two days later, much to my relief and that of Louise. Our first daughter had just been born and we had recently moved into our first proper home at Killearn, a village fifteen miles to the north of Glasgow.

Shortly afterwards I was promoted to run the Collins Diary department, which was very profitable. I became something of an expert on diaries of all types, eventually becoming chairman of the Diary Publishers Association. In those days Collins Diaries were considered somewhat less prestigious than those of Letts and T.J and J. Smiths. However we had the volume commercial business from the large Trade Unions and companies like ICI. Our head salesman was an extraordinary little man with a face like a turnip and a Kojak hair cut. He was without exception the ugliest man I have ever seen. He wore a bow tie, spats and a bowler hat. He operated out of a scruffy little office in Covent Garden near Bow Street Police Station. You had to push past the cases of oranges and bananas to gain entry. But as no customer was allowed near the place it did not matter and it had the merit of being very cheap. Horace Rissen, for such was his name, claimed that the police called him in to line-up for identification parades once a month, but so idiosyncratic was his appearance that his chances of being wrongly identified must have been nil. He was a keen Mason, telling me that I had no chance of success with our Trade Union customers unless I became one too. He took me into the Masonic Hall close by the Connaught Rooms, making a serious effort to recruit me. I had assumed that this was contrary to Masonic practice and it put me off for life. So far as I am aware I have suffered no disadvantages since.

Large quantities of whisky and Scottish shortbread were distributed to customers at Christmas. I thought this rather a waste of money, naively preferring to believe that customers bought on quality and price. After Rissen retired I decided to cut the practice out, saying that we would be happy to give to charity instead if our customers wished. I had a frantic call from his successor, Bob Oyler, to the effect that the buyer for the Transport and General Workers Union, our largest single order, would unhesitatingly place the order elsewhere and had in fact only recently complained that our cigars the previous year were not up to standard! I wrote to the General Secretary, Frank Cousins, but took the precaution of sending a blind copy to Bob Oyler first, suggesting he might like to show it to the buyer before I posted it. I never did have to post the letter to Union Headquarters. We retained the order for many years.

A less successful venture was my attempt to establish a range of distinctive diaries in the United States. The Americans have never really cottoned on to the peculiarly British habit of carrying pocket diaries about with them. I appointed an agent who was enthusiastic, though in the course of time he proved unreliable. He loved Manhattan as only New York Jews can with an endearing passion; he was keen to show it off to me on my first visit. Laurence Myers met me at Idlewild Airport one evening (President Kennedy had not by then been assassinated to give his name to JFK International) before driving me to his home in the smart suburb of Scarsdale. 'Do you mind going up in a small aeroplane?' he said, 'I would like to show you Manhattan from the air.'

It was January. The next morning found us at Westchester Airport on a day of diamond brilliance with the thermometer far below freezing. His friend who owned the plane was called Al. 'Hi Dave,' said Al. 'Welcome aboard.' As he started the engines I asked Laurence Myers for his surname. 'He's called Abbott Bugaliser and he's the largest importer of musical instruments into the United States,' came the unlikely reply. We flew north over the Rockefeller residence towards the Hudson and then down the river over the palisades with the spectacular Manhattan skyline ahead. Our call sign was '70 dollar' and we flew at only 3,000 ft.

while air control drew our attention unconcernedly to commercial planes taking off from Idlewild or La Guardia. We seemed so close to the Empire State, the Chrysler and Pan Am buildings glistening in the sun. It was of course long before the construction let alone the destruction of the twin towers of the World Trade Centre. On we went over the Statue of Liberty and Statten Island before circling back across the East River and over Jones Beach and Long Island. Two hours later we were driving into New York at Cadillac level but the geography and atmosphere were indelibly printed on my mind. Years later I calculated that by walking really fast from downtown Manhattan to 52nd Street I could manage to cover a block a minute. There was for a while a helicopter-transfer from JFK International to the top of the Pan Am building before security concerns made it impractical. It only took seven minutes and you felt as if you could touch the skyscrapers as you came in to land. But I have never forgotten the kindness shown in giving me such an unforgettable introduction to New York.

The decade of the Seventies was a miserable one for British management. It was easily the most difficult of my own business life. Britain's reputation for quality, service, delivery and competitiveness reached an all time low. The oil crisis of 1973 and the first of the catastrophic miners' strikes induced the Heath Government to introduce the three-day week. I well remember two stony faced civil servants appearing unannounced into my office one morning to spell out the dire consequences under the law for my colleagues and me, if we did not instantly comply. Jan Collins showed great initiative in buying a large generator from the USA, which we flew into Prestwick Airport by Hercules. This enabled us to run some parts of the printing works on the two days when the use of our mains power supply were forbidden without breaching the government regulations. In 1974 the Heath Government collapsed having gone to the country too late following the miners' strike. Inflation burst into double figures, where, off and on, it remained for nearly twenty years. A Labour government under Harold Wilson was returned with even worse consequences for British industry. The three-day week, the miners' strike and constant industrial disputes in our own printing industry remain etched indelibly on my memory. Throughout the decade there were a series of mandatory pay freezes, with the inevitable subsequent pay explosion in the eighties.

For the previous ten years my colleagues and I had been striving to move the Collins factories and warehouses from their Victorian premises in the city of Glasgow to modern buildings on a greenfield site at Bishopbriggs six miles to the north. We needed new facilities to house modern machinery, to introduce modern working practices and technology and, as we mistakenly thought, to provide greatly increased capacity for ever increasing sales volumes. The exercise was successfully completed by 1976 but at a crippling cost just at the moment when demand was turning down and fiercely competitive prices started to bite. Trade Union militancy was at its height. To compound these problems there was grave management conflict at the top, partly over the correct strategic path to follow and partly over succession. Basically the publishing side of the business was profitable whereas the manufacturing side was not, and there was conflict between the family members of the Board and the non-family executive directors. Billy Collins died during the year. His younger brother Ian, who had been my boss, and his cousin Hope Collins had both died a few years earlier.

Ian, widely known as I.G., was a remarkable character. Most members of the Collins family were outstanding athletes and I.G. was the most celebrated of all. He reached the final of the Men's Doubles at Wimbledon with Gregory in 1929, being beaten only by the legendary French pair of Cochet and Borotra. He represented Britain in the Davies Cup. He made seventy-odd playing cricket for Oxford against the Australians and also got a Blue for football, but broke his leg very badly. This subsequently seemed to accentuate his rather angular, craggy appearance. For he was by no means a natural or graceful mover but was possessed of an eagle eye for a ball and an iron determination to win. Curiously he was an indifferent shot with a shotgun. He was extraordinarily kind to Louise and me from the moment we arrived in Glasgow in 1954.

I well remember my first interview with Billy Collins in St James's Place in 1953. I must have seemed to him both naïve and arrogant. I said that I could not come to work for Collins unless I was paid at least as much as I was getting as a Captain in the army (hardly a fortune in those days but more than one might have expected to start on in industry as an unqualified trainee) and would need an undertaking that I should become a Director within five years. To both requests Billy said that he would need to consult his brother Ian and that I would need to go to Glasgow to see him. This I did. As I walked up Buchanan Street for the very first time, amidst the horde of Glasgow pedestrians in their lunch hour, a very contrasting figure rushed past downhill in a loud check tweed overcoat. He had a thick dark head of hair and a strikingly angular jaw set in a face full of character. An hour later I was ushered into the Vice Chairman's office in Cathedral Street and this same man stepped out from behind his desk to shake my hand. Somehow it seemed to be assumed that I would start as soon as I could get my discharge from the army. He knew John Head who was Secretary of State for Defence and would write to him. We never looked back.

I did become a Director of the main operating Board in 1959 and of the top Holding Company Board in 1967. Shortly afterwards I was fortunate to be allowed by the Collins Board to develop some outside interests, becoming a non-executive director of Scottish United Investors in 1970 and General Accident based in Perth, the UK's second largest composite insurer, in 1971.

My first involvement with the Public Sector came rather surprisingly in 1975 when I was appointed to the Scottish Industrial Development Advisory Board. This quango was charged with advising Ministers on the disbursement of loans and grants under the Industry Act to Scottish companies. I do not know which civil servant recommended me but my friends were surprised, knowing my lack of sympathy with the then Labour Government, that I was appointed by Tony Benn, then President of the Board of Trade, and was responsible to his even more left wing Minister for Industry, Eric Heffer. I sadly never met Tony Benn and what contact I had at ministerial level was with a Scottish Minister, Gregor Mackenzie, whom I liked and respected. A few years later I happened to be dining in Westminster and was taken into the House after dinner to listen to a censure debate on the maverick MP for Leith, Ron Brown. In a gesture of protest against the recently elected Conservative government he had picked up the Mace and dropped it, doing some minor damage. It was a classic piece of parliamentary drama. Tony Benn made a fine speech. I remember the oratory better than the contents. Then Eric Heffer was called. He claimed that the sentence proposed for Ron Brown, one month's suspension from Parliament, as I recall, was draconian and totally disproportionate to the crime. He claimed that 'this unfortunate Member had inadvertently dropped the Mace due to an old industrial injury to his hand' . . . and that 'the sentence was like taking a sledgehammer to crack a . . . A NUT, A NUT!' roared the Tory backbenchers in delighted glee as they finished his sentence for him!

I suppose it was my growing involvement with external affairs that must have drawn my name to the attention of the CBI in Scotland. I had joined the Scottish Council and by 1976 had been approached with a view to taking over as Chairman in 1979. I have to admit that my ambition needed more scope than that which could be provided by someone else's family firm, however prestigious. When I left the army my uncle had deliberately refrained from offering me a job in the Nickson business, not wishing me to repeat the mistake he felt he himself had made. But the remark he made at the time still rankled: 'Good God, boy, what the hell do you think you're playing at, giving up a regular commission in the Coldstream Guards to go to work in someone else's bumf factory in Glasgow?' I had secretly watched the progress of some of my army contempories with envy, conscious that I could at least have kept pace. For years I could not watch the Trooping the Colour ceremony without suffering pangs of nostalgic regret for the career I had abandoned. I also remember thinking that I would like the opportunity to follow in Hope Collins' trail. He was a first cousin of Billy and Ian's, the third member of the triumvirate who controlled the business in the Fifties and Sixties. He was the son of Sir Godfrey Collins who had been a Liberal Secretary of State for Scotland. Hope had been very active in printing industry politics and had been President of the Glasgow Chamber of Commerce. I had always found him very encouraging and supportive. As my role in Collins was by no means mainstream by that time, the chance to spread my wings at the CBI for two or three years was attractive, and I have no doubt that it was quite welcome to one or two of my colleagues to have me fully occupied elsewhere for a while! I had caused enough trouble by creating flutters in the dovecot.

But in 1979 Collins made its first loss in over 150 years. The banks were unhappy. Management succession issues, long rumbling like an angry appendix, came to a head in a series of miserable rows. Our non-executive directors played an anchor role. Dick Troughton and Robert Smith were imperturbable, wise and decisive. The Trustees of one of the two largest family Trusts supported management and not the family. In August 1979 I was asked if I would take over as the managing director, while Jan Collins remained as Chairman. I had twenty-four hours to write my terms, in which I included the option to retire on full pension two years later. I was fifty at the time and this suited me well. I believed that I could work with Jan, provided he had a strictly non-executive role, and with my great friend and more senior colleague Ian Chapman, who had been unwilling at that time to accept the job subsequently offered to me.

It was extremely sad that the long friendship I had with Jan should have gradually disintegrated into the bitterest of business disagreements. I am sure there were mistakes on both sides. He was a man of huge if eccentric charm. He had been a brilliantly successful and popular schoolboy at Eton, President of Pop, and winner in successive years of the Squash, Rackets and Eton Fives championships before going on to gain a Tennis Blue at Oxford. He had married, even younger than we had, Sara Hely-Hutchinson. They were our closest friends and wonderfully kind to us when we first came to live in Scotland. Jan was Godfather to our eldest daughter Felicity. We had enormous fun together on a personal level. But the sad fact was that all of us in the business eventually found it almost impossible to work with him; we did not consider he was the right person to succeed his father, and took a diametrically opposite view on the way forward. This was the background to the unhappy events leading to the demise of Collins as a family business, and the takeover, which led to the formation of HarperCollins as part of the Murdoch Empire. I am happy to say that it is all now well in the past, and twenty years later, Jan and I have been able to resume our earlier friendship celebrating with great pride our respective Golden Weddings in the last couple of years.

But by the time I was asked to take on the new task at Collins I was already committed to the CBI. John Methven was Director General at the time. He had come from the Office of Fair Trading after a distinguished career in ICI. I took the opportunity after a dinner in the Caledonian Hotel in Edinburgh to ask for a word after the other guests had departed. I told him that because of the Collins situation I would be unable to take on the Scottish CBI Chair. I realised that I was letting him down and that it would be very difficult to find anyone to take my place at such short notice. 'Let's go for a walk,' said he. So we set off out of the 'Cally' up Randolph Street just after midnight. John took me by the arm. 'Now look,' he said 'If you turn down the CBI, yet do a good job as managing director of Collins and help to save your company, no one will take a lot of notice. Lots of managers are faced with similar crises every year. But if you take on the chairmanship of the CBI in Scotland, make a success of it, and at the same time succeed in saving your company the world will sit up and take notice. After that almost any opportunity will be open to you.'

Well, I took his advice; and there followed the two most worrying and difficult years of my life. I have been blessed in countless ways, not least by robust good health and abundant energy. In the months that followed, for the first and only time I felt continuously unwell. I had a number of medical checks. They were all negative. I now know of course that I was suffering from what is fashionably recognised as work-related stress. At the time I regarded such weakness as something that only happened to other people!

Collins pulled itself together and a united management team started to sort out the major problems. By 1981 it seemed time for Ian Chapman to take over as executive Chairman. He had had a brilliant career, starting in Glasgow; he became responsible for the publishing of all Collins Bibles. He was such a high flier that he was recruited by Billy Collins to help him to run the sales and editorial side of the business from St James's Place in London. He became Chairman of the Publishers Association. He and I were in harness together as joint managing directors from 1967 onwards. We saw eye-to-eye on most issues and enjoyed each other's company. It was always clear that he was the right person to head up the business once the family dynasty had collapsed. My role had been as caretaker to get the show back on the road after the crisis. I wrote a letter to the Board to this effect. It had more or less unanimous approval. But it put Mark Collins, Jan's younger brother, in a very difficult position, until the issue was resolved in a most unhappy way and he also felt compelled to cast his vote against his brother.

When the proposal eventually came that Jan should retire as non-executive chairman, and that Ian should succeed him, the trustees of the family trust, which supported Jan, sold their 31 per cent shareholding, without telling the Board, to Rupert Murdoch's News International. He simultaneously made a takeover bid for the company, as he was bound to do under Stock Exchange rules, and though this was defeated with the help of the city and the support of all Collins authors, he was left with a holding of over 40 per cent. Ian Chapman duly became Chairman but we had Rupert Murdoch and Ted Pickering, another News International director, on the Board, and the writing was on the wall. I exercised the service agreement, which I had negotiated two years earlier, stayed as a non-executive director until 1985 and then resigned.

Two years later Rupert Murdoch bid again for the company and despite a valiant fight, he won as he was bound to do. Collins became HarperCollins and Ian's long, honourable and distinguished career at Collins came to an end. A number of our good friends and colleagues left with him. One story in the light of subsequent events is worth recording. During the first struggle for control Robert Maxwell, who owned Pergamon Press and the British Printing Corporation, built up a holding of 7 per cent. We were between Scylla and Charybdis! A meeting took place with our merchant bankers, Schroder's and Bob Maxwell. He said that he was either 'part of our problem or part of our solution'; in the latter case he would increase his shareholding and take two seats on the Board. 'But what about the problem?' we said. 'You surely would not sell to Rupert Murdoch?' (They were known to hate each other's guts.) 'Sell to that shit – never in a thousand years!' He had sold out to Murdoch before midnight that same evening.

Years later he entered my life again in my CBI role along with another infamous businessman, Ernest Saunders. But that is another story. I met Rupert Murdoch a few times in the context of Collins Board meetings. He appeared to have little time for social niceties, cutting through the undergrowth of Board agendas and reports with ruthless incision, cross-examining the unfortunate presenter in adversarial style on any points that interested him, without any pretence of 'going through the Chair'. But it was indeed fascinating to hear at first hand his plans to take on the militant printing unions by establishing his printing operations in secret at Wapping! That triumph would probably not have been possible had Margaret Thatcher not come to power.

So ended my first thirty years as a businessman. Now I can look back on everything at Collins with affection and nostalgia, thinking how fortunately life has turned out for my family and myself in Scotland, as a direct result of that approach from Jan over fifty years ago.

CHAPTER 4

Chairman CBI for Scotland
1979–1981

I<small>N DUE COURSE</small> I did become Chairman of the CBI in Scotland in
September 1979, four months after the new Conservative Government
had been elected. The first Minister I was to meet was Jim Prior,
Secretary of State for Employment. He came to Glasgow to meet Trade
Union Leaders. I was impressed by his approach and in sympathy with
his political stance. At the time I did not appreciate how he would later
become characterised and criticised by right wing Tories as one of the
archetypal 'Wets'. My political credo such as it was (I was never any sort
of politician nor did I ever have any political aspirations) was very much
that of the 'One Nation'. So it was Jim Prior whom I invited to be the
principal speaker at my farewell CBI dinner when my term of office
came to an end two years later. By that time he had lost favour with
Margaret Thatcher. I remember him saying to me that if the Press
speculation that he was about to be moved to Northern Ireland was
correct he would refuse to go. Shortly afterwards he was indeed
appointed as Secretary of State for Ireland and loyally accepted, going on
to do a splendid job.

I was present on one or two occasions at meetings and dinners when
the Prime Minister visited Scotland. There were always fireworks of
some sort. On one occasion at a private dinner at Ingleston, the
Headquarters of the Royal Highland Show, Bruce Patullo, later Governor of the Bank of Scotland, suggested that interest rates and therefore
the exchange rate were too high for Scottish Industry. He might as well
have lit the blue touch paper but he had no slit trench into which to
retire! On another occasion she made a speech in a Glasgow Hotel to a
large assembly of businessmen and trade unionists. I remember being
startled, not to say rather shocked, to hear her say, 'People talk about
government by consensus. I don't know what they mean. I believe in
government by consent.' Later in her career such a remark would have
surprised no one, but it shows how conditioned I still was to the idea
that no effective management measures could be taken without prior
Trade Union agreement!

My first meeting with Margaret Thatcher occurred in 1978. She was not the first Prime Minister I came to know well. For over twenty years I used to shoot with Alec Douglas-Home at Crawfordjohn, one of the bleakest and most exposed villages in Lanarkshire. I often stayed at Castle Mains, which had been the factor's house before Douglas Castle had been blown up before the War. It was without exception the coldest house I can remember. The only form of heating was one small single-bar electric fire in each bedroom. Temperatures in January were often well below zero outside and seemed even colder inside. Paddy Dickson, the Constituency Chairman for Alec's Perthshire seat, and I used to pack our thickest shooting stockings to wear in bed the moment the coveted invitation to shoot arrived. There were usually two or three other people staying, often his younger brother Edward and on two or three occasions Willie Whitelaw. The atmosphere apart from the temperature inside and out was always very friendly and congenial. A less pompous man than Alec Home could not be conceived.

I first stayed there in November 1962 when he was Foreign Secretary. I collected him from the Conservative Headquarters in Glasgow where he had a speaking engagement. My invitation had come in a handwritten letter from Elizabeth Douglas-Home, starting with the words: 'You won't know who I am but I used to know your parents at Eton.' She had gone on to ask me if I could possibly do her a great favour by collecting her husband, the Foreign Secretary, after a dinner in Glasgow, driving him down to Douglas and 'perhaps I would like a day's shooting there the following day?'

Her father Cyril Allington had been Headmaster of Shrewsbury when my father and my Eton housemaster Jack Peterson were boys. He had followed their progress and recruited them as young beaks when he became one of the most famous Eton Headmasters of the twentieth century. My own life would have taken a very different course but for that bit of headhunting in the 1920s.

In fact Alec Home was not the first member of the Cabinet I came to know well, for Rab Butler had been a friend and contemporary of my father's at Pembroke. He was often in my parents' drawing room at Eton since all three of his sons, Richard, Adam and James, were in my father's house. I saw something of Richard later on when he was the distinguished President of the National Farmers Union and I was at the CBI.

Thus it was that I turned up in the middle of Glasgow in my black Hillman Minx car, by no means in its first youth, with my yellow labrador, Crisp, moulting profusely on the back seat. It was starting to snow heavily. I met the great man, installed him in the front seat and his detective, in a blue suit amidst Crisp's white hairs, in the back seat. Eventually we arrived at Douglas only to find that I had inadvertently collected an additional suitcase belonging to the then Chairman of the Scottish Conservative party, Menzies Anderson. 'He won't have a very comfortable night, poor fellow,' said Alec. The next morning it was still slowing heavily. All the other guns were snowed up. After Alec had dealt with various telephone calls from the Foreign Office two Land Rovers full of keepers drove up to the front door. We set off together to have a splendid day's shooting in a full blizzard. We got about forty head. I noticed that the Foreign Secretary slew everything that moved and some things that did not, such as the old cock grouse that was unwise enough to wait just too long before flying from the corn stack on which it was feeding.

The next year he became Prime Minister. I did not return to Douglas until January 1965 by which time he was Leader of the Opposition following the Labour victory in the 1964 election. Willie Whitelaw was there on that occasion. I well recollect a discussion about the method of selection for the next Conservative leader. Alec certainly felt that the way that he had been chosen, following Macmillan's illness when the traditional 'soundings' were taken among the senior figures in the party, was no longer appropriate. A new more open and democratic system of election must be devised. In due course Edward Heath was indeed elected as his successor, becoming Prime Minister in 1972.

I was at Douglas once again in 1974 following the miners' strike and the re-election of a Labour government. Once again Willie Whitelaw was present. It was clear that Heath would go as leader of the Conservatives and, with Alec's encouragement, Willie certainly aspired to be his successor. In the first leadership election under the new procedures that followed in 1975 it was of course Margaret Thatcher who came top of the ballot. Willie had not chosen to stand against Heath out of loyalty to his leader. But once Margaret had beaten Heath the way was clear for him to oppose her in the next round. As Cecil Parkinson reminded us in a recent television programme, 'It is easy to forget, thirty years on, how jaw-smackingly, gob-droppingly startling it was when a woman was elected as Conservative party leader.' Her political opponents saw it as a Tory suicide pact. Many in her own party took the same view. Even Norman Tebbit admitted that he would definitely have preferred a man with similar qualifications. 'It was widely felt that once she had lost the next general election, nature would return to its course and a man would take over as leader of the party,' said Matthew Parris, then a young researcher. 'The nickname we all used for her was Hilda, mocking her lower middle class origins, and it was not meant kindly.' But of course she did not lose, and like Tony Blair eighteen years later, she led her party to a resounding victory almost against their better instincts. When Jim Prior heard her extraordinary 'Where there is discord let me bring harmony' speech outside No 10 on the day following her election, he recalled that he was nearly sick on the spot!

One of the Collins family trustees who supported the management during the 1970 disagreements was a wise old lawyer, Alan Rees Reynolds. In 1978 he invited me to a small gathering in the City chaired by John King, the chairman of British Airways and a long-time admirer and supporter of Margaret Thatcher. She came to address this small invited gathering. She spoke for some forty minutes without a note expounding her vision for a Britain shorn forever of socialism and trade union domination. She looked marvellous. She had the technique of speaking alternately to right and left and looking directly into the eyes of the friendly face in the chair at 45 degrees. This happened to be me. I was vastly impressed. This was just before I was due to become Chairman of the CBI in Scotland. At the very first CBI conference in 1977 I had successfully moved a motion in favour of proportional representation. I believed that the entrenched and hostile attitude of 'bosses' and 'workers' was mirrored and accentuated by the political divide and that we needed to change the political structure if we were ever to achieve consensus and better industrial relations. How naive I was! When Mrs Thatcher finished speaking the first questioner asked about PR. She demolished him with, in my view, all the wrong arguments against PR. Her looks changed. All the charm, feminine appeal and sparkle of her earlier manner changed to the 'hand bagging', laser-eyed look and headmistress style for which she became so famously feared and caricatured. The contrast was startling. 'She can't get away with that,' said I to my host. 'I strongly advise you not to pursue the subject!' said he, shifting his chair well away from me. But I was unwise enough to ignore his advice, and shortly after asking a clumsily phrased supplementary question on the same topic received my first, but by no means my last 'Exocet' at the hands of The Lady.

Afterwards I was introduced to her for the first time. 'That is an important job you are going to do in Scotland,' she said, but then remembering her importunate questioner of a few minutes before and wagging her finger in that threatening way she had – 'but remember no more of that PR nonsense, no more of that PR nonsense!'

I had listened with fascination but with incredulity to her agenda for tackling socialism and militant trade unionism. Having been brought up in the printing industry I did not believe that those entrenched and powerful trade unions could be tackled head-on with success. It took several years and finally the miners' strike of 1985 to prove that she was right and that a whole generation of British industrial management, and many Conservative politicians too, had lacked the confidence, the courage and the belief to implement the Thatcher revolution.

The CBI had been formed in the 1960s by a merger of the two largest employers' organisations. It was seen as an essential counterbalance to the increasingly influential TUC in the Harold Wilson era of 'beer and sandwiches' at No 10. But by the early seventies it needed modernising and streamlining. The then President, Harold Watkinson, Chairman of Cadbury Schweppes and a former Minister in Harold Macmillan's Cabinet, charged two other distinguished members, Edwin Plowden and John Partridge, with producing a strategy. This was to set the pattern for the organisation for the next twenty years. It was known as the Plowden–Partridge report produced in 1974–5. This was the moment when I joined the council of the CBI for Scotland and for the next fifteen years I was increasingly involved in CBI affairs. At the time I knew neither of these great men, but our paths crossed later. I succeeded Lord Plowden as Chairman of the Senior Salaries Review Body responsible for advising the Prime Minister on top public servants' pay; and, as the seating round the General Accident Board table was arranged alphabetically, I was placed next to Sir John Partridge, then Chairman of Imperial Tobacco. He frequently seemed to have to leave meetings early, so passed his questions to me to ask after he had left. As a result I suspect that I got the credit for making far more intelligent and better informed points than I could have originated on my own!

In 1977 the CBI held its first National Conference at Brighton. This was designed to claim the attention of press and media after the party political conferences and to compete on equal terms for coverage with the TUC conference. But it was a learning experience. Businessmen were relatively unused to, and untrained in, the need to put their views across on radio and TV. Most of them were pretty bad at it; 'I worked my way rather than talked my way to the top' was a common attitude. The discipline of speaking succinctly, relevantly and effectively for no more than three minutes during a debate was a new challenge. The decision was taken not to invite senior politicians to speak at the early conferences on the grounds firstly that the CBI should be seen to be apolitical and secondly and more pragmatically that they would grab the headlines rather than the business leaders. Nevertheless the first conference was seen as a success and as I write these words twenty six years later the 2003 conference is taking place in Birmingham and I have just been listening to one of my sons-in-law, Melfort Campbell, as the incoming Chairman of CBI in Scotland, speaking on the radio. I am very proud of that. Rather depressingly though, so many of the issues on competitiveness being addressed today seem remarkably similar to those that worried us a quarter of a century ago!

At that first conference I spoke for the first time, little dreaming that I would be presiding as President ten years later. The firemen's strike was on at the time, one of the endless sequence of public sector disputes. I spoke about that but also managed to mention Scottish Devolution and my belief in Proportional Representation as a better electoral system than First Past the Post. I saw the institutionalised adversarial attitudes in industrial relations mirrored in adversarial two-party politics and yearned for the centre ground (so successfully captured from the Conservatives later on by Tony Blair's New Labour). I once got a private motion passed at a CBI conference to this effect, when I suspect everyone who would have opposed it was out having a coffee break. Someone told me that it was the only CBI resolution about which Margaret Thatcher was faintly interested. I was surprised at the time but judging by her violent reaction to my question on this topic, I should have known better.

The Institute of Directors had for a time held their annual jamboree in the Albert Hall every year, filling it with 5,000 people by attracting world class speakers. I attended once or twice before committing myself to the CBI. Basically the IOD represented small business. By and large it did not attract the key players, and was too politically right wing for my taste. But the Albert Hall certainly had the edge over Brighton and Blackpool and listening to the Governor of California, one Ronald Reagan, or HRH Prince Charles, brilliantly and funnily making his first major public speech aged about twenty, certainly had the edge on listening to a lot of the boring fare served up at early CBI conferences.

The CBI claims to be the voice of British Industry. By and large this is correct. It suits the press and media to have one acknowledged spokesman. Chambers of Commerce can be very effective locally but that is their role. They have no influence collectively. Organisations that are specific to individual industries such as the Engineering Employers Federation or the Retail Consortium have their own vital sectoral agendas. But on national issues it is the CBI that has and will continue to have the greatest influence and authority, and to whom Governments, Oppositions and their officials will wish to speak. The CBI has three separate roles. It acts firstly as a forum for debate among its members to exchange opinions and to form policies. Where this debate is in public as at the annual conference it also helps to inform and influence public opinion. Secondly it acts as a lobbying organisation. The visible side of this is in public too, through press and media, through meetings with politicians and through its policy pronouncements. But just as important is the work that constantly goes on behind the scenes with officials in Whitehall and the devolved assemblies to influence and correct bills and regulations during their passage through the legislative and government machinery. Many a subsequent government amendment to government bills has originated by CBI officials quietly and patiently explaining to civil servants the implications if alterations are not made. Finally the CBI provides a service to its members through advice and guidance on policies, legislation, regulations, the economy, foreign markets and industrial affairs. It serves British Industry well and has in its turn been well served by a succession of outstanding Director Generals.

This then was the organisation in which I became increasingly involved. I succeeded Alan Devereux as Scottish Chairman in September 1979. He had a penchant for outrageously colourful ties and an ability to make equally startling soundbite quotes, very different from me! We had a problem early on because Alan Stewart, the Scottish director, had been selected as Conservative candidate for West Renfrewshire and was spending far more time nursing his constituency than pursuing his CBI job. He was duly elected and later went on to become a Minister in the Scottish Office, where roles were reversed and he twice became my ministerial boss, once when I was Chairman of the Countryside Commission for Scotland in 1985, and once when I was Chairman of the Scottish Development Agency during its transition to becoming Scottish Enterprise in 1991. Here we crossed swords. He was deeply suspicious of the political motivation of one of the senior officials at the Agency and conducted something of a personal witch-hunt. He took to telephoning me late at night at home, and finally told me to sack the official concerned. I replied that he was welcome to sack me but that I had no intention of dismissing someone who was doing a very competent job. I went to see the Permanent Secretary at the Scottish Office and asked him to make sure that the Secretary of State for Scotland, Ian Lang, was aware of the circumstances. I heard no more of the matter.

As the replacement Director for the Scottish CBI Alan Devereux and I chose John Davidson, who made an outstanding success of the job for ten years until his early and tragic death from a heart attack in 1989. I gave the address at his funeral and recalled his splendid reply at his job interview. He too had had political ambitions and we did not want a second man to take his eye off the ball. I had asked him to assure us that he had no further intention to go into politics. His reply was that if he could become a junior minister right away he possibly would, but he had no intention of becoming a backbencher! Thus he neatly gave us his assurance while leaving us in no doubt about his self-confidence in his own abilities.

I learnt a lot during my two years as Chairman, meeting politicians, becoming involved with the Civil Service for the first time, somehow surviving the endless press, radio and TV appearances without apparently falling flat on my face, becoming more knowledgeable about the wider industrial and economic issues and always fighting the Scottish corner at Centre Point usually with the support of the splendid Director of CBI regions, Sonia Elkin. She could be quite formidable but met her match in my mother. Sonia once rang me while we on a fishing holiday on the Conon. My mother answered the telephone and made it very clear that no one, least of all someone from the CBI, was to bother me while I was on holiday. Few others would have dared to speak to Sonia in those terms!

The CBI had given up their rabbit warren of a building at Tothill Street, so convenient for Westminster and Whitehall, for the more sophisticated and much more expensive option of Centre Point, inconveniently situated for almost everywhere. If Sonia could not be persuaded of the special importance of Scotland on any particular issue then I would form a Celtic alliance with Sir Phillip Foreman of Short Brothers in Northern Ireland, who conveniently had a company aeroplane, and Emrys Evans, the Welsh Chairman. Few at the CBI could resist this combination, and they soon learnt to stop referring to Scotland, Northern Ireland and Wales as 'regions' like the various areas in England! Of course there was the social side too. It was not all work and Louise and I enjoyed the new experiences of dinners at Holyrood and endless other less prestigious social occasions. In between whiles we married our eldest daughter, Felicity, continued our happy family life at Renagour, and somehow survived the trials and tribulations at Collins.

By the autumn of 1980 British Business was becoming very disenchanted with the economy. North Sea oil had pushed the £/$ exchange rate to uncompetitive levels. Geoffrey Howe's budget with the introduction of VAT at 15 per cent to replace the old purchase tax but on a far wider range of goods was regarded as a disaster. John Methven had tragically died after a minor operation earlier in the year. I remember attending his memorial service in Westminster Abbey, the first occasion I had been to a service there.

He had been succeeded by Terry Beckett, formerly Chief Executive and then Chairman of the Ford Motor Company, who had caused the CBI Council some embarrassment in the seventies by granting high pay awards to Ford workers in breach of the Government's pay policy. His right to do so had however been stoutly defended by John. The CBI conference in November was very flat. Terry was about to make the traditional Director General's winding up speech. At a breakfast PR meeting some of those present said that his draft speech needed pepping up to send CBI members home in a more cheerful frame of mind. Terry's carefully crafted speech had contained the phrase: 'If we don't get what we want from government then we must go on knocking on their door.' 'Too weak,' said Michael Edwardes, the punchy little South African of British Leyland and 'Red Robbo' fame. 'You need something that will grab the headlines.' Thus was born the infamous phrase: 'We will give the Government a bare-knuckle fight.' Terry came to regret this and the Conservative leadership never forgave him. Indeed I detected some of the continuing suspicion when I became President myself six years later.

On his retirement in 1986 Terry was appointed a much-deserved KBE (he had been knighted in 1978 for his work at Ford's). I rushed across the corridor between our offices in Centre Point to congratulate him, only to find that he was bitterly disappointed that he had not been elevated to the House of Lords, as General Secretaries of the TUC such as Len Murray had been under the Labour Government. Terry was a longstanding champion for British Industry and despite his plain speaking a staunch supporter of most Conservative policies. In 1974 a previous Director General, Campbell Adamson, had been blamed for helping to lose the General Election by an injudicious remark and it is sad that perhaps this one remark of Terry's will be the one for which he is best remembered. He would have made an outstanding contribution to the Upper House.

I enjoyed my two years as Chairman of the CBI in Scotland, becoming increasingly involved with both politicians and civil servants. I became a member of the Scottish Economic Council where I probably learnt more than I contributed. The need for politicians to hear the blunt truth of current business experience and to be able to balance this against the fluently expressed views of the more esoteric economists is a very real one. I started to see for the first time the activities of other industries apart from the printing industry. North Sea Oil was coming on stream. Visits to the BP Forties oil rigs by helicopter were exciting. The sheer scale of the technology and the volumes of crude oil made a lasting impression. The benefits to our economy were obvious. Less apparent at first was the accelerating value of the pound against the dollar, at one point threatening to rise to three dollars to the pound. The 'petro-pound' as it was called made vast sections of traditional British manufacturing industry uncompetitive in world markets, sucked in imports, and led to the massive increase in unemployment in the eighties.

Visits to the nuclear power stations at Hunterston 'B' and Torness were equally fascinating. I remain of the view that nuclear power could have been the best long term answer to our energy requirements, and in this, as in much other public sector investment, we could have profitably followed the example of the French.

Throughout this time industrial relations continued to dominate my business life. At Collins' factories and distribution centres, where we were seeking to cut costs dramatically in order to survive, the powerful left-wing printing unions met us in bruising and exhausting confrontation. I have never had much stomach for conflict, always preferring compromise and negotiation, but there was no alternative. I did not enjoy it. At the CBI we were anxiously involved in seeking to influence the new Government's series of measures designed to prevent damaging strike actions by the Trades Unions. Sympathy strikes and secondary picketing were a menace. And yet I still did not fully understand or believe that the change that Thatcherism came to achieve was remotely possible.

I learnt to speak in public with confidence, rather enjoying the challenge posed by TV and radio interviews, conferences, seminars and dinners, though I lacked the intellectual ability ever to be original. Reading some of those speeches now they seem dated and dull. I probably took myself far too seriously. I have often felt privately that I was a bit of a fraud, pontificating second-hand views with an authority that led people to think that I was much abler than I actually was. As a result I found numerous approaches coming my way, as it became known that I was leaving Collins and would finish my two-year stint as CBI chairman in 1981. My last job of any significance at Collins was as Chairman of Pan Books. This was a role that rotated every year between the three joint owners, Heinemann's, Macmillan's and Collins.

Ambition is a curious emotion. I imagine that it must affect people very differently. My own experience is that I have never had any long term, visionary ambition for my life and career. I have been opportunistic in generally believing that one should almost always say yes to new openings and opportunities, go into them with wholehearted enthusiasm and commitment, enjoy the new challenges, do one's best, and hope that in so doing promotion, recognition and reward may follow. But I have always felt the need to be appreciated and hate doing poorly or being criticised. To that extent I suppose I am competitive. At Eton I vividly remember the moment when I became aware that I must stand a chance of being elected to 'Pop'. I minded about it very much. I would have been bitterly disappointed if it had not happened. But I kept this ambition very privately to myself, not even daring to mention it to my parents. At Sandhurst I went through the same emotions over being made the Senior Under Officer to my company. Again I was fortunate. In the army at platoon commanders' courses at both Hythe and Warminster I hoped for and eventually got the coveted 'A' gradings, which I was told would be influential to one's career. Then I left the army, and though for every family and personal reason this brought much happiness, a wonderful lifestyle and better prosperity, working for some one else's family business, where there was no possibility of ultimately getting to the top, did not satisfy my need for outside recognition. For years I watched with secret envy my army contempories being promoted and recognised. Secretly I knew that I might have hoped to become a General. Very privately, and not at all commendably, I was resigned to the fact that my ambition bug would not be fulfilled. So I would be less than honest if I did not admit that I was keenly aware that both my predecessors as Chairmen of the CBI in Scotland had been honoured with the award of a CBE. It was a great delight when I too received the CBE in the 1981 Birthday Honours.

The great point about honours is that they do indeed bring great joy to family, colleagues and friends. Everyone was exceptionally kind about it. I received hundreds of lovely letters often from people I had not seen for years. My father was eighty and only had a couple of years to live. I think his pride and that of my mother meant more to me than anything. In the event she was able to come with Louise and me to Buckingham Palace in November. Our daughters had their opportunity six years later!

At the Investiture you are herded with huge courtesy in the grandest imaginable surroundings into the appropriate 'pen' behind scarlet ropes, like priceless pedigree cattle in an auction market. There is time to spare before Palace officials brief you with charm and humour about the day's proceedings. Naturally you look around at the paintings and gilded ceilings before, as is human nature, you glance with discreet curiosity at your fellows, none of whom you have ever seen before. On the whole they looked a dull lot. No doubt they thought the same of me! Then at last I recognised someone. It was Peter May, the best cricketer of his generation, captain of England and a hero to all cricket lovers. I remembered seeing him make an exquisite late cut as a schoolboy playing for Charterhouse against Eton on Agar's Plough. I was a small thirteen-year-old passing by on my way to some undistinguished junior game. I had hero-worshipped him ever since. He looked as nervous and apprehensive as I felt. He was on his own so I went up to introduce myself. We sat down on two gold chairs and had a fascinating discussion about cricket for quarter of an hour. It was the only time I ever met him and he died all too young, but it is a memory I greatly treasure.

Thus, when I left Collins and finished my two years as Chairman of the CBI in Scotland, my career as an executive came to an end at the age of fifty-two. I did not know what path my life would take. Certainly I had no idea that by far the most interesting, varied and rewarding twenty years of my business life lay ahead.

CHAPTER 5

The Countryside Commission for Scotland
1983–1985

O NE DAY, when we were struggling with Collins' defence against Rupert Murdoch's takeover bid, I was in Ian Chapman's office in 14 St James's Place when a telephone call came through for me from a senior civil servant in the Scottish Office. Thinking that this must be connected with the bid I took the call, only to be asked whether I would be interested in becoming Chairman of The Countryside Commission for Scotland in succession to the very experienced and well-qualified Dr Jean Balfour. I knew little about this quango, which was charged with conserving the beauty of Scotland's countryside and providing facilities and opportunities for increased public access to it. It had been established by Act of Parliament in the 1960s along with its much larger sister The Countryside Commission for England and Wales. Its headquarters were in a large country house set in a beautiful garden at Battleby near Perth. It had a full time staff of about sixty.

The Director, almost since its inception fifteen years before, had been the well-liked and widely respected John Foster. Both he and Jean Balfour, who had been in joint harness for over ten years, welcomed this unknown and inexperienced import from the world of business with great courtesy and patience. For my part I was excited to be given my first chance to work in the public sector in an area which greatly appealed to me. Both Louise and I had an abiding love for Scotland's wonderful scenery and derived constant and lifelong joy from it, considering ourselves extremely fortunate to live in such a marvellous country. The opportunity, as I thought at the time, to give up a city commuter's life in my early fifties, to actually work in and for that environment seemed highly attractive. I saw myself with a part time job moving happily towards retirement and spending much more time at home. How wrong I was!

I had been a non-executive director of Scottish United Investors (subsequently the Edinburgh Investment Trust) and of General Accident, Scotland's largest composite insurance company, for several years, and felt that I would be able to cope with one or two other non-executive directorships. Almost simultaneously I was approached by Peter Balfour, the Chairman of Scottish and Newcastle (as it happened and by complete coincidence brother-in-law to Jean Balfour) and by Sir Robert Fairbairn, the Chairman of the Clydesdale Bank. Nowadays all non-executive appointments seem to have to be made at arm's length via headhunters and nomination committees of the board. Approaches directly by Chairmen in this way would be seen as politically incorrect and part of the 'old boy network'. I doubt if the more cumbersome and impersonal modern practice produces any better results, nor did I feel that my own independence to act in the interests of shareholders was in any way prejudiced by these personal approaches. I accepted both offers (little imagining that in time I would go on to become Chairman of both these companies) with the proviso that I could not take up my place on the boards until I retired from the CBI in September 1981. I also became a director of Radio Clyde, the new independent sound radio company for the West of Scotland, and here perhaps the relationship was a little incestuous for the Chairman was Ian Chapman, my friend and colleague at Collins. The Chief Executive was Jimmy Gordon, now Lord Gordon of Strathblane.

Another but rather different approach came from John Bute, Chairman of the National Trust for Scotland. He had enjoyed a highly successful partnership with the long serving and much loved Director Jamie Stormonth Darling. But he wanted to retire and hand over to a successor before the time came for Jamie to retire a year or so later. He indicated to me that I was the preferred choice and sought my reactions before taking discussions further with the Council. They wanted someone with a business background who had not previously been too much involved with the Trust in order to put the organisation on a firmer footing. I think that of all the opportunities I have had this would have given Louise the most interest and satisfaction. She loves history and heritage and would have enjoyed visiting many of the Trust's properties. But I did not feel that I was the right man for the job. I was too much of a philistine, insufficiently interested in the arts. In any case I had decided by then to accept the Countryside Commission, though my appointment had not been publicly announced.

It took effect on 1 January 1983. It was not long before I was plunged, almost literally, in at the deep end. The Falklands war was won in 1982. It did not take the Ministry of Defence long to conduct their post mortems and to conclude that Britain lacked a homegrown training area with suitably rugged terrain for training for the next Falklands war. Knoydart, that wild and magical stalking estate on the west coast of Inverness-shire, was on the market. It filled the bill perfectly. The MOD announced their intention to bid. John Knott was Secretary of State and Jerry Wiggin the Minister responsible. There was an instantaneous outcry in the Scottish press and media from environmentalists, hill walkers and Uncle Tom Cobley and all. The Ministry countered by claiming that some of the best conservation took place on Salisbury plain as the public had restricted access to field firing ranges. They seemed a little hurt when it was pointed out that there were considerable differences between Wiltshire and the West Highlands.

Anyway the upshot was that a site visit was arranged for everyone with an axe to grind. About thirty of us assembled on Mallaig pier on a wild wet January morning prior to embarking on the *Western Isles*, colloquially known, as it was a Sunday, as the 'Minister's boat'. After a violent tossing some very seasick passengers were deposited on the jetty at Inverey. The Laird, Nigel Chamberlayne-Macdonald, met us. He swept the Minister and his VIP guests, Jean Balfour and Jamie Stormonth Darling, off to the Kirk. It did not appear to me that I was to be included in this exalted company. The rest of us were invited to queue in drenching rain outside the factor's office, waiting to be assigned to our billets. I was near the back. It was very wet. At last I reached the desk. 'Name?' 'Nickson,' I stuttered between chattering teeth. 'Oh. You shouldn't be here. You're in the big house.' So there I found myself in due course standing in front of a roaring fire, glass of sherry in hand, feeling much happier, when the others returned from the Kirk.

For the next thirty-six hours we were well entertained and well educated on the precarious finances of a remote highland estate. It had previously been owned by the Brocket family and, before them, by the Crosthwaite-Eyres, before it was bought and sold on quickly by Lord Hesketh. The Chamberlayne-Macdonalds had owned it for about ten years. It clearly had strong historical appeal quite apart from its value as a magnificent deer forest, for Nigel was indeed Macdonald of the Isles. He told us that when he had bought the estate it had an annual loss of around £100,000. The management plan had been to spend another £1 million over the purchase price on capital improvements, including its own hydroelectric plant and a refurbished boat, in order to achieve a break even after five years. Now, some eight years later, with inflation through the seventies in double figures, the capital expenditure had been £5 million and the revenue deficit had risen to £250,000! This brought home to me very forcibly the reason why most highland estates change hands every generation and why they are completely unviable without the constant annual input of wealth from industry, the city or from overseas. Much was made of the welfare of the seventy or so crofting families on the Knoydart peninsula should it be purchased as a field firing range. It was pointed out that only two or three of these families were indigenous crofters with roots going back for more than one generation. The rest were all recent incomers.

At one moment I was taken by car across a rough track by Nigel Macdonald to the far side of the peninsula. The other occupants were John Foster, the Director of the Countryside Commission, and Alan Sellars, the Provost of Inverness. The rain continued to teem down. I was more interested than I should have been in spying some of the heavy stags we saw than listening to the endless discussion on the future of the peninsula. I had already made up my own mind that it would be a disaster for this uniquely rugged and beautiful mountainous area to become a live-firing army training area. Nor could I believe that it would be wise for the National Trust for Scotland with their limited and stretched management and financial resources to assume such a huge liability. Then we got a puncture. We were hours from the house on foot. So the two ex-guardsmen, Chamberlayne-Macdonald and Nickson, proceeded to change the wheel, still in a drenching icy cold downpour, while John Foster and the Provost sat in the back seat.

The next morning the gale had reached such a pitch that the Inverey pier could not be used. The boat crept in a mile further west under some shelter and hove-to while we were boarded three at a time from a rowing boat. Margaret Denny, a septuagenarian veteran of the National Trust with a gammy leg, put us all to shame with her remarkably cheerful fortitude. I then drove Nigel at a furious pace to put him on the London train at Crianlarich before arriving back at Renagour wondering if the rest of my time at the Countryside Commission was going to be quite as exciting. We had reached no firm conclusions on the future of Knoydart, though there was little support for the MOD. A few days later some of us were summoned to a meeting at the Army Headquarters at Kirkliston. I was actually en route when I was telephoned to say that Michael Heseltine had succeeded John Knott as Secretary of State that morning and had immediately ordered his officials to drop the whole idea! He realised at once that the political downside in Scotland was considerable and the military advantages at least questionable. Knoydart was subsequently sold privately and split up into two or three separate estates.

This was an exciting introduction to the Countryside Commission. Life did not often continue at that pace. I had a good board comprising a wide variety of talent and experience in rural affairs. We met once a month at Battleby. I probably spent one other day a week there interspersed with visits to Country Parks, long distance walking routes such as the West Highland or Southern Upland Ways, and project sites where we were being asked to invest public money. I often wondered whether it was right for me to be paid out of taxpayers' funds to have so much fun and to have the opportunity to travel anywhere in Scotland usually in delightful company and always in superb scenery. John Foster was a wise, thoughtful and dedicated Director. Always considerate of such an inexperienced Chairman his advice was invariably sound. For the first time I had to cope with the vast volume of paper generated by the public sector. When Civil Servants have to look over their shoulders to the Audit Office and the Public Accounts Committee it seems necessary to cover every possible eventuality on paper in advance. Relatively minor projects require ten pages where a single sheet would suffice in the private sector to provide Board members with all the facts they need to make up their minds. As a result the time necessary to prepare conscientiously for meetings places a greater burden on members of Public Boards even if the real responsibility for direct control of the issues involved may be much greater in the private sector.

The main topics during my short time at the CCS were the development of the network of Country Parks, Regional Parks and the ever present long term ambition for National Parks for Scotland; the creation of long distance walking routes; the funding of the Countryside Ranger service; and in cooperation with Local Authorities the provision of facilities for improved public access and visitor interpretation. We were frequently consulted on planning issues. There was a reasonably close relationship with the Nature Conservancy Council, a UK body with a Scottish Advisory Committee, and discussion on policy issues with the much larger Countryside Commission for England and Wales.

My views on National Parks were conditioned by John Foster. He had been director of the Peak District National Park and clearly saw the advantages of combined planning powers where areas of outstanding natural beauty lie close to areas of high population. I believed that there was a strong case for a Scottish National Park for Loch Lomond where there were two Local Government Regional planning authorities and no fewer than four District authorities making it almost impossible to achieve any degree of consensus. But I was much more doubtful about the advantages or necessity for other areas like the Cairngorms or Kintail. My view was that the then Conservative government could easily have brought in the necessary legislation with a fair measure of public support for a Loch Lomond Park while putting the question of other Scottish Parks on the back burner for ten years. This could have had political advantages, while providing Loch Lomond with all the much needed advantages of Park status ten to fifteen years earlier than Donald Dewar's eventual decision when Labour came to power in 1997. Much could have been learned about the operation of a National Park in the Scottish context, and perhaps some of the controversy and mistakes made in establishing the Cairngorms National park avoided.

In a different way my views on the running of the countryside met with a quicker response. It seemed strange to me that by accident of legislative timing there were quite separate bodies with responsibility for conserving the beauty of Scotland's countryside, while encouraging and managing access, and for the fauna and flora that existed in that countryside which were subject to the pressures created by that access. In most countries of the world the same authority controls wild life and parks. The year after I retired from the CCS I was asked by Jamie Bruce, then Scottish Chairman of the Royal Society for the Arts, to give a lecture in the Burrell Gallery entitled 'A vision for Scotland's Country-side in the future'. I chose 2020 as my vision year on the grounds that I would not be around to be proved wrong! Among other topics I floated the idea that the CCS should be merged with the Nature Conservancy Council in Scotland. This caused some surprise to my successor Roger Carr and his colleagues, who were in the audience, but I hoped they took what was a kite flying exercise in good part!

However the very next morning I was attending a meeting of the Scottish Economic Council in St Andrews House in Edinburgh. Gavin Macrone, the economic adviser, asked me how I knew that secret meetings were already taking place on this issue in the Scottish Office. He was convinced that I had been put up to making an inspired leak in modern approved 'spin' fashion. A few moments later Malcolm Rifkind, who had recently succeeded George Younger as Secretary of State, entered the room and said to me with his delightful grin, 'It does not take some Secretaries of State twenty five years to make these decisions, you know!' Much later he told me that Nicholas Ridley, who was Secretary of State for the Environment, had been strongly advised by his officials and by the Nature Conservancy Council not to allow responsi-bility for nature conservation within the UK to be split up. A hen harrier, for example, should be under the same authority either side of the Scottish border, ran the argument. But Nick Ridley said he was fed up with the Scots, who were always troublesome, and if Malcolm Rifkind wanted to go it alone, let him have his head. So the two Secretaries of State jointly took the matter through Cabinet. Shortly afterwards Nick Ridley had to resign following some trenchant remarks he had made about the Germans. Chris Patten succeeded him. The Civil Servants and the NCC returned to the attack, seeking to reopen the issue, but Malcolm Rifkind responded robustly by saying that the decision had already been taken in Cabinet and it was too late. Thus was Scottish Natural Heritage born. My involvement was actually marginal and coincidental. But some of my friends did not believe this at the time, and there are certainly those today, judging on its current performance, who may not now feel that its conception was altogether a good idea!

I was keen that the Headquarters of the new body should be at Battleby, which is ideally situated for a countryside agency in beautiful surroundings and as convenient as possible for travel from all over Scotland. I suggested this to the first Chairman, Magnus Magnusson, when he came to lunch with me at Scottish Enterprise on taking office. He expressed the view that it was vital for SNH to be based in Edinburgh for easy communication with Ministers and Civil Servants. I wonder if he or his successor would now agree following the recent extraordinarily idiotic political decision to relocate in Inverness. If they had kept the Headquarters at Battleby in the first place they would probably still be there!

William Wilkinson was Chairman of the NCC. He had been appointed in 1983 after his predecessor Ralph Verney had been unfairly sacked by Michael Heseltine over his defence of the Severn Levels. His appointment was a great joy to me for his father, Denys, and mine had been close friends as housemasters at Eton. Denys had taken over his house from another of my father's great friends, John Upcott, and had married someone with an even brighter classical brain than his own. So it was scarcely surprising that William had a brilliant intellect, becoming Captain of the School at Eton and Major Scholar at Trinity. He was two years younger than me but as boys we had shot partridges together with our fathers near Eton and wigeon and white-fronted geese on the marshes opposite Llanelly where the Wilkinsons had a cottage on the Gower peninsula. His father had taught me for my last two years at school in a class called 'Classical General', which meant you were not clever enough to be a proper classical scholar. I now remember far more

of what I learnt more from him about birds and how to play bowls on
his lawn at Keate House than I do about Homer or Virgil.

Since those early days William and I had lost touch. He had a
distinguished career, first at Borax, then at Lonrho where he had
famously and courageously stood up to Tiny Rowland; then, later, he
became a director of Kleinwort Benson. He was treasurer of the RSPB
where he put the finances on a firm footing from which they have never
looked back. So we met again as colleagues nearly forty years later and
for the remainder of my time at the Countryside Commission for
Scotland we resumed our old family friendship and saw a lot of each
other. It was a dreadful tragedy that he went blind after heart surgery
while still in office and died in 1996. He had been knighted in 1989, two
years after me. (We felt that our fathers might have been pretty surprised,
had they known this lay in store for us, when we were two small boys
learning to shoot together.) William of course was in favour of a
continuing UK wide role for Nature Conservation and felt strongly that
it was a mistake to hive off the Scottish responsibility to SNH. So on
that subject we did not agree.

I was present when he opened the Ben Eighe Nature Reserve in 1985
and we had a delightful trip to the Isle of Rhum together in company
with John Arbuthnot, former Chairman of the NCC Scottish Advisory
Council and a colleague of mine on the Board of the Clydesdale Bank.
By that time I was Chairman of Scottish and Newcastle and they thought
I might have some ideas as to what to do about their celebrated white
elephant Kinloch Castle! We had fun looking at the nesting colony of
shearwaters and the red deer on the hill but found no solution to the
problem of the castle. I was amused to see on TV only recently, twenty
years later, that the castle featured as one of the BBC's 'Great Restoration'
projects with an estimated bill of over £5 million. It should never have
belonged to the public sector in the first place and thus become a burden
on overstretched conservation budgets. It was a magnificent demonstra-
tion of Victorian affluence derived from a Midlands textile fortune. How
poignant to see hinds grazing peacefully round the Parthenonesque
mausoleum on the south side of the island where two generations of the
Bullough family are buried.

Another trip with John Foster was to Shetland, prospering dramatically
as a result of North Sea Oil revenues. Louise came with me on this
occasion. We stayed at Busta House. I visited the old walled stables for
the Shetland ponies, the remains of the great herring processing factories
from the heydays of the herring industry, the Mousa broch, all of which

had received or needed funding for the conservation of heritage sites, and of course Sullam Voe, the mighty oil terminal which most assuredly did not. On one expedition to the isles of Yell and Unst in a Shetland Islands Council Range Rover we were driving south in thick mist. I was in the back seat when, glancing out of the window at the endless expanse of bleak and barren landscape, I thought I saw a snowy owl standing beside a rock. I knew there were one or two on the neighbouring island of Fetlar so it was not totally improbable. 'Stop!' I shouted to the astonishment of the Shetland Island officials. John Foster was by then somewhat more used to what he would have termed my 'unchairmanic' behaviour so was less surprised. It was politely pointed out that we would miss the last ferry to Yell and condemned to spend the night on Unst. I said I couldn't care less. I wanted to realise a lifetime's ambition to see a snowy owl. 'But our snowy owls are on Fetlar,' they said incredulously, 'and we've never seen one ourselves.' 'Well you will now,' I replied, 'otherwise I'll get out and swim home.' They turned about and there she was only fifty yards from the road and so beautiful. My stock went up a bit after that. We caught the ferry with seconds to spare. The next day I was off duty. Louise and I hired a car and drove all the way back in the hope that we could find the owl for her to see. Alas, it had gone. We spent the day trudging gloomily about in the driving drizzle.

I never got to St Kilda. The National Trust for Scotland invited me to take a spare seat on their helicopter trip one July. I was very excited at the prospect of seeing the island. I left our house in Ross-shire at 6 a.m. only to find that Inverness Airport was in thick fog. We sat about gloomily for two or three hours until eventually the trip was cancelled.

By 1985 I had been Chairman of Scottish and Newcastle Breweries (as it then was) for a couple of years and had been asked if I would succeed James Cleminson as President of the CBI, though this was not public knowledge. My career seemed almost irresistibly to be leading me back into industry. I was finding it less and less easy to find the time to devote to the Countryside Commission which the role demanded. I had only been there two years and was only just beginning to acquire the necessary knowledge and experience. Clearly the time was coming when I was likely to be appointed for a second term. Equally clearly it would be an impossibility to accept the CBI job and still to remain at the CCS. John Foster had retired and his successor was not turning out too promisingly. Sadly I came to the conclusion that I should ask George Younger, the Secretary of State, to let me stand down at the end of my third year. I went to see him and he was his usual charming and understanding self. I was sad to say farewell to a job that was after my own heart and to colleagues who had been so kind and helpful to me. Roger Carr, my Vice Chairman, succeeded me and did a fine job until the eventual merger with the Nature Conservancy Council to form Scottish Natural Heritage.

CHAPTER 6

Scottish and Newcastle plc
1981–1989

Y ARRIVAL AT my first Scottish and Newcastle Board meeting at
their Head Office at Holyrood, where the new Scottish Parliament
building is now being constructed at astronomical cost, was scarcely
auspicious. From time to time throughout my life I have suffered from
back trouble. Occasionally this has been dramatic. I was aware that I had
tweaked my back a few days before. Sometimes this would right itself
after a few days, sometimes it was a prelude to something more serious.
As I rose to acknowledge Peter Balfour's welcoming words to his new
Non Executive Director I was seized by a violent spasm and finished up
writhing on the floor under the boardroom table. Doctors and nurses
were summoned and I was sent home lying flat in the back of a Mercedes
shooting brake with a staff nurse in attendance in the front seat. She
seemed somewhat cold and monosyllabic until I asked her if she had ever
had back problems herself, whereupon she confessed to having been
invalided home from Kuwait by air when, serving as a matron, she had
joined the nurses doing a can-can during the Christmas party and also
finished flat on the floor! After that the ice thawed and we got on much
better.

It soon became clear to me that there had been more to my
recruitment as a director than was first apparent and that I was being lined
up as Peter's successor as Chairman. The company was in the doldrums.
The share price languished and the dividend yield was high. It was hard
to find a kind word about the company or its management in the
financial press. We were touted at least once a week as the next prime
takeover target. We were the smallest and most vulnerable of 'the big six'
national brewers. The others were Bass, Allied, Whitbread, Grand
Metropolitan and of course Guinness. Later on after I became Chairman,
these major competitors cautiously eyed me up as Peter Balfour's
unknown successor. The old establishment represented by Derek Palmer
of Bass, Derek Holden Brown of Allied and Charles Tidbury of
Whitbread regarded me as a potential ally against the perceived
ungentlemanly competitive attitudes displayed by two other incomers

from outside the industry. These were Ernest Saunders of Guinness, who had come in from the Swiss giant Nestlé, and Allen Sheppard of Grand Metropolitan, now Lord Sheppard of Didgemere, who came from the motor industry. They all realised quite soon that I intended my role to be strictly non-executive and that any threat to their established positions by S&N would come, not from me, but from the young turks who succeeded to the senior executive positions. Nevertheless the brewing industry in those days was still highly congenial and both from the 'big six' and the larger regional brewers such as Greenall Whitley, Vaux and Greene King, and from Bulmers the cider company, I received kind welcomes and hospitality. The brewers seemed to spend much time taking or owning good shooting for the purpose of corporate entertaining. But far from inviting customers they seemed mostly to entertain each other. I gradually came to realise the somewhat incestuous nature of the industry in that they were indeed all each other's customers anyway. This certainly never stopped me from accepting and greatly enjoying the many shooting invitations that came my way!

S&N had been very successful in the sixties and early seventies marketing its brands to the free trade, but it lacked a tied house estate outside Scotland and the North East, traditional beer consumption was falling, it lacked an established lager brand and had serious industrial relations problems. Above all there was a lack of confidence in the Chief Executive who had been recruited from outside the industry to succeed Peter Balfour. Many difficult decisions had already been taken, such as the dispersal of distribution depots to weaken the hold of the Union militants, the creation of new lager brands and the acquisition of Thistle hotels. But future strategy was unclear, borrowings were high, and above all there was dissension within the Board and considerable unhappiness among senior executives.

I asked a great friend of mine, Gordon Simpson, who had been deputy chairman of the Stock Exchange, for his advice about taking on the Chairmanship under these circumstances. 'Well,' he said, 'you are either much braver or even stupider than I know you to be.' Moral: don't ask advice if you don't intend to take it!

We had an unhappy few months. There were leaks to the press directly after Board meetings, a most uncomfortable situation for us all as we eyed up our colleagues, most of whom were still unknown quantities to me. The only other two Non Executives were David Airlie, then the head of Schroder's, our merchant bankers, and subsequently my Chairman at General Accident, a man of huge distinction, Lord

Chamberlain to the Queen and countless other high offices, related by marriage to Peter; and Lewis Robertson, at that time Chief Executive to the Scottish Development Agency. He would have been the obvious candidate to become Chairman and, I suspect, would have liked to do so but in the circumstances was not acceptable to our colleagues. Peter consulted us before taking the brave decision to sack the Chief Executive, require the suspect 'leaker' to resign from the Board and to reassume the Chief Executive's role himself for at least a year. I was due to go on a farewell trip with Louise to say goodbye to our colleagues and friends in Collins following my retrial as an executive. Peter asked me to agree to being named as his Vice Chairman and potential successor along with other announcements during my absence abroad. This I did.

The question was who should succeed Peter as Managing Director? I had ruled myself out from the start. I knew nothing about the brewing industry and did not seek another executive career. Another appointment from outside so soon after a spectacular failure was never a starter. So we were back to the four inside executive directors who were considered possibles. Two of them had been in the company for a relatively short time: Bernard Kilkenny, a man of great experience in brewing and considerable intelligence, but had he the leadership qualities? And Chris Chalmers, the financial director, he was young, very bright, very ambitious, but did he know enough about the industry and could he take his colleagues with him? Two had been in the company all their working lives, both as it happened Etonians, almost the only two who had survived the 'politically correct' purge of traditional young brewers carried out through McEwen Youngers and Newcastle breweries by an overzealous personnel department in the seventies. Gavin Reed had strong family ties in the business and had, I was told, been viewed as the front-runner until a health hiccough a few years before. He had great style, great enthusiasm and was an extremely nice man. But was he tough enough? Finally there was Alick Rankin, the marketing director. He was certainly tough enough, had wide experience in the company, was financially astute, never afraid to state his mind and indeed had just given David Airlie a torrid time for failing to get a grip of the situation as a Non Executive. He had lots of friends in the City of London, but could he be too volatile?

Over the next few months I came to know them all and spent time with each of them. Eventually I went down to stay a night with Peter Balfour at his home outside Edinburgh after a Board meeting to discuss the issue. I thought he would favour Christopher Chalmers. I ran through the pros and cons for each of the four candidates in turn, eventually concluding with my firm recommendation for Alick. Peter was silent for a few moments. He could look very formidable. Eventually he said, 'I agree with every word you have spoken.' So Alick it was. The rest is history. Alick showed outstanding flair and leadership, pulling Scottish and Newcastle up the Brewers league table, restoring its fine reputation, taking it into the FTSE 100 and eventually fighting off a bitterly contested Australian take-over bid. It was widely acknowledged that he was the outstanding Scottish businessman of the decade. All his colleagues reacted loyally to his appointment and each of them gave him outstanding support. When I took over the Chair from Peter in September 1983 I inherited a united Board, firm in their resolve to succeed and to retain the company's independence. And so it remained for the next six years until, on reaching the agreed retirement age of sixty, I handed over to Alick.

We had our difficulties. Just before Peter retired he was approached by James Gulliver of Argyll, the drinks and supermarket chain, asking us to agree to a merger. Alick and I had dinner at Prestonfield House with James Gulliver and his financial director Alastair Grant (who went on to run Safeway and eventually to become Governor of the Bank of Scotland and indeed Chairman of Scottish and Newcastle in succession to Alick, before they both so tragically died from cancer within a year or two of each other). James Gulliver was a buccaneer with a lifestyle to match; but he had a successful reputation in the City. We replied to his none too delicate propositions that we were both new at the helm of S&N and were determined to go it alone. Shortly afterwards he bid for the Distillers Company, thus triggering the celebrated counter bid from Guinness and the ultimate downfall of their Chief Executive Ernest Saunders and a number of his financial allies. But that is another story.

Peter Balfour had initiated the strategy to tackle the institutionalised trade union militancy of the 1970s by seeking to break up the large distribution depots into smaller more decentralised units, and to him should go the credit for the steady improvement in relations with the unions and the workforce through the 1980s. But the culture of knee-jerk heavy-handed strike action to any dispute remained. The anticipated capitulation by management had usually followed. By 1984 we were starting to see profitability improving, levels of borrowing set to fall and the prospect of channelling much needed new investment into our Thistle Hotel chain. Suddenly the new Executive was faced with a game of Russian roulette. A supervisor at a soft drinks plant outside

Newcastle caught an operative urinating against a tank in the building. It was one man's word against another's. The operative was fired. The Transport and General Workers Union backed him. The Newcastle Brewery and all the distribution depots went on strike. On a different pretext all the Scottish operations came out two days later. A week passed before our next Board meeting. We were told that the cost to the company would be over £1 million a week if the strike continued. We could see our hard won improvement in profits vanishing like snow off the proverbial dyke, plunging us once more into crisis. The management under Alick never even blinked. It was showdown time. Three days later the TGWU officials backed off. Never again was there a confrontation on this scale.

Thistle Hotels began to prosper under Ian Hannah. The beer businesses continued to provide good results under Gavin Reed, Bernard Kilkenny and Alastair Mowatt. Eventually we acquired the 'third leg' that was part of our strategy by buying Pontin's holiday camps and with them the services of a quite remarkable entrepreneur called Trevor Hemmings.

Growth by acquisition started to become a possibility. One of our first targets was the North Eastern brewery of Camerons owned by Ellermans. The Barclay brothers, David and Fred, then relatively unknown, prior to the building of their huge empire including the Ritz Hotel and, more recently, the *Daily Telegraph*, were involved. They were just as secretive and shy of publicity then as they are now. I was told that they required a meeting with the Chairman before they did business with us. So Gavin Reed and I met them in a private room for dinner at Brown's Hotel. We had a reasonably congenial evening and were just getting down to concluding our discussions when they each produced two of the largest cigars I have ever seen, nearly a foot long. The room became shrouded in smoke. Suddenly we were deafened by the hotel fire alarms shrilling throughout the building. Waiters rushed in and everyone was very publicly hustled into the street. We stood there chatting amicably away until the Barclay brothers' Rolls Royce appeared. They did not seem at all put out by any loss of privacy!

Our next venture was in the North West. We bid for Matthew Brown. This was fiercely contested by their Chief Executive Pat Townsend and rapidly became a very political and public struggle. It developed into a trial of strength between two equally combative Chief Executives with all the public sympathy in favour of the underdog. The Office of Fair Trading examined the bid prior to a possible referral to the Monopolies and Mergers Commission. Alec Fletcher was our Edinburgh

MP but he was also the Minister responsible for competition policy at the Department of Trade and Industry. He arranged for Alick and me to see the Secretary of State, Norman Tebbit, who had only recently returned to duty after being seriously injured by the IRA bomb in Brighton. We were his first appointment that morning and we saw him limp into his office as we waited outside. He greeted us courteously by saying that he was prepared to listen to our arguments as to why the bid should not be referred to the MMC but we should not expect him to make any response or comment whatsoever. He would take advice and consider the matter. I kicked off before passing the ball to Alick. He said that we had been most careful to seek advice both from our sponsoring Ministry, the Ministry of Agriculture, and from the Scottish Office, neither of whom had given us any reason to think that competition policy would be infringed if our bid were to proceed. Norman Tebbit instantly banged the table, silencing Alick in mid sentence. 'MAFF and the Scottish Office,' he spat out contemptuously. 'What the hell do you think they know about my mind on competition policy! You might as well come here and ask me when to plant your spring barley!' The IRA had done nothing to quench his inimitable style.

Eventually the bid proceeded. We were told by our advisers as the closing date approached that it would be very close. Many institutional investors and most private shareholders in the North East would be loyal to Matthew Brown. We lost by less than 1 per cent. A few thousand shares would have done the trick. We were downcast. The Press were jubilant. Alick had staked his reputation on this bid and worked tirelessly to achieve success. Thinking that like Drake before the Armada he had done all he could he took the previous day off to shoot in Hampshire. Perhaps one more effort in the City might have done the trick? I knew this but I don't think he was ever aware that I knew! The next morning he came into my office and offered his resignation. I refused to accept it. He persisted. I agreed to consult Hew Hamilton-Dalrymple, the Vice Chairman, who was a tower of strength to me until his retrial in December 1985 and for whom we both shared great respect and affection. Hew agreed with me. So rather unusually I won an argument with Alick and he withdrew his resignation.

A year later, from the base of our substantial share holding, bought during the course of the bid, we were successful in acquiring Matthew Brown. I have always thought that if a bid fails it is rather unfair on the management, who have successfully defended, that the aggressor should be able to bid again from a large shareholding base twelve months later.

Like snakes and ladders I believe the bidder should go back to square one! But I am well aware that this would not wash with the City or institutional shareholders. I think I was conditioned by Murdoch's eventual takeover of Collins. I certainly had a secret sympathy for Matthew Brown but I was at pains to disguise this from my colleagues. This was our first successful breakout from the strategic straitjacket in which the company had been held. From this moment on all our efforts started to meet with success, management's tails were up and they started to believe that by following Alick's confident leadership anything was possible.

Michael Falcon was one of Matthew Brown's non-executive directors. He was the Chairman of the Norwich Union, our own largest shareholder. Early on in my chairmanship I had called to see the investment manager at their grand headquarters in Norwich. I had certainly failed to contradict the assumption that I had come down from Scotland especially for this purpose. Michael came in to lunch and we immediately hit it off. Afterwards he volunteered to show me out to my car via the impressive boardroom and staircase. 'Tell me,' he said as we walked down the stairs, 'where are you shooting tomorrow? Nobody comes to Norfolk on a Friday unless they are shooting somewhere on the Saturday!' Of course he was right. We became firm friends on the spot and, despite being on opposite sides during the takeover battle, have remained so ever since.

Three other S&N executive directors should be mentioned. Henry Fairweather was the first person to achieve Board level having joined the company through the graduate recruitment programme in the early seventies. He became Human Resources Director. His wise head and unruffled manner created calm and trust not only throughout the group in his own area of responsibility but also round the boardroom table.

Christopher Chalmers swallowed any disappointment he may have felt over not getting the top job, backed Alick to the hilt with sound financial advice but never lost his belief in his own potential. Tragically he contracted cancer in his early fifties and died all too suddenly. Shortly before he became ill I had a conversation with him about his future career. He wanted operating responsibility for one of the major divisions. I said that this was certainly a possibility but that in my opinion it would be wrong for him to combine this with his present role of financial director. Alternatively, if his mind was set on becoming the Chief Executive of a major plc, sad though we would be to lose him, he would need to look outside S&N. I asked him whom he would recommend as his successor as financial director if he did decide on an operating role. I expected him to mention one of a number of able accountants in the beer companies. Unhesitatingly he named Brian Stewart. So when Chris became ill and died, we were able to tell Brian that he was not only the Board's choice but also that of his predecessor. Brian at that time was a young accountant in corporate planning, very bright, imaginative and creative with a delightful smile and sense of humour, but he was nobody's pushover. Not surprisingly he made a huge success of the job, eventually following Alick as Chief Executive and in due course Chairman and, later, to a CBE and then a well deserved Knighthood. He became Chairman of Standard Life and holds many other appointments.

By 1988 the company was prospering and gaining a good reputation in the City at long last. Thistle Hotels were earning a good operating profit and we were proud of their performance, but their asset value had escalated out of all proportion. So we were ripe for the next round of takeover speculation. Sure enough it arrived in the form of John Elliot of Elder's, the Australian company that had acquired Courage from Imperial Tobacco. His stockbroker, Richard Westmacott, asked me to meet him in his offices in St James's Street, only a hundred yards across the road from our own London office at No 7 St James's Place. He explained that in his view neither Courage nor Scottish and Newcastle had the strength or the brands to compete alone with the other big brewers but that together they certainly could. He said that he had no sufficiently experienced senior management and that our senior people would run the business and could more or less write their own blank cheques for remuneration and share options. He did not say that Elder's holding company, Harlin, was seriously over borrowed and they needed to strip out our assets!

I undertook to consult our board, which I did. The reaction was immediate and robust. We told them that we were not interested in further discussions. We prepared for action stations. Sure enough the early morning telephone call came before long. I remember taking it before I was dressed beside my bed at Renagour and immediately afterwards John Elliot telephoned Alick. Seconds later we were talking to each other and calling an immediate board meeting. The strategy was clear. Our first line of defence was to play the Scottish card. Control of Scotland's largest commercial company headquartered in Edinburgh, could not be allowed to pass to Australia. Politicians, press and public were rallied behind the demand for an Office of Fair Trading enquiry followed by a referral to the Monopolies and Mergers Commission. Alick cleared his decks, handed over all operating management to his colleagues and proceeded to mount a brilliant campaign, which led eventually to the referral and six months later to a ruling from the MMC against the takeover. We had great support from Ian Lang, the Secretary of State for Scotland, and through him no doubt some sympathy from the Secretary of State for Trade and Industry and possibly also from No 10. We also had very good advisers, merchant bankers, stockbrokers and financial public relations consultants but in retrospect the prize for effective performace must go to our legal advisers Linklaters, so ably partnered by our quiet, calm and delightful company lawyer and secretary Michael Peary. All Elder's intelligence had anticipated a green light for their bid. Elliot's comment as reported to me later by Alec Fletcher was, 'My God, they've crucified us!' And this was indeed the effect both on Elder's as a company and John Elliot as a businessman, for their unorthodox financing and certain legal enquiries in Australia came home to roost. Whether we would have survived if the bid had been decided in the marketplace we shall never know.

For Alick it was a personal triumph. Both he and S&N continued to prosper. Thistle Hotels were sadly but inevitably sold at the very top of the market and one third of the proceeds reinvested in Centre Parcs to produce the same operating profit, thanks to the influence and business contacts of Trevor Hemmings. Eventually we were able to acquire Courage's brewing business to create the new brewing division of 'Scottish Courage' so turning the tables on our former aggressor. My own time as Chairman came to an end in 1989 and I retired on my sixtieth birthday as I had always said that I would. But I was asked to remain on the board as a non-executive for a further five years, so I was able to enjoy at first hand seeing my colleagues continue to enjoy increasing success under Alick's chairmanship.

Two very different personal memories of the takeover battle remain with me. In both I was sitting alone late in the evening in the office that Alick and I shared in St James's Place when the telephone rang. On the first occasion it was a correspondent from *The Times*. 'Would I comment on the fact that National Australia Bank, the owners of the Clydesdale Bank of which I was a director, were part of the underwriting syndicate for Elder's bid?' 'That is the first I had heard of it.' 'Would I resign immediately?' 'I will have to consider the matter.' My problem was not whether I would resign from the Bank; it was clear to me instantly that I should do so. But Eric Yarrow, the Chairman, was at that moment in mid air flying out to a board meeting in Melbourne. I knew I could not

Chairman: Scottish & Newcastle Breweries plc 1983–89

contact him for twenty-four hours and felt I had to tell him first. Overnight I spoke to Nobby Clark, the Chief Executive of the National Australia Bank. He confirmed, somewhat apologetically, that the Bank was indeed supporting John Elliot in Australia. I told him that I was resigning from the Clydesdale but it was too late to avoid *The Times* headline next morning: 'CHAIRMAN OF S&N DITHERS OVER RESIGNATION.'

It was very large minded of NAB and Eric Yarrow not only to invite me back onto the Clydesdale board some eighteen months later, but also to appoint me Chairman in 1991 and onto the main NAB board in Australia.

The second call was of a very different nature. A woman's voice asked if I was aware that I was ruining her marriage! Her husband was a director of the famous merchant bankers who were handling our defence. She had hardly seen him for three weeks. They were due to fly off on their first holiday for three years. He had said it was impossible for him to leave in the middle of the takeover. If he did not show up at the airport she was going to divorce him and would hold me personally responsible. My efforts at marriage guidance counselling were remarkably unsuccessful. Finally I said that I would speak to the Chairman of the Bank and leave the decision to him. No! I was to tell nobody about the conversation. On no account was her husband to know that she had called me. This did make it rather difficult. I was able to speak to the Chairman, who as it happened I knew, and who was a great personal friend of Alick Rankin's. He undertook to produce a replacement by 8 a.m. the next morning and was as good as his word. The story had a happy ending. Two or three years later I was in the Ladies side at Boodles and recognised the merchant banker concerned, whom I had not seen since. I said hello and he turned to his wife with the words: 'Darling, I don't think you've met David Nickson who was Chairman of Scottish and Newcastle.' She looked at me in horror and put her head momentarily in her hands, but neither of us said a word.

John Elliot had undoubtedly recruited a board in waiting among the Scottish establishment. I don't know exactly who they were but one or two of our business friends did look a little sheepish for some time afterwards. The most prominent was Alec Fletcher who acted as Elder's spokesman. This was embarrassing for me, if not for him, because I was by then Chairman of the Scottish Development agency and he was one of my board members. He was also an Edinburgh MP. He and I were 'door-stepped' by the press at the entrance to the SDA offices and found ourselves as antagonists in front of the TV cameras. Alec was a nice man, who had not quite made the grade as a junior minister. I had an evening in Brussels with him a few months later and was able to make friends again, while he told me some of the inside story from the Elder's camp. Tragically he died from a heart attack only weeks afterwards. Another embarrassment was when Bill Hughes, the current Chairman of the CBI for Scotland, agreed to host a reception for Elder's. This was a grave misjudgement. We were one of the largest CBI members in Scotland. I left him in no doubt of my views.

I may have joined S&N in 1981 with some misgivings and knowing none of my future colleagues. I retired from the board in 1994 with immense pride and satisfaction leaving a wonderful collection of friends. It had not always been easy commuting from Aberfoyle to Holyrood. Our Head Office was part of the old Holyrood brewery just across the road from the gates to the Palace. Now it is all a memory. For the jumbo of all white elephants, the new Scottish Parliament building, is nearing completion at a cost to the taxpayer rapidly approaching £500 million. For a time we owned a nice spacious flat in Great Stuart Street in the New Town, but we did not use it enough after our youngest daughter, Rosie, married and went to live in Greece. We should have kept it. It would have proved a superb investment.

The relationship between Chairman and Chief Executive is always potentially tricky. A lot does depend on personal chemistry. But I have always gone on the principle that a non-executive chairman should never, ever interfere in executive matters, and in return should expect to be constantly briefed by his Chief Executive so that he has the opportunity to discuss policy and appointments in advance and is never surprised by events. It is of course an oversimplification but when it comes down to the basics a chairman's job is to preside at board meetings and to hire or fire the Chief Executive. Alick Rankin and I had a good six years based on these fundamentals. It would not have worked otherwise. In the course of it he became one of my greatest personal friends. It was a huge sadness when he became seriously ill with cancer in 1999 and died in August in his mid-sixties at the height of his powers and reputation. It was one of the greatest privileges of my life to be asked by his widow, Suzetta, to give the address at his memorial service in St John's in Edinburgh.

CHAPTER 7

Family life

IN THE LAST four chapters I have attempted to describe my business career over some thirty years from the mid fifties to the mid eighties. Throughout this time we lived a full and happy family and social life with our three wonderful daughters and many firm friends. Louise was not by nature or inclination the typical corporate wife, following in her husband's footsteps to endless conferences and business trips. She was instead a superb homemaker and a wonderful mother. She it was who 'kept the home fires burning' while I was away. She provided the security and sanctuary of the homes to which I returned. She supported all my activities with great outward loyalty even if she was less than mildly enthusiastic about some of them in private! She put up nobly with endless trials of her patience and good nature. It is high time I recorded a part of our lives together that was fundamental to our happiness and to our children's upbringing and of far greater importance than my efforts as a breadwinner.

Our first home was in a bungalow at 22 Stamperland Drive on the south side of Glasgow. We were thrilled to have a roof over our heads with some prospect of staying there for a while after the turbulent start to our married life. We had bought our first small car, an A30 baby Austin. Everyone in Collins was kind and welcoming to us. It was May and the west of Scotland seemed incredibly beautiful after the Canal Zone. One evening we drove out to the north for the first time up the old A82 road along Loch Lomond. We sat on the shore and gazed at the view. We felt very excited to be starting out on a new life in such a beautiful country.

Apart from the Collins family and Humpo and Dee Philips who were distant cousins of Louise's we knew few friends but we rapidly started to make them. Eddy McGrigor had been Captain of my father's house at Eton. After serving in the Rifle Brigade during the war he had married Mary Edmonstone, the eldest daughter of the distinguished family from Duntreath Castle a few miles north of Glasgow. They were living in a house on the estate, which Eddy was looking after following his father-in-law's death, and while Mary's brother Archie was doing his

National Service. They asked us for several weekends and suggested that
we might like to move into another house on Duntreath called Lettre
Cottage. This was really the dower house and had quite a provenance
because a former Edmonstone, Alice Keppel, a mistress of Edward VII,
is reputed to have stayed there when he was a guest at Duntreath. It was
a low white house lined inside with pine in the manner of a Scottish
shooting lodge. It had not been lived in for a year, was in a state of some
disrepair and the garden was head high in grass and weeds. It seemed to
us a magical suggestion. We had no furniture to speak of, and no carpets
or curtains, nor could we afford to buy much, but the prospect of living
in the country was irresistible. We moved on 16 September 1954. The
night before Gwen Edmonstone, Mary's mother, most kindly had us to
stay at Duntreath. This was of course in the huge old Castle before
Archie sensibly reduced it in size a few years later. We awoke to a
fairytale morning with thick white hoar frost on all the trees as the sun
slanted through. Never since can I remember such a hard frost so early
in the autumn.

Two happy years at Lettre Cottage followed. We survived the cold
winters with no heating, climbing into the attic each morning to break
the ice on the water tank before going to work. I used to catch the blue
bus from Killearn dressed in my one city suit and a bowler hat. Old habits
die hard and I still wore a stiff white collar too. It was not until the mid
sixties that the bowler hat as an essential accessory for every professional
businessman died a sudden death. At Lettre Cottage we met for the first
time Peter Joynson and later Kate Douglas before they became engaged
in 1955. They have been our close friends and neighbours for fifty years.
To them, to the McGrigors and to the Collins we owe the initial
introductions to the wide circle of friends throughout Scotland with
whom we have enjoyed so many happy times. Eddy used to ask me to
shoot and fish. In those days there were grouse on the oat stooks beside
the main road into Killearn, where long since there have been houses,
and coveys of grey partridges dusting under our sitting room windows,
and rabbits galore until myxomatosis struck for the first time in 1956.

In June 1954 Humpo and Dee Philips asked us to stay for a weekend
with them at Glen Cassley Castle. This was our first of many trips to the
north over the years. We drove up in our little car after I got home from
work on the Friday evening. It was pouring in Glencoe. We were
awestruck by the glowering splendour of those hills seen for the first
time. As we drove on past Inverness the skies cleared. Sutherland was
bathed in late evening sunlight. The yellow flag irises were everywhere.

It was still light as we arrived just before midnight. Scotland looked unbelievably beautiful. We were thrilled that it had become our home.

Two more great friends came into our lives at Lettre Cottage. Louise had been a bridesmaid to Pam Joyce with whom she had grown up at Ashstead in Surrey before the war. Pam had married Graham Mackrill, a Wykehamist whose home was in Yorkshire. He was in Glasgow on business and came to stay for a night. Pam and Louise were concerned that their respective husbands might not hit it off. They need not have worried! We have spent fifty years in each other's company, fishing, shooting, drinking claret (mostly from Graham's high class cellar) and talking far into the night with undimmed enthusiasm and enjoyment. The other was also a Wykehamist. I have nothing against them! Peter Ansdell had done his National Service in The Coldstream in Malaya. He had been sent up to Glasgow by his family firm to work in Glasgow. Someone had suggested that we should get together. How right they were! Peter became a regular visitor to Lettre Cottage and to Buchlyvie before meeting and marrying his wife Sue. They and their family are also lifetime friends. For a few years Peter joined Collins and lived not far away, before buying an historic Elizabethan house in Gloucestershire.

But far and away the most important event at Lettre Cottage was the birth of our first daughter Felicity Sarah on 3 November 1955. For that reason above all others that, at the time somewhat neglected, house will remain very dear to us. A year later Archie Edmonstone married and Gwen naturally wished to do it up as a home for herself before he moved into Duntreath. So we were on the move again. We were determined if we could to stay on the north side of Glasgow as close to the Highlands as possible. We did not think we could afford to buy until, with great generosity, Louise's parents said that they would lend us the sum of three thousand pounds. This may seem nothing today but to put it into perspective it was probably two thirds of their total capital and two thirds of the price we eventually paid for The Cottage, Buchlyvie.

Five happy years there followed. Buchlyvie was and remains a delightful friendly farming village set in the Stirlingshire countryside with fantastic views to the Perthshire hills to the north. It is a happy coincidence that our youngest daughter Rosie and her husband Alastair Campbell have made Redlairdston, another house near Buchlyvie, their home and are bringing up their own small boys there. So life has turned full circle. Her elder sister Lucy was born in a Glasgow nursing home in July 1959. She arrived a week early. I was in the south for Collins' sales meetings and was actually playing cricket for the annual game against our authors at Marlow, and was blissfully unaware of the impending event. A large police sergeant in shirtsleeve order strode onto the field just as Billy Collins was running up to bowl. I was keeping wicket and turned to first slip with the words 'Someone is for it now.' Suddenly I realised that the policeman was heading straight for me. 'Are you Mr David Nickson? Congratulations! Your wife has just given birth to a daughter in Glasgow.' As he walked off the spectators asked him what crime I had committed. He gave nothing away, saying with a deadpan expression, 'It's official. I can't tell you.' My sister Mary, with whom I was staying at Sunningdale that night, having heard the news had rung the police, and with her accustomed enterprise and charm had told them to go and search for her brother on some cricket field in Marlow. I wonder if the police today would have been so obliging. I beat a hasty retreat to London Airport and just managed to see Louise and get my first glimpse of Lucy that evening.

I was given permission by the farmer on the edge of the hill above Buchlyvie to shoot over his land. I had great fun there walking after the odd covey of partridges and wild pheasants with my yellow Labrador, Crisp; and leaping out of bed to rush up the hill to flight the pinkfooted geese as they came into the potatoes before I rushed back to drive to Glasgow in time to avoid being late for work. From Buchlyvie too I made weekend sorties to Lochdochart to shoot grouse and try to stalk the odd stag. On one occasion I had crammed two stags into the boot of my Hillman Minx after shooting them at midday, dragging them singlehanded down the hill, one by one all afternoon in a blizzard of hail, and arriving home long after dark. Poor Louise, what a time she has had from a husband so passionate about his shooting and fishing.

Nanny Wilson arrived, shortly after Lucy was born, to help look after two small girls. She was with us for nearly ten years. She had many good qualities but was a strangely mixed up woman and it was only later that we fully realised how besotted she was with Lucy and how unkind she often was to Felicity. Fortunately it does not seem to have done either of them any lasting harm! Her arrival meant that once again we were on the move because our house at Buchlyvie was not big enough to accommodate a growing family. We had heard that Ronald and Marion Orr-Ewing were moving to their family home at Cardross from the house they had bought at Aberfoyle when Ronald had left the Scots Guards. They offered to let it to us on a ten-year lease. We were pretty daunted by the size and state of the house but did not think we could afford to buy a large enough house for our purposes. By the time they changed their minds and decided to sell after all, because they had found extensive dry rot at Cardross, we were committed. Eventually we obtained a mortgage, sold The Cottage, Buchlyvie for what we had paid for it five years earlier, and bought Renagour for £8,750. It was our much-loved family home for the next forty years until we sold it in 2001 for nearly one hundred times what we paid for it!

Renagour had originally been a small farm on the Montrose Estates in the Pass of Aberfoyle. It lay on a peninsula between the Afon Dhu burn out of Loch Ard and the Duchray river. These two streams meet at the point of the Renagour land to become the infant River Forth at the start of its long winding journey to Stirling and so on to Edinburgh. The house had been built onto many times to become a shooting lodge with three or four thousand acres on the south side of Loch Ard. It had been let for many years for stalking and grouse in common with half a dozen other lodges on the Montrose estates around the loch. In the nineteen twenties all the land had been sold to the Forestry Commission to form what is now the Queen Elizabeth Forest Park. The house had fallen on hard times in the war and had been the home of scores of evacuee children to escape from the bombing of Clydeside. The Orr-Ewings, knowing that for them it was only a temporary home, had taken it much as they found it. It had no central heating, an extensive and vulnerable roof and very antiquated plumbing. Twice in the first few years after installing central heating we had outbreaks of dry rot, involving heavy expenditure on treatment and redecoration.

In the hard winter of 1963 the frost started on Christmas Eve and the thaw did not come until 6 March. We had seventy-two continuous days of frost and snow. The main water supply to the house, running under the bridge over the Afon Dhu, froze. For several weeks we had to bring all our water by garden hosepipe for two hundred yards from a stopcock on the main road. This was the year of the 'Grand Match', the outdoor curling competion with teams from clubs from all over Scotland coming to the Lake of Menteith. There were over two thousand people on the ice and you could hear the roar of the stones from miles away. Hundreds of skaters took to the ice every day. Patricia Cunninghame-Graham, wife of a celebrated local admiral, taught Felicity aged seven to skate by using an old kitchen chair. I drove my Jaguar car onto the ice towing a sledge behind me. What on earth an insurance company yet alone the Health and Safety Executive or the police would say nowadays I hate to think! There were other cold winters but the only comparable one was in 1979 when the only other postwar *bonspiel* took place on the Lake on 11

February. My diary records that the frost that year lasted until 26 February. But the coldest if not the longest winter was 1982 when we had many consecutive nights with the temperature below minus fifteen degrees Centigrade and one night it reached minus twenty (thirty-six degrees of frost in Fahrenheit).

On the night of 13/14 January 1968 a great gale swept across central Scotland creating a swathe of havoc fifty miles wide from Ayrshire to Fife. So loud was the howl of the storm in the early hours that it drowned the crashes of the falling trees. We lost over a hundred large trees round the house. They fell higgledy-piggledy like a giant game of spillikins and took months to clear away. The girls and the animals crept into our bed in terror as the chimney pots crashed down outside.

For forty years I enjoyed keeping a record of the rainfall at Renagour in an amateurish and somewhat spasmodic way, since I was frequently away from home for many days at a time. We soon learned that Aberfoyle was a very wet spot catching all the clouds as they swept westwards along the Trossachs. In the 1960s the average annual rainfall was about 65 inches a year but as global warming began to take effect so it rose; and by the 1990s it had reached 75 inches, with several years of over 80. The wettest years were 1990 and 1998 with over 87 inches. Every year at Gordon Simpson's traditional New Year party I used to compare notes with John Muir of Blairdrummond. Doune is only fifteen miles from Aberfoyle but the rainfall is usually about half. No wonder we moved to Doune in 2001!

Our greatest friends and closest neighbours at Renagour were the Joynson family from the Glassert and Kate's parents Archie and Cicely Douglas who lived at another house on Loch Ard called Laraich. At first Peter's parents lived at the Glassert, another Montrose shooting lodge on the shores of the loch with stupendous views to Ben Lomond. Here they had enjoyed wonderful sport for four generations. Here I shot my first stag as a guest of Peter's father Will. He was a great character and very kind. He had won an MC in the First War. I never saw Peter's mother Mary without a hat even informally at home. They lived a splendid Victorian style existence, little having changed in their regime since the twenties. From the Glassert or from Laraich we set out every twelfth of August to walk the hill towards Ben Venue for grouse. Many too were the days pheasant shooting I enjoyed along the lochside, where the walking gun was rowed along the side of one wood in a boat and pheasants planed down at impossible angles from the almost vertical hillsides above. The Douglases were equally kind in every way to us and to our children. It was one of the great privileges of my life to be asked by Kate to give the addresses at their funerals in St Mary's Church, Aberfoyle to two such wonderful and generous people.

Every house on the loch had a boathouse. Ours was on Little Loch Ard. We used to row up through the narrows past Laraich to the Glassert on the big loch on countless fishing and picnic expeditions, the girls playing 'Swallows and Amazons' while I invented improbable stories about Duke Murdoch and his castle on its romantic little island. Early on we abandoned the kitchen garden we had inherited and, in its place, put down a hard tennis court: the scene of countless family games and some pretty competitive matches in the local interhouse tennis club. The house and garden were full of livestock of various kinds; bantams and pigeons in the steading, guinea pigs and kittens in the kitchen, dogs and puppies sometimes in the kennel but as often as not leaving their hairs and other things in the drawing room. The Jardines' spaniels in particular were notorious for rushing into the house and relieving themselves on the drawing room carpet within seconds of their arrival.

Dogs have played a permanent role in our family life. We have never been without one or two, sometimes three. Often they seem to have dominated our lives to the exclusion of other considerations. They have been a joy and a delight as well as sometimes bringing sadness and anxiety. We have had a succession of Labradors, all much loved, some more successful than others as gun dogs. Twice I have succeeded in training black Labradors to an acceptable standard myself. More frequently I have failed and had to resort to the professionals. Ten years ago we embarked on a Norfolk terrier, and for our Golden Wedding our family gave us another. Norfolks and Labradors are a splendid combination. They are completely different in character in every way. What the terriers lack in size they more than make up for in assertiveness and independence!

Renagour was on the edge of the Queen Elizabeth Forest Park. We could walk out of the garden along Loch Ard or up the river Duchray for miles; or set off up the hill above us to climb Craig Mhor with its secret Covenanters' cave; all wonderful settings for children's expeditions or for walking dogs. In 1986 before taking on as President of the CBI I decided that I had better realise a long held ambition while I still had the energy. This was to walk out of the house to the summit of Ben Lomond and back, a round trip of some twenty-six miles. I set off on a glorious May morning with the woods alive with the song of willow and wood warblers. I was glad to be alive. It took me ten hours there and back.

Two Labradors and I were pretty tired and Louise was relieved to see us safely home. After suitable refreshments we watched the BBC news bulletin before going to bed. 'There is no danger of radioactivity in this country from the fall-out from Chernobyl,' the newscaster said, 'except for those who have drunk snowmelt over three thousand feet.' I had drunk pints from the snowfield near the summit to quench my thirst! Fortunately I have so far suffered no ill effects nearly twenty years later!

All four of our parents and my sister and brother-in-law, Charlie Sheepshanks, and their children enjoyed visiting Renagour. It was the scene of many happy family gatherings, birthday parties and Christmases. Louise's father only saw it for a couple of years before he died in 1963 at the age of eighty-three. My own parents and my mother-in-law Jane were regular visitors for over twenty years. All three girls were married from Renagour at our church in the village, St Mary's: Felicity to James Lewis in 1980, Lucy to Melfort Campbell in 1983 and Rosie to George Petronanos in 1988. Later she was happily married again in Edinburgh in 1992 to Melfort's eldest brother Alastair. Marquees became almost a regular occurrence on the lawn. We had our own Ruby Wedding party there in 1992. The last great Renagour occasion was on Boxing Day 1999 when we had a family Millennium photograph with thirty-one members of my sister's and our family ranging in age from myself at seventy to James Campbell aged one: Nicksons, Sheepshanks, Lewises, Campbells, Coxes, and Shirleys all laughing in front of the drawing room fireplace. A most fitting farewell to a family house that gave us, and so many of our friends, much happiness.

In 1963 Peter Joynson and Andrew Stainton invited me to become a partner with them in the grouse moor at Doune. This gave us superb sport for over twenty years until the grouse in West Perthshire started to go into terminal decline. I tended to fill the house in August and September with all my old Coldstream friends and their children for shooting weekends, Jardines, Windsor-Clives and Napiers in particular. This was hard on Louise who was not only coping with all the extra work of children's summer holidays but also had to provide endless dinners and picnic lunches. Nevertheless she managed magnificently despite not being too keen on shooting herself; and we were all younger then and more able to burn candles at both ends! And looking back on it now we both agree we did all have enormous fun on the hill at Doune and the girls in particular adored it. I have continued to be the shooting tenant for pheasants on the low ground at Doune and have now been shooting there continuously for over forty years.

To start with Lucy and Rosie went to the village school in Aberfoyle as the little school where Felicity began in Callendar had closed. Later they all went to St Mary's, Wantage. We had been attracted to this because it was run by Anglican nuns and had an excellent reputation. Nowadays it would seem crazy to send girls so far away to school, but at that time we felt that, living in Scotland, it would be good for them to go to school in the south. On the whole it did them well, though it was on the decline by the time Rosie went there, and I don't think any of them have any regrets.

'St Mary's' was often on our lips because it was also the name of our Episcopal Church in Aberfoyle. We started to worship there when we were at Lettre Cottage in 1954 and both played an increasingly active role in its affairs. I was secretary to the Vestry for seventeen years from 1963 until 1980. Louise was busy organising the flowers and other events, and we both continued to serve on the Vestry at various times and in various capacities. St Mary's congregation and its Rectors had their ups and downs, as do most parishes, but it became very much woven into the fabric of our lives for forty years. We were and remain very attached to the church and very fond of its congregation, despite the fact that we now worship at St Modoc's, Doune, which is in walking distance of our house.

We had a cottage attached to the house at Renagour. To this in the mid eighties came a couple from Yorkshire, Jean and Neil Sykes. She was to be our housekeeper and he a part time gardener. They also became our trusted and well-loved friends. It was a great tragedy that poor Neil developed cancer within a few years of their arrival and died in 1989. Jean stayed with us until we left for Doune in 2001, and we felt, and hope she did too, that she was part of the family; her son Mark continued to help us with the garden.

The garden at Renagour extended to about seven acres though a lot of it was woodland. There was a great deal of grass to cut. The soil was acid, it lay in a frost pocket at the bottom of the hill and the rainfall was high. We gradually discovered that although we could grow hardy azaleas and rhododendrons we were wasting our time with our amateur efforts to grow most other plants. So over the years we planted many trees in the garden and in the two fields which we had taken into the 'policies'. These gave us much pleasure and we were as sad to leave them as we were to leave the house itself. The largest field in front of the house ran across to the River Duchray, which in turn became the River Forth at the junction with the Loch Ard burn at the point of the other field. The river provided marvellous scope for children for paddling, 'pooh sticks' and picnics in the summer. It gave me endless amusement as I walked my dogs and tried to train them to the gun. Every winter it flooded dramatically with the water covering the field and encroaching into the garden. In 1984 we decided to excavate a pond in front of the house from the boggy area at the limit of the winter flooding. This was a success. It improved the view, extended the garden and on occasions I stocked it with trout to encourage grandchildren to fish.

On the morning that the bulldozer was due to arrive to start digging out the pond I had agreed to give an interview at home to a journalist from the *Glasgow Herald* on the work of the Countryside Commission for Scotland of which I was currently the Chairman. As we sat on the terrace drinking coffee and I was expounding on the importance of conservation there was a ghastly noise and the digger cruised into view with a transistor blaring away at full volume. I had forgotten it was due to arrive so thought it best to ignore it in the hope she would think it was some agricultural activity and nothing to do with me. The article was duly published and concluded with the comment that she was left with the conclusion that David Nickson could not make up his mind whether he was a businessman-developer or a countryman; because during the interview a large machine appeared and proceeded to rip up the countryside in front of his eyes and he appeared not to notice! I have always enjoyed the definition of the difference between a developer and a conservationist. A developer is someone who wants to build a cottage in unspoilt countryside: a conservationist is someone who has already got one.

Louise and I took great delight from the birds at Renagour. During forty years we recorded one hundred species seen in or from the garden, of which thirty-five nested with us. Every year we noted the arrival dates of all the migrants, swallows nesting in the outhouses, martins under the eaves on the house, garden, willow and wood warblers, chiffchaffs and blackcaps and both spotted and pied flycatchers. Every year we watched the geese flying overhead as they arrived in the third week of September and departed again on their long flight to Iceland in late April. We had many nest boxes in the garden and along the riverbanks. It was always a particular thrill when we attracted a pied flycatcher or a redstart instead of the more usual blue and great tits. We had a few unusual visitors for central Scotland. Once a fulmar, presumably sick, crash landed in the hayfield and hissed at the dogs and bit my thumb when I tried to rescue it. Louise once saw a lesser grey shrike. On another occasion we saw a capercaillie flying along the forest edge. Occasionally there was a water rail in the pond and once a green sandpiper. We fed in a number of mallard in the winter and occasionally a goldeneye and once a pair of teal favoured us with a visit. One day in May Rosie shouted to me while I was shaving, 'Dad, there is a duck in the hall and it has made a mess all over the place.' I went downstairs to find a female goosander flying around that had come down the chimney while looking for a nesting site. Another less surprising visitor that chose to arrive in similar Father Christmas fashion was a tawny owl.

Siskins and great spotted woodpeckers were a regular delight, the latter demonstrating a surprising and unattractive characteristic by breaking into the nest boxes to feed baby blue tits to their own young. Woodcock nested with us a number of times. Once the hen carried her downy young across the burn and once one of our Labradors retrieved a chick to Louise while she was on the loo upstairs. It was quite unharmed, I am glad to say.

Red deer often came into the field at night from the forestry and roe deer were usually with us in the garden. Once or twice we saw red squirrels but regrettably far more frequently there were grey. Sometimes a salmon spawned in the garden burn and we hoped to find it before the dogs revelled in that most attractive to them, but to us most revolting of all smells, a really rotten kelt.

Renagour was our launching pad for countless family holidays to Argyll, Sutherland and Skye, to Yorkshire and the south of England, to Italy, France, Portugal, Norway and Spain, to Corfu and Venice and later further afield to Kenya, Namibia and South Africa. Sometimes Louise was able to accompany me on business trips to the United States, Australia and New Zealand. I have been fortunate to see so many places often at other people's expense! I was away a lot and often very late back from the office. She held the fort at home, looking after everything so well. We always had one golden rule, that if I had to be home later than eight o'clock in the evening, I would ring her to say so. Often it must have been hard on her to see other husbands, on a comfortable nine to five stint, getting home in time to help put the children to bed. But she was wonderfully uncomplaining and this proved a recipe to avoid much unnecessary anxiety.

In the mid seventies I realised a lifetime's ambition to own a beat on a Scottish salmon river. I bought with two friends the Upper Fairburn beat on the River Conon in Easter Ross. This has proved the best investment I have ever made and has given great enjoyment to our family and friends for nearly thirty years. For the first few years, when we were there on holiday, we lived in the cottage near the river. Then we decided we wanted a more permanent second home. Thanks to Louise's determination we went up one bitter February day to look at a house that was about to go on the market. We bought Tigh-na-Fraoch, the 'House in the heather'. It has been a constant delight to us, to our family and our friends now for nearly twenty years. It has an incomparable view to the north over Ben Wyvis and is a marvellously secret and remote place. We have travelled up and down the A9 constantly in the summer between Renagour and TNF, as we call it in the family, because the correct pronunciation of the Gaelic name is pretty testing.

By the late 1990s I was retiring from most of my commitments, all our children were happily married and away, and we mutually agreed that Renagour was a little too large for our old age. We also tacitly knew that when either of us was left on our own we would not wish to stay there. We wanted to move to Doune, a village we both liked and an area where we had many friends, in particular Colin and Caroline Stroyan. They had heard that other friends, the Steins, were planning to move from the house they had built in their own garden in 1979. Eventually we were able to buy it and moved in 2001. It has been an outstanding success. We love the house, enjoy a much more user-friendly garden, revel every day in our incomparable view of Doune Castle and I am in the centre of my shoot and can walk out of our garden gate to fish the River Teith for salmon.

We have been immensely blessed to have enjoyed such a wonderfully happy family life with the sound of laughter seldom absent for long.

CHAPTER 8

President of CBI
1986–1988

A ND SO, after that most important and enjoyable diversion into family life, I must return this narrative to the last and perhaps most significant part of my business and public life.

Just after the new year in 1985 my secretary at Scottish and Newcastle, Maureen Hall, told me that Sir James Cleminson, the President of the Confederation of British Industry, would like to meet me in London. He would not tell her the purpose of the meeting. He was also Chairman of Reckitt and Colman, headquartered in Norwich, and my first reaction was that this must be to discuss some business opportunity between our two companies. We were very sensitive to takeover threats at the time but for the life of me I could not see any obvious synergy between a major food and household product supplier and a brewer. Perhaps he wanted my advice as a former regional chairman of the CBI on some Scottish matter? But as I had had no involvement for four years this too seemed unlikely. An appointment was made for some three weeks later. Before leaving Renagour for the London plane I mentioned to Louise over breakfast that among various other engagements I was due to see James Cleminson at Centre Point and could not think what he wanted to talk about. We had actually met him once before socially many years before when he lived in Yorkshire. 'Well,' said Louise at once, 'perhaps he wants you to succeed him as President of the CBI.' I laughed, dismissing the idea out of hand. But on the plane I suddenly had the chill feeling that her woman's intuition might be right. The prospect was both daunting and challenging, always an irresistible combination for me.

I had always assumed the CBI selected the President from one of the top twenty or thirty companies inevitably based in London. The two Presidents I had known best during my time were Sir John Greenborough, Chairman of Shell, and Sir Ray Pennock (later Lord Pennock) of ICI. They had both been supportive while I was doing the Scottish job, as had Sir Terence Beckett, the Director General. James Cleminson's predecessor had been another Scot, Sir Campbell Fraser of Dunlop. So far as I knew no former regional chairman had previously been offered the top job and certainly it had never gone to a Scottish company. Perhaps it was thought a good idea to give Scotland a chance, and one of these great men had had a sufficiently high opinion of me to suggest my name!

James welcomed me and immediately came to the point. I said I would need to think it over and mentioned the obvious problems. I was Chairman of the Countryside Commission and was only approaching the end of my first three-year term. My home and my office were in Scotland. I had no base in London. At that time S&N did not even have a London office and there was no company flat. I had no car in London let alone a chauffeur. It would cost my company at least £100,000 a year in expenses to enable me to be in London for the necessary three or four days a week. I had no idea whether my board would be prepared to let me do the job and did not know what my wife would feel! Altogether not a very encouraging response from his point of view, but he must have realised that I was personally flattered and excited. In the event my colleagues at S&N were hugely supportive saying that it was just what the company needed to help put them on the map in London and at Westminster and Whitehall. Louise as ever was immensely loyal and supportive, however unattractive the prospect of an increased corporate existence was to her personally.

A week later James and Judy Cleminson took us both out to lunch at the Berkely Buttery to talk us through the personal implications. They were wonderfully kind to us from the outset and have become great personal friends with whom we share many common interests. But Judy did not help matters to start with by telling Louise that it was a seven-day a week job (not inaccurate) and that she would see little of me for the next three years. James whispered that he still managed to shoot and fish and had only had to cut his hunting down to one day a week! With his usual unassuming modesty he did not say that he had made a huge success of his company and was rated an outstanding CBI President. He is one of the most conscientious men I have ever met. Shortly afterwards I had a long talk with Terry Beckett and it was agreed that I should become Vice-President in May at the AGM and take over from James in May 1986. S&N kindly provided a driver and a car in London plus a suite on the top floor of the Lowndes Hotel that would always be available to us.

In June my first duty as Vice President was to host a reception in Scotland for the Premier of China, Zhao Ziyang, who was on a week's State visit to the United Kingdom. Never before or since have I been on the receiving end of such an impressive motorcade of police outriders on motor bikes as I stood in solitary loneliness waiting to receive him on the steps of an East Lothian hotel.

The next year was a learning curve with attendance at Council meetings and the President's Committee whenever I could, but James and Terry were thoughtful in sparing me too many other commitments. James took me to call on the Prime Minister at No. 10 with whom he had an excellent relationship. She always saw one upstairs in a sitting room very informally, unlike John Major later on who always saw me in the Cabinet room. I hoped she had forgotten our first meeting seven years earlier when she had taken me to task over my advocacy of proportional representation!

I attended and spoke at the CBI conference at Harrogate in November and got my first experience of dealing with the Japanese when the Kaidanren, the nearest equivalent to the CBI, brought a large delegation to Centre Point. But my main memory is of 'Spring Sunningdale', at the Civil Service staff college in May. This was an annual get together over a weekend between all the Permanent Secretaries and Senior industrialists invited by the CBI. Robert Armstrong (now Lord Armstrong of Ilminster) the Cabinet Secretary was in the chair and I met many others with whom I was to have dealings later. Robin Butler, who succeeded Robert Armstrong in 1988, was at the Treasury, as was Peter Middleton; Kerr Fraser of course from the Scottish Office I already knew, Brian Hayes from the Department of Trade and Industry, Michael Quinlan from the Department of Employment, until he went to Defence and was succeeded by Geoffrey Holland, all played a big part in my time as President or in the years shortly afterwards. Antony Acland, a friend and contemporary from Eton days, was head of the Foreign Office in 1986 but he was then appointed Ambassador to Washington, so sadly I did not see much of him. It was very useful to meet them all in the informal atmosphere of a weekend seminar for the first time.

Later I arranged a dinner for Permanent Secretaries with CBI officials and luminaries for the same reason. The following year Spring Sunningdale took place in early June because of the General Election on 11 June 1987. All the Permanent Secretaries had already written their briefs for whichever party came to power and were in a very jolly and relaxed mood. We had a fascinating discussion as to why it was apparently so difficult to produce 'joined up' government policy with all departments working much more closely together. Everyone let their hair down in agreeing, in this pre-election hiatus, that this was highly desirable in theory, but extremely difficult to achieve in practice once individual ministers arrived, flushed with success at their new appointments, and determined to pursue their own political ambitions and pet policies!

Of course I also met most of the senior figures in industry, many of whom played their part as members of the CBI President's Committee, among them Adrian Cadbury, Denys Henderson of ICI, Peter Walters of BP, John Raison of Shell, George Jefferson of British Telecommunications, Austin Pearce, originally from Esso but by then of Smith's Industries and many other companies, Eddy Nixon and later Tony Cleaver of IBM, Ron Dearing of the Post Office, Richard Lloyd of Hill Samuel, David Plaston of Vickers, and four who were all later to become CBI Presidents, Trevor Holdsworth of GKN, Mike Angus of Unilever, Colin Marshall of British Airways and John Egan of Jaguar.

In due course I moved into the President's office in May 1986 under the benevolent guidance of Beatrice Gilpin who had cared for and protected all my predecessors. Somehow she always produced the answer from behind the largest and untidiest piles of files and paper I had ever seen. She may not have appreciated the benefits of modern technology for she took dictation onto a marvellously antiquated black box but she was a master of etiquette, charmed everybody and was a very dear lady. She was most capably assisted on the top floor by another lady of great charm and elegance, Anne Marten. I have been hugely fortunate in being looked after by a string of quite delightful and immensely efficient secretaries, Anne Macquarrie and Lyndsey Ross at Collins, Maureen Hall at S&N, Sandra Pollock at Scottish Enterprise and Ellison Simpson at the Clydesdale Bank, all of them brilliant in every way, but the doyenne of them all was Beatrice. She, Maureen and Sandra were all honoured at some stage with the award of MBE.

A few selected extracts from my diary for 1986 perhaps gives a flavour of the varied life I led. In June Louise and I were at Holyrood as guests of John Arbuthnot who was High Commissioner. I visited the Prime Minister at No. 10 for a general chat on taking office. We gave a farewell dinner at the Tower Hotel for James and Judy Cleminson to mark his retiral. Slightly to my consternation we could hear from the penthouse suite the jeering of the printing union pickets outside Rupert Murdoch's Wapping plant nearby. I went to Brussels for my first meeting of UNICE, the association of European employers' associations and my first experience of multilingual simultaneous translation. I flew back to take part in 'Any Questions' at Sturminster Newton in Dorset. I did not distinguish myself; and suffered from the fact that as the only non-politician I had no political partisans in the audience to cheer my less than inspired answers. I was not invited back. On 27 June I was made an Honorary Doctor of Stirling University.

In July Her Majesty the Queen visited the CBI at Centre Point. In August I attended the Commonwealth Games in Edinburgh, which in typical fashion Robert Maxwell had tried to take over once they ran into financial difficulties. We dined with Pat and Mary MacLellan at the Tower of London. He was resident Governor and an old friend from my days in the Coldstream. The last time I had been there was when I was on Guard and took part in the Ceremony of the Keys way back in 1950. On 23 April 1988 I greatly enjoyed making the St George's Day speech for him at the Guildhall.

In September I made the main speech at the CBI in Scotland dinner, a nostalgic occasion of course since the last time I had attended had been my own farewell. I called on Giles Sheppard at the Savoy and Nigel Broakes of Trafalgar House at the Ritz, in both cases trying to persuade their boards of the importance of becoming CBI members. Recruiting is normally considered a staff matter but I lent a hand when I thought, quite wrongly as it turned out, that snob value and the prestige of the President's office might do the trick. On the 29th I dined at No. 10 for some overseas industrial occasion and sat on Margaret Thatcher's left. As my family knows I am notoriously clumsy and talk too much. Gesticulating to make some point I knocked my glass of white wine right across the Primeministerial place. She was magnificent and instantly became the solicitous hostess she could be on occasions. 'Don't worry at all,' she said. 'Look, not a spot has gone onto my dress. This is what we do.' She rolled up her table napkin in a flash and placed it under her plate before summoning a waitress to mop up. She could not have put me more at ease and rough though she was with me at other times I worshipped her for that.

In October I dined with the Army at Millbank and lunched with the Bank of England in the City. In November I made the speech for the Royal Warrant Holders' Dinner in Grosvenor House to a capacity audience of twelve hundred guests and presided over my first CBI conference as President in Torquay. The last time Louise and I had been there was for the first three days of our honeymoon in 1952! Finally I shared a platform with General Peter de la Billiere of SAS and Gulf War fame in Cardiff Castle for the Welsh CBI dinner. The acoustics were abysmal and some well oiled Welsh members talked with increasing crescendo over my pretty dull speech that they could not hear even if they had wished to do so. In between times I attended the monthly meetings of the CBI's regional councils round the country, getting to know the all important regional Chairmen, whose influence is so vital.

And so one shuttled about between Scotland, London and elsewhere, making several speeches a week, attending meetings, lunches and dinners, travelling by plane or car with at least two black despatch cases and trying desperately to keep up with the accumulating mountains of paperwork. I am afraid I was a poor attender at non-executive board meetings of General Accident, the Clydesdale Bank and Edinburgh Investment Trust during this period and S&N took up what spare time remained.

Terry Beckett was a tower of strength and support. He had been Director General for seven years by then and knew it all. He guided me through my early months, prepared me meticulously before every meeting in the thorough Ford Motor Company management style, which of course was his own background, and saw that I was competently briefed on the political minefields. But he was getting tired and becoming increasingly unwell. It had been agreed that he would retire in the mid-term of my Presidency. His deputies were John Owens, Brian Rigby and Ken Edwards, all with different areas of responsibility.

Early on Ken came to see me with a pile of letters that required action or response. 'I expect you would like me to deal with this one from the Army,' he said, passing it across the table. I glanced at the letter from the General UK Land Forces suggesting a joint Army/Industry seminar and saw that it was signed by Jimmy Glover. He had been my immediate predecessor as Senior Under Officer in Normandy Company at Sandhurst and I jumped at the opportunity to meet him again. I also had my own agenda. I was concerned that so many able young officers were leaving the army for the high salaries offered in the City. Mindful of my own background and believing that a few years as a regular soldier was a superb training for general management I was hoping to develop a scheme whereby major companies would guarantee places in industry under their graduate recruitment programmes. After meeting Jimmy Glover the MOD did consider the idea carefully but rejected it on the understandable grounds that they did not want to offer any further incentives for able young officers to leave the services. By then I had secured a number of offers from large companies, so added the further carrot that they would require their army intake to serve a further five years in the Territorial Army. This foundered on the grounds that the Territorials were by definition entirely voluntary and any element of compulsion was unacceptable.

So my hobbyhorse fell at the first fence but we went ahead with Jimmy's seminar. He said he would order all his UK generals to attend. I said I could order no one to do anything, but would invite senior industrialists. Ken Edwards suggested to me that the whole motivation on the Generals' part must be to parade themselves in front of my guests in the hope of employment on retiring from the Army. I thought this extremely cynical and told him so. At the seminar, and the highly congenial dinner that followed, Jimmy gave a superb presentation, without a note, on global defence issues. Not long afterwards Peter Walters invited him to become a non-executive director of BP! (I suspect that in this capacity he may have played a critical role later on when Bob Horton was required to resign as Chief Executive.) Anyway Ken Edwards claimed afterwards that his cynicism had been justified.

The next year I lectured at the Royal College of Defence Studies, by invitation from another old friend and Coldstream General, Mike Hicks, who was Deputy Director. I floated my scheme again but to no avail. Incidentally both Pat MacLellan and Mike have recently been called to give evidence before the Bloody Sunday Enquiry into the tragic events of 1972 when Pat was commanding the Parachute Brigade and Mike the Coldstream Battalion. It must have been a great ordeal to have to try to recall the events of thirty years before with any accuracy. It remains to be seen what this fantastically expensive enquiry will say. It makes me wonder, as I write this without the aid of any contemporary diary, how correct my own memories are of events far more mundane.

The first major heffalump trap into which I fell was entirely of my own making, but it began with memories of the left wing dominated Trade Unions from the printing industry. The other senior executive at Centre Point was Keith McDowall, the Director of Information. He was very experienced having worked for both Jim Callaghan and Willie Whitelaw while they were Secretaries of State in Northern Ireland. He was a delightful character who appealed to me at once. But early on in my term of office I was at a presentation on Industry Year at the Royal Society of Arts at which HRH the Duke of Edinburgh was giving the introduction. I found myself sitting next to Brian Redhead who was at that stage John Humphrey's equivalent on the 'Today' programme.

'Hello,' he said, 'I was out with Keith and Brenda last night.'

'Keith?' I replied obtusely.

'Yes,' he said, 'he works for you as your Director of Information. Didn't you know?'

'Oh of course,' I replied, 'but Brenda? I did not know he was married.'

He looked at me, realising that I was pretty square, and explained that everyone knew Keith and Brenda, and that she was General Secretary of SOGAT, the largest printing union. I said nothing, not wishing to expose my ignorance further, but was concerned that the man responsible for all CBI publicity was quite as close to the boss of such an important Trade Union.

Shortly afterwards Paul Channon (now Lord Kelvedon), the Secretary of State for Trade and Industry, asked to see me. The Financial Services Bill was going through Parliament. This was admirable in concept, designed 'not to achieve the impossible task of protecting fools from their own folly but to protect reasonable people from being made fools of.' But it rapidly became far too bureaucratic and complicated. We had pointed out that many of the clauses in the Bill as drafted would affect the normal day-to-day routine treasury operations of commercial companies who had nothing to do with the financial services industry. We were starting to make quite a song and dance about this. Paul asked me to lay off our news hounds, saying that the Government fully appreciated the validity of our case and were intending to table a raft of Government amendments in the Lords, but that Willie Whitelaw, then the Leader of the House, was getting tetchy about the pressure of business so they could not do anything quickly. 'Would I kindly agree to refrain from referring to this or from adverse press comment for four or five weeks?' I gave my assent but may have failed to make this sufficiently clear within the CBI.

Shortly afterwards I was trying to clear my desk on a Friday evening before flying to Inverness for a weekend at our family fishing house in Ross-shire. I initialled my approval on an apparently satisfactory press release about the Financial Services Bill, which, though not particularly complimentary, in no way breached the undertaking I had given to Paul Channon. On Sunday morning all hell broke lose. The Sunday papers were full of the CBI's hostile criticism of the Government's handling of the Bill with verbatim quotes in my name! My telephone started to ring. My first and wholly unjustified reaction was that Keith McDowall had stitched me up. It was soon pointed out to me that I had in fact seen and approved every word that was printed. And so in one way I had. In my haste to catch my plane I had turned over from page one to page three of the press release, totally missing the offending paragraphs and quotes on page two. There was only one thing to do: catch the first plane to

London that night and appear on the steps of the DTI to apologise first thing on Monday morning. The Under Secretary of State with responsibility for the Bill was Michael Howard, now Leader of the Opposition. I had never met him before. In the circumstances he was charming and appeared to understand. I was very grateful to him for this, but it is not an episode on which I look back with any pleasure.

The only other dealings I had with him were two years later when he was Minister of State at the Department of the Environment with responsibility for the Poll Tax. Again the CBI was strongly opposed but this time on the grounds that it would be a disaster for the Government because the tax would be not only unpopular but also inefficient and impossible to collect. We had our own proposals. This time Michael Howard gave us the rough side of his tongue, saying that it was in their Manifesto and it was no part of our role to criticise the method of raising domestic taxation. So, although both episodes took place nearly twenty years ago, I can appreciate those who say that the new Leader of the Conservatives can be both very generous and charming but that he is also a formidable and tough adversary.

The other sequel to this story is that I came to trust and admire Keith McDowall. He was enormous fun to work with and a wise and experienced operator on the Whitehall circuit. He never let me down. Some months later he asked me out to dinner to meet Brenda Dean and it was a great pleasure to be asked. She was delightful; in due course I was a guest at their wedding. I now see her occasionally in her distinguished career in the House of Lords as Baroness Dean of Thornton-le-Fylde.

The Financial Services Bill duly went onto the Statute Book but the initial rules drafted by the Securities and Investment Board were ridiculously bureaucratic and created an outcry in the City. I was actually sitting beside Kenneth Berrill, the first Chairman, at a meeting in the Bank of England when Lord Young, by then Secretary of State, very publicly sacked him and replaced him with David Walker from the Bank in the presence of the Governor, Robin Leigh-Pemberton. It seemed to me a curiously callous and public way to dismiss somebody.

The crucial issues during my two years of office from 1986 to 1988 were the economy and the background to our delayed entry into the ERM: the level of business confidence and investment; UK competitiveness; the effects of Big Bang in October 1987 and the crash in world stock markets so soon afterwards; the continual struggle over pay and inflation; the changed situation in industrial relations and the power of the unions following the miners' strike and the consequent new legislation. But this book is not intended as a serious record of these events nor as a commentary on economic policies. Rather it is a personal record of the people I have met and with whom I have worked. Anyone who wants to read a first hand account of all the economic and business issues that preoccupied us during these two years at the CBI should study Nigel Lawson's comprehensive autobiography *The View from No. 11* published in 1992.

Nigel was far the most open and approachable of all the cabinet ministers in the Government. As he says in his book: 'I made a practice of telling each incoming CBI President that my door was always open whenever there was any aspect of Government policy that was troubling them and which they wished to discuss with me, frankly and in private. They invariably took me up on this.' But Nigel did much more than this. He made it clear that he thought the CBI, its policies and its members really mattered. In particular he was ever keen to know the results of the regular CBI forecasts on business confidence and activity, trusted in them and was always keen for more subjective anecdotal evidence to support them. It was often at his request rather than mine that I would turn up for a gin and tonic at No. 11 around 6 o'clock. Sometimes he telephoned me at home in Scotland. Louise likes to tell the story of one of our granddaughters rushing into the garden shouting, 'Papa, Papa, telephone, telephone, it's Nigel.' The Chancellor of the Exchequer meant nothing to her! He often confided in me over his difficulties with his neighbour through the wall in No. 10, and particularly in 1988 when he was so near to resignation he really let his hair down.

The CBI after sitting on the fence for a long time finally adopted joining the ERM as its official policy in 1985, so I inherited this. Nigel had long advocated it as a key mechanism for controlling inflation and the Exchange rate. Geoffrey Howe at the Foreign Office and a former Chancellor made no secret of his view in favour; Robin Leigh-Pemberton and the Bank of England recommended it. It must have been intensely galling for him that Margaret Thatcher was influenced so strongly by the advice of her unofficial economic guru Alan Walters instead of by the almost unanimous views of her senior economics ministers. The crunch came in November 1985 when Nigel recommended that the moment was ripe for joining at a parity of sterling to the Deutschmark of 3.70. The Prime Minister left the meeting saying that if we joined the ERM it would be without her. The subsequent decline in the value of sterling to DM 2.85 by December 1986 meant that the opportunity had been lost and the rate at which we eventually joined in 1990 contrived to create the crisis of September 1992 when we had to leave so precipitously and ignominiously. Throughout my time at the CBI Nigel's policy was unofficially to shadow the Deutschmark at a parity of DM 3.00 to the £ as a surrogate for the ERM. In this he had the CBI's support. Today's arguments about the Euro might have a rather different complexion had we been able to join the ERM at the right rate in 1985 and successfully maintained our membership. His vindication in his book of his subsequent record as Chancellor reads very convincingly to me.

He made the main speech at the CBI dinner in May just before the 1987 General Election. The service at Grosvenor House was so slow that by the time he was due to get to his feet it was clear that the TV coverage would miss his speech, so I reversed the order and invited him to speak before me. I think he was pleased. The next day I left for Tokyo leading the CBI delegation to talk to the Japanese. A giant of a man, Fred Warner, a former Ambassador to Japan, who was an adviser to the CBI, accompanied me. In those days one flew via Anchorage. As we left the plane in transit on Sunday morning Fred said, 'I must go and worship. Follow me.' He swept through the airport, brushing aside numerous assorted Asians who scarcely reached his knee level, to the fur section where he stopped in front of a vast stuffed polar bear. He bowed three times to the bear that dwarfed even his 6 ft 8 inch frame, and stood in silence. When I asked him what on earth he was doing he replied that on every trip to Tokyo he always prayed to the polar bear. His prayers were invariably answered.

'What were you praying for?' I asked.

'That,' he said, 'is a secret between the polar bear and me.' Much later I learnt that he had asked that both his sons should pass their 'A' levels and catch their first salmon in the summer holidays. They did.

I was lucky to be staying at the very grand British Embassy building, and in the VIP bedroom too. The week before the Election was announced I had been sitting next to Geoffrey Howe at a Foreign Office lunch. He knew I was going to Tokyo and was due there himself later that week. 'Make sure you are clear of the Embassy to make way for me,' were his parting words. But the General Election gave me a free run. John Whitehead, our ambassador, and his wife were the most charming hosts. The main items on our agenda were set-piece meetings with the Kaidanren and the Nikairen, the major employment organisations. The removal of trade barriers especially on Scotch whisky was our prime aim. I had been well briefed by my old army friend Bill Bewsher, who after a distinguished military career was Director of the Scotch Whisky Association. I doubt if our efforts were anything like as effective as the representations of the Association itself or of Margaret Thatcher, whose favourite tipple it was, but we did our best. Eventually the duty was halved in 1989.

We had a fairly punishing programme and I was rather jet-lagged. On the only early night I went to bed with a sleeping pill. I was in a deep sleep when the Ambassador entered my room to tell me that the Chancellor was on the telephone. I knew I must be having a nightmare. I had visions of the 1974 election when the Director General at the time, Campbell Adamson, was blamed for contributing to the Conservatives' defeat by saying that British business would fare better under a Labour Government. What clanger had been dropped this time in my absence? Eventually Nigel's voice came on the line. 'Oh, David,' he said, 'there is something important I want to ask you . . .' then suddenly CLICK . . . and we were cut off. I wiggled the receiver. No result. A Japanese operator came on the line. I could not understand a word. More and more disastrous reasons for the call flooded into my drugged brain. I decided the only hope was to find John Whitehead. The whole Embassy was in darkness and I could not find the light switches. I groped my way along the upstairs landing shouting, 'Help, Help. Is anyone there?' John Whitehead emerged from his room and calmly reconnected me, though the line was far from clear. Nigel wanted to know if I could tell him what the CBI monthly forecasts due out the next day would say about business confidence levels! I told him I was in Tokyo and it was two o'clock in the morning and that I hadn't a clue. Afterwards I discovered that he was electioneering in a factory in Scotland with the reporters all around him and had just said to his Private Secretary, 'Get me David Nickson on the telephone.' He had no idea I was in Japan. He thought I was in Scotland too. I went back to sleep, a much relieved man.

The only other Japanese occasions worth recording were when Mr Sargy, the Chairman of the large drinks group Suntory, asked to meet me. S&N were doing some business with them in Japan and as a matter of protocol it was apparently important he should entertain me on a visit to London. We met at the Suntory restaurant in St James's Street, formerly Pruniers. There were just the two of us. We had a private room and squatted uncomfortably with our feet under a low table. Kimono-clad Japanese girls waited on us bowing to the floor each time they entered the room. As there were no fewer than seventeen courses they took a lot of exercise. We built up through a range of raw fish dishes to the climax, which arrived about course twelve, when they carried in the largest lobster I have ever seen, the size of an average dachshund. By this time it was three o'clock. I had to leave for another CBI meeting, thus breaching all Japanese etiquette. As a non golfer my knowledge of the Suntory golf sponsorship was negligible. We had had no other topic of conversation of any mutual interest. I did not feel that the lunch was a success or that I had done anything to promote Scottish and Newcastle's interests.

The other occasion was at a CBI Annual Conference when a live satellite link was established with Tokyo so that I could carry on a conversation from the conference platform with the Chairman of Sony for the benefit of the delegates and the BBC audience on live TV. Of course timing was precise and carefully rehearsed; and the questions and answers were scripted. The trouble was that he answered my questions so fast and fluently that I soon realised we were going to finish at least two minutes early. So to the consternation of CBI officials and to the evident surprise of my Japanese friend I started to ad lib until I knew we were off the air. So far as I know no lasting damage was done to international relations.

Once a month the meetings of the National Economic Development Council (NEDC or NEDDY) took place in Millbank. Nigel was ex officio in the Chair. It had been founded in 1961 under the Macmillan Government in an effort to achieve consensus between representatives of the Government, the CBI and the TUC on the measures necessary to improve economic performance. It supervised the work of numerous 'little Neddies' for individual industries. These did have a real role to play, but with the abandonment of any pretence of a Corporate State under Maggie Thatcher, the meetings of the NEDC had become a waste of time. The TUC used them to try to provoke the Chancellor, and any other members of the Cabinet who attended for agenda items covered by their Departments, into commitments or indiscretions, and then gave a slanted press conference immediately afterwards. Nigel gave at least as good as he got by baiting the TUC and did not try to disguise his irritation. The CBI and the six independent members including the Governor, Robin Leigh-Pemberton, and the Chairmen of the Nationalised Industries such as Coal and Electricity tried to take it all very seriously and spectated at the dog fights, which could be quite good value!

Norman Willis was General Secretary of the TUC. He clearly had little time for Clive Jenkins of ASTMS. At one meeting Nicholas Ridley, a chain smoker, was attending. He lit up at once. Clive Jenkins immediately raised a point of order that it was a 'No Smoking' meeting in a rather aggressive way. In those days it was quite uncommon to have such regulations. Nigel looked uncomfortable, clearly not wanting to embarrass Nick Ridley. Nick puffed resolutely on. There was some inconclusive muttering. Whereupon Norman Willis, whom I had never seen smoke at a meeting before, very ostentatiously took a packet of cigarettes out of his pocket and lit up. That concluded the matter. Clive Jenkins looked daggers. Nigel got on with the business. Norman Willis went up in my estimation.

General Accident had had a long running dispute with ASTMS over Union recognition. As a Non-Executive Director on the Staff Committee of the board I was well aware of the details and mentioned this to Clive one day as we were leaving the meeting. 'Come and have dinner one evening and we'll discuss it,' said he. In due course he followed this up and a date was arranged. To my astonishment his chosen venue was the House of Lords. I had at that time never set foot in the House and of course he was not a Peer. 'Oh,' he replied to my query, 'I find it very useful to have my Assistant General Secretary there for entertaining'! This was Muriel Turner, Baroness Turner of Camden, who had been ennobled in 1985 and was the Labour opposition spokesman on Social Security. I now know of course that she is a highly respected and well-liked Member of the House but on that occasion she never appeared, as she was busy in the Chamber all evening. Clive met me in the Peers' bar, we went into the Peers' dining room where a table had been booked in her name for three, and he proceeded to order in an overloud voice as if he was in his own club.

'Let's drink champagne,' he said. 'Waiter, bring a bottle. I'll open it myself.'

This he proceeded to do with a loud pop. By this time heads were turning all around. I could see what they were thinking, 'That's Clive Jenkins all right. He's not a peer so he must be a guest of that new bad mannered young peer who we've never seen before who must be entertaining him.'

Muriel Turner never appeared. We resorted to the Peers' bar for coffee where Harold Wilson and Lady Falkender, his Political Secretary during his last unhappy two years as Prime Minister from 1974 to 1976, came to sit beside my 'host'. He did not introduce me. An argument began almost immediately. 'Marcia,' said he to her, 'I think the way you behaved the other day was absolutely despicable.' Sparks started to fly. I decided to make my exit as rapidly as possible. It was the most embarrassing evening I have ever spent. It never crossed my mind that one day I would be entitled to entertain in the House of Lords myself!

After the 1987 Election Nigel asked me to call in to discuss the future of NEDDY. He wanted to make some changes. 'What did I think?' I said that he might as well scrap it altogether for all the good that it did, but he should retain the office (NEDO) to administer the 'little Neddies' which continued to do valuable work for individual industries. His book describes what happened. He was for abolition but surprisingly it was Margaret Thatcher herself who, apprehensive about Union reaction, insisted on a less drastic compromise. Nigel flatteringly describes the episode in his book.

> I had taken the precaution, meanwhile, of sharing my thinking with David Nickson, the then CBI President. David was not only a highly successful Executive Chairman of Scottish and Newcastle, the brewing and hotel group, but a businessman who combined to an unusual extent a clear understanding of the climate needed for business success with a keen sense of public duty. This made him one of the best Presidents the CBI has ever had. He undertook to deliver the compromise proposal that had emerged.

This was overgenerous but it was very kind of him to say it.

Of course I had dealings with most other members of the Cabinet at the time, but usually on a one-off basis over particular issues: Douglas Hurd at the Home Office, an Eton contemporary, Geoffrey Howe, over Europe with whom Louise and I lunched at Chevening on one occasion; Kenneth Baker at Education; Cecil Parkinson at Energy and John Macgregor at the Treasury; David Young at Employment and then Trade and Industry; and George Younger at the Scottish office before he took over from Michael Heseltine at Defence after the Westland affair. I felt it was important to be able to discuss current industrial and political topics in an informal and confidential atmosphere without officials being present. The CBI staff were, I think, rather surprised when I persuaded most of the Cabinet to accept an invitation to dine with me in the lovely Georgian room at Boodles. I have no idea whether this practice has continued under my successors.

Relations between the City and Industry were pretty strained in the mid eighties. The series of large takeovers involving in some cases questionable tactics, the doubt as to whether the Stock Exchange could ever be capable of self regulation, the perceived lack of support for and investment in British Industry, all conspired to create considerable distrust in the City. Voices were raised at CBI conferences and critical motions tabled. Nicholas Goodison, the Chairman of the Stock Exchange and the architect of 'Big Bang', was concerned. Many CBI members sought a more constructive dialogue. After my first conference in November 1986 I suggested to Terry Beckett that we set up a City/Industry task force to explore the issues and to make recommendations. We had almost as many members in the Banking and Financial Services Industries as we had in Manufacturing so it was not difficult to recruit a pretty distinguished committee. We met under my chairmanship throughout 1987 and produced our report for the conference. I wish I could say that it had had any lasting impact. Its recommendations were too anodyne owing to the impossibility in finding enough common ground. Its publication coincided with Black Monday in November 1987 when the stockmarket collapsed. We were at pains to say that in fact industrial profitability and confidence remained high demonstrating the artificiality and fickleness of financial markets. I fear my well-intentioned task force achieved little.

There were many enjoyable functions and outside activities in which the CBI President could become involved if time permitted. One of them was to be part of the judging panel for the Queen's Awards to Industry. Robin Butler, whom I came to know well later on, chaired this. The applications had been well sifted in advance. I particularly enjoyed reading the applications from small firms and meeting three representatives from the successful companies at a reception at Buckingham Palace later on which was always very well supported by many members of the Royal family.

On a very different note I had dealings with two notorious characters during my term of office. Robert Maxwell suddenly started to take an interest in our proceedings and to come to CBI meetings. It was never clear to me what his motivation was, but his company was a member, and ironically he seemed interested in printing a magazine for pensioners! I was placed next to him at a dinner in the Guildhall on 11 February 1988 to celebrate the centenary of the *Financial Times* just after his autobiography was published. Our place numbers were A12 and A13. I was glad he was number 13, not me!. We were wearing white ties and in full fig. To my utter astonishment he had a plastic bag under the table containing three copies of his book. He proceeded to tell me his life story referring to illustrations in the book once or twice. What an Ego! What a Showman! Later during the takeover bid for S&N I was travelling by car from some conference in Cambridge back into London when Maureen Hall came on the telephone to say that Robert Maxwell's personal assistant wanted me to call him. I had recollections of his role in the Collins takeover battle with Rupert Murdoch. My heart sank. Were we going to have to contend with him in some capacity as well as John Elliott? I told Maureen to ring his PA, say that she was my PA which indeed she was, and if Mr Maxwell wanted to speak with me he could call me himself. A short while later the telephone rang again. His booming voice came on the line. 'David,' he said, 'I'm due to make the speech to the Aberdeen chamber of Commerce next week. I know you did it last year and I want your advice on what line to take.' What an anticlimax! Little did I imagine the extraordinary and mysterious end to his life soon afterwards when he was facing financial ruin.

The other was Ernest Saunders. Guinness were of course important CBI members. His nickname in the brewing trade was 'Deadly Earnest'. Whatever qualities he may have had a sense of humour was not among them. It was in the wake of the controversy over their takeover of Distillers. Investigations were under way. He asked me to use my influence with the DTI to explain that he had a company to run, with vital world markets being neglected because he could not do his job as Chief Executive. He said the Secretary of State Paul Channon was in baulk because of his Guinness family connections. This was true. No one else in any position of authority would talk to him. 'Who do you want to speak to?' I asked. 'The politicians or the civil servants?' He suggested that it should be the civil servants. I rang Brian Hayes, the Permanent Secretary, explained the position and asked if he would spare ten minutes to see one of our important members. He readily agreed. Ernest Saunders went straight round to the DTI, unburdened himself, and subsequently wrote me a nice handwritten note thanking me for my pains.

Some months later the investigation into the Guinness affair was drawing to a close and the net was closing in. Once again Ernest asked to see me urgently. By this time he was operating out of a suite in the Inn on the Park overlooking Park Lane. We met at 7.30 a.m. as I was on my way to Heathrow. He was haggard, unshaven and looked pretty desperate. Scottish and Newcastle had a whole range of outstanding issues with Guinness on purely operational matters waiting for decisions. I brought a typed shopping list with me that I gave him. This had been my main reason for agreeing to see him. He said, 'The Authorities need a scapegoat who is not in the City. They are determined to get me. I need to speak to the Chancellor of the Exchequer. Please can you arrange

it.' I told him that I had already played that card for him once and was
not prepared to do so a second time. I never saw him again. Shortly
afterwards he was arrested.

The search for a new Director General to replace Terry Beckett was
naturally of critical importance. I asked my predecessors James Cleminson, Ray Pennock and John Greenborough for their collective wisdom.
We appointed Kit Power of Spencer Stewart to do the Executive Search
and he came up with an impressive shortlist. James and I did the
interviewing and were in no doubt that we had found an outstanding
candidate in John Banham. He had been the youngest director of
Mckinsey ever appointed and was currently Controller of the Audit
Commission, aged 47, a man of outstanding intellect and ebullient
charm, huge self-confidence and a headline grabbing turn of phrase. He
sailed into the organisation like a gale of wind from his native Cornwall.
There could hardly have been a greater contrast in management style to
the thorough, painstaking Ford trained Terry Beckett. I had quite
enjoyed the short interregnum because it had enabled me to act as a
Chief Executive again for a short time. If my first year was relatively crisis
free under the protective, steady, guiding hand of Terry my second was
infinitely less predictable under the colourful creativity of John Banham.
He had a phenomenal work rate and his brain worked so fast that it was
often difficult for staff let alone the President to keep up with him! We
had one or two problems when we said differing things to the press at
the same time. His were always infinitely more quotable than mine. This
was especially true at the time of the Black Monday stockmarket crash
in November 1987 during the CBI conference in Glasgow. But he was
enormous fun, we became great friends and no one could deny that his
five years in the job put the CBI on the map as never before.

Finally the time came to choose my own successor. Again this was
done in consultation with previous Presidents and I was most fortunate
in persuading Trevor Holdsworth of GKN to follow me as President
from May 1988. He was slightly older than me, and a man of great
distinction and industrial experience. It is sometimes said that music and
mathematics go together so perhaps it is no surprise that apart from being
an accountant he was an amateur pianist of professional concert standard.

Having worked in Glasgow most of my working life it was a great joy
to me when the CBI chose that city as the venue for my last conference.
But an issue of protocol arose. Whereas the conference was in the City,
over which the Lord Provost presided, it also came within the boundaries
of Strathclyde Region. It was well known that the Convenor of

Strathclyde and the Provost of Glasgow were pretty jealous of their respective territories and that if a turf war over the conference did not actually exist, careful diplomacy was needed on the CBI's part to avoid one breaking out. The organisers hit on the brilliant solution that the Convenor should open the exhibition in the Strathclyde Exhibition Centre the night before, but the Provost should welcome delegates to the conference the next morning. All went well until I visited the VIP suite to spend a last penny before taking my place on the platform. There I found to my horror the Convenor of Strathclyde, unattended, clad in all his finery with chains of office, clearly with every intention of taking his place on the platform. I knew there was no place for him! Everybody else had already taken their seats. The TV cameras were about to roll.

I found a slip of paper and scribbled a note to Trevor, who as Vice President was already on the dais, saying, 'Move at once to the front row of the stalls. Leave your seat NOW. Explanations later.' I gave it to a member of staff to deliver if she could. We entered to a fanfare of trumpets and to my huge relief there was an empty seat for the Convenor. The Lord Provost did his stuff and a Scottish Diplomatic incident was avoided!

At my final dinner as President in Grosvenor House on 12 May 1988 I spoke about Industry's relationship with the City of London and also the perennial hot potato of Europe. But *The Times* City Diary the next day ignored my weighty conclusions and instead printed a rhyme I had quoted about the merchant banking community:

> The Lazards came from New Orleans, the Morgans from New York;
> > The Guinness Mahons from Dublin town and not from County Cork;
> The Montagus (sans Capulets) from Italy perchance;
> > The Higginsons from Boston and the D'Erlangers from France.
> The Barings with the Schroeders and the sons of William Brandt
> > May well have read philosophy with old Emanuel Kant.
> The Hambro who left Norway's shores was formerly a Dane,
> > While Nathan Meyer Rothschild came from Frankfurt on the Maine.
> The Kleinworts who left Cuba when with Spain it still was one
> > Reached London – as the Samuels did – by 1831.
> The Seligmans, the Warburgs and the Halbert who joined Wagg
> > May not appear in Domesday but they've got it in the bag.
> So, if you fear for Britain by 1992
> > And do not want to act as other countries do,
> Just look around at London and the merchant banking set.
> > It's the most Uncommon Market the world will ever get!

I have left to the end of this chapter my meetings with and anecdotes about Margaret Thatcher during my time at the CBI. She will go down in history along with Winston Churchill as the most famous, most influential political leader of the century. To have known her and had some dealings with her, however trifling in the context of her own career, must be worth recording. I have related one or two already. There was always a sense of apprehension before meeting her. You had to have your wits about you. I was always nervous. She was never anything but welcoming and charming on arrival but you never knew when the balloon might go up! This was quite different to visits later on to see John Major, where I felt as if I was going to a business meeting with a very important but never daunting senior solicitor. She was extraordinarily kind and generous to me, giving a dinner in my honour at No. 10 on 30 September 1987 to which I was asked to pick most of the guests. She also wrote to me in the most generous terms when I retired in May 1988.

She had also written me a kind personal note when I was appointed a Knight of the British Empire in the Birthday Honours list of 1987. This of course was an enormous thrill and to pay a second visit to Buckingham Palace for another Investiture, this time with Louise and Felicity and Lucy, was the highlight of my career. Most CBI Presidents have already been knighted for previous endeavours before they are asked to take on the job and don't necessarily get any additional recognition for it. I certainly had not expected to be honoured after only a year in office so it came as a most delightful surprise, and to be given a KBE rather than become a Knight Bachelor was the icing on the cake. For the Birthday Honours you receive a letter dated 1 May from the Private Secretary, in this case Nigel Wickes, saying that 'the Prime Minister has it in mind to submit your name to the Queen for . . . before doing so she would be glad to be assured that this would be acceptable to you.' This is a clever formula because until the day of the publication of the list you don't know that she may not have changed her mind in the meantime or that it may have proved unacceptable to the Monarch! So apart from one's wife there is a strong incentive not to tell a soul.

The list was published on Saturday 13 June, two days after the General Election when the Conservatives had been returned for another five years. Louise and I were attending the Trooping the Colour on Horseguards Parade so we had a wonderful day of nostalgia and celebration. It was thirty-seven years since I had taken part in the parade myself. The investiture took place on 29 October. The Household were very kind in arranging for Louise and the girls to have particularly favourable seats. Louise took some time to come to terms with her new title and she preferred for a long while to remain Mrs Nickson, especially when doing her weekly shop in the Co-op in Aberfoyle. For the next few weekends I struggled to answer nearly seven hundred letters of congratulation by hand but eventually had to admit defeat and resort to signing my name on a typewritten message of thanks.

My family know well that I am one of the clumsiest people around. True to form my sister came up with the following offering:

ST CLUMSY

I thought you were a brigand always armed with rod or gun,
    But the papers say you're 'flawless' and take on work for fun.
The 'erudite' Sir David (how delighted Pa would be)
    Is set to make the Highlands shout 'whah-hey for Mrs T . . .'.
The corridors of power, it's true, are filled with birds of prey,
    But to see the rarer species you still need to hide away.
If you discard your old tweed cap to wear a gloriole
    Will you have time for humming-birds or golden oriole?
Haloes become uncomfortable (the hatbands get too tight)
    Don't let the nursery friend I love get buried out of sight!
We're Oh! So proud to have a Knight, but don't become a saint
    If Maggie has you canonised I may come over faint!

Louise and I lunched at Chequers on a Sunday several times. On the first occasion we were rather too early; indeed the first arrivals, Mrs Thatcher and Dennis, came out onto the steps. She welcomed Louise while Dennis said in true 'Dear Bill' fashion, 'Thank God you've arrived on time. Now I can have a drink.' But on another occasion I was standing in front of the fire, sipping sherry and talking quietly to Nicholas Goodison, when she suddenly remembered some recent press comment we had made about the privatisation of the Central Electricity Generating Board under Walter Marshall. She came sailing across, eyes blazing, wagging her forefinger at me and launched into a tirade starting with the words: 'I am so angry with the CBI,' and continuing for several minutes while the assembled company retired to a safe distance to watch the fun. Louise feared for my survival. Eventually she finished with the words: 'And that behaviour is typical, absolutely typical of the CBI.' Since I had gone out on a limb at the 1986 Conference to make a far more political speech than CBI presidents were supposed to do, and had generally been pretty supportive of the Government, I found this hard to take and said,

'Prime Minister, that is unfair and you know it!' As we left after lunch Charles Powell, her private secretary, said, 'Well, you took your medicine like a man. It's the only way.'

Shortly before John Banham's appointment was announced Paul Channon said to me that he had heard rumours that John was going to be appointed as the new Director General. He sought to warn me that, if true, the appointment would be very unpopular at No. 10. The next day I received a further warning in much more specific terms from Nigel Lawson. We were about to make the announcement so I thought I ought to go and face the music. I asked for an appointment to tell the Prime Minster personally about the announcement before it became public. She saw me without delay. I had not been in and out of any office so quickly in double time since being on Commanding Officer's Orders at the Guard's Depot! She was much displeased and let me know it. That was my second serious handbagging. Apparently John, never a man to mince his words, had produced some pretty critical stuff at the Audit Commission and to compound the crime it was known that he had once been invited, but had not stood, as a Liberal candidate in the West Country. He certainly did not qualify as 'one of us' at the time.

On another occasion we were invited to lunch at Chequers during a weekend conference with the Russians at Brocket Hall. I was co-chairing this event with a Russian in the context of President Gorbachov's recently announced *Glasnost* and *Perestroika* policies. The opportunities for openings for British companies were important. It was a complete coincidence that Louise and I had to leave the proceedings to lunch with Margaret Thatcher, but I did not let the Russians know that, and it did wonders for the CBI's reputation. Lord Brocket and his American model wife gave a dinner for us the last evening to which Foreign Office Ministers and diplomats came. Little did I know that he would so soon come to grief with the Inland Revenue and the police, and much later in 2004 receive much publicity as one of the finalists in the ITV show 'I'm a Celebrity. Get me out of here'! At dinner his wife was placed next to a very Slavic character, who looked to me like Breshnev. She was a very striking looking girl, taller than me, and would not have looked out of place in a James Bond film. As we said goodnight I thanked her for coming and said that I feared she must have had a dull evening. She looked down on me rather haughtily, I thought, and said, 'What makes you think that?' showing me at the same time the reverse of her place card, on which her companion had written 'From Russia with Love'.

I had further dealings with Margaret Thatcher during the last two years of her Premiership, but they fit more appropriately into a subsequent chapter.

Looking back on my two years at the CBI my main recollections are how lucky I was to have been asked to do the job, how fortunate I was to hold office during a period of relative business prosperity at a time when the country was benefiting from all the changes made possible by the Thatcher revolution, and how grateful I am for all the support and encouragement from members and staff. I enjoyed it.

CHAPTER 9

A visit to Windsor
March 1988

O N A FRIDAY EVENING in early February 1988 Louise and I were
sitting by the fire at Renagour when the telephone rang. It was Sir
Paul Greening, Master of the Household, ringing from Buckingham
Palace to say that he had been commanded by the Queen to invite us to
dine at Windsor Castle on 28 March and to stay the night afterwards. A
few days later a letter arrived confirming that we were invited to dine
and telling us to arrive between 6.45 and 7 p.m. that evening. We
subsequently learned that this was one of three or four evenings on which
the Queen entertained during her stay at Windsor each April. They were
known colloquially in the Household as invitations to 'Dine and Sleep'.
Beatrice, my PA at the CBI, who knew all about these matters, said we
were very lucky to be asked because it was ten years since a CBI
President had received such an invitation, and this year they were only
having two such evenings because of the impending State Visit from the
King of Norway, and because the Queen and Prince Philip were shortly
departing for Australia.

We did not know who our fellow guests were to be; but by chance I
had a meeting with Robin Butler in the Cabinet Office earlier in the day
to tell him that I was accepting the invitation to chair the Top Salaries
Review Body. He told me that the Prime Minister and Dennis Thatcher
were also due to stay at Windsor that night. Louise and I had flown down
from Scotland that morning. She went to see her mother in her flat at 15
Chiltern Court in Windsor, while I was driven up to London. I collected
Louise in the late afternoon and we were driven up the familiar road to
the Castle. Many memories flooded back as Louise recalled her girlhood
at 8 Lower Ward and I remembered days on Guard duty and all the
kindnesses shown to me by her parents during our courting days. We both
thought about our wedding in St George's Chapel thirty six years before.
This time however, instead of turning left through Henry VIII's Gateway
into the Lower Ward, we swept straight on up the hill to the Quadrangle.

We arrived at 6.45 p.m. to find footmen standing outside the doors
on the right of the Quadrangle. Our rooms were in the Augusta Tower.

Paul Greening, the Master of the Household, and Tim Lawrence, the Equerry, who was to marry the Princess Royal a few years later, were there to greet us. Our apartments were on the first floor. They comprised a bedroom, sitting room and dressing room, all looking out onto the South Front of the Castle towards the Copper Horse. We met our valet, Stephen Roberts, and lady's maid, Sylvia Lister. After a quick wash we were taken along the corridor to the Green Drawing Room where other guests were starting to assemble. The corgis were much in evidence up and down the corridor. In the middle were two delightful children's pedal cars, waiting no doubt for the grandchildren's arrival for Easter.

Our fellow guests were the Ambassador of Paraguay, a businessman and his nervous little wife; I suppose they had been nominated by the Foreign Office, as also the High Commissioner for Grenada and his wife. They were both black. At dinner Louise sat next to him and I sat beside her. They were both pleasant and easy companions. Then there was the Bishop of Gibraltar in Europe, John Satterthwaite. He was a charming and a splendid Bishop – a pity more Bishops are not like him! His diocese consists of the whole of Europe outside Great Britain. There was then a rather mousey-looking couple from Oxford. He was the architectural expert on Royal Palaces. She was a splendid bluestocking, extremely well read, particularly on Trollope, and talked a lot about Bishops. I suggested that it must have been a pose for Harold Macmillan to let himself be found reading Trollope before Cabinet meetings. Susan Hussey, the lady-in-waiting, disagreed saying that it was the best relaxation she knew.

Ted Hughes, the Poet Laureate, and his wife were the next guests. He was nice, friendly, interesting and very easy to talk to. He and I shared a passion for the salmon and he wrote a special poem for the Atlantic Salmon Trust of which I was to become Chairman the following year. In the Library after dinner special exhibits had been prepared, reflecting the particular interests of each guest; the angling material laid out on a table was designed to appeal to us both. She was his second wife (his first of course had been Sylvia Plath), younger by several years, tall, dark, with hair parted severely down the middle. After dinner it was evident that she was much more interested in the exhibits to do with poetry and had little time for fishing. I must have bored her stiff.

The final outside guests were the Warden of Radley, Dennis Silk, and his wife, both equally charming. Louise had a good chat to them both after dinner. Members of the Household not already mentioned were Sir William Heseltine, the Queen's private secretary, and his wife, both Australian; Geoffrey de Bellaigue and wife, he is the surveyor of the

Queen's works of art; the Queen's librarian, Oliver Everett and his wife – he was a former Private Secretary to Prince Charles. They now live at the Garden House, where the Morsheads once lived and where Louise did lessons with their daughters, Mary and Phoebe, in the War. They were most friendly, pressing Louise to go back the next day to see the house. Robert Fellowes, the Deputy Private Secretary, and Blair Stewart Wilson, both already known to us, made up the party.

The Prime Minister was having an Audience with the Queen, so shortly after we were all assembled, the Duke of Edinburgh came in on his own. We were presented to him in turn and he circulated, chatting round the room. A little later the Prime Minister swept in looking terrific. I happened to be talking to Mrs Colvin, the expert on Trollope, who was clearly nervous and had been mentally rehearsing her curtsey for the Queen. Maggie's appearance triggered her reaction and she curtseyed deeply. The Prime Minister did not look in the least surprised or displeased, shaking her head slightly and smiling kindly. I wondered if it often happened to her!

When Louise made her curtsey a little later the Queen said, 'Hello, back to your old haunts again.' In another conversation before dinner Prince Philip and the Bishop were discussing a book titled *Jesus Identified*. This, on the evidence of the Dead Sea Scrolls, was seeking to prove that it was historically impossible for Our Lord to have lived in the first century AD. The conversation became somewhat confused and animated, with the Bishop, I judged, winning marginally on points. But, not to be outdone, before we went in to dinner Prince Philip rushed off to his bedroom to get the book for the Bishop to read overnight.

I had quite a long talk with Margaret Thatcher standing in front of the fire. We talked about the political scene in Scotland. When we had lunch at Chequers a few weeks before she had asked my view as to whether or not she should attend the Scottish Cup final at Hampden and present the trophy. I had said that I thought with her present unpopularity there it might be a considerable risk. Amazingly she had remembered the conversation in detail. She told me she had decided to attend, but not to go out to meet the teams on the field beforehand. She would present the Cup in the stand after the game. She was very worried about the political scene for the Conservatives in Scotland and talked about it whenever I saw her. We also spoke about the recent decision by Fords to withdraw from their proposed electronics factory at Dundee because the Transport and General Workers Union would not give them the Industrial Relations guarantees which they were seeking in advance of finally

Our Golden Wedding at the River House, 18 October 2002

At one of the last parties on the Royal Yacht Britannia *before she was decommissioned*

Beatrice Gilpin's retirement party in 1988 after serving as PA to eleven presidents of the CBI
Back row from L to R: Sir Ralph Bateman, Sir James Clemison, Sir Campbell Fraser, Self, Lord Pennock, Sir John Greenborough, Viscount Watkinson
Front row from L to R: Sir Arthur Norman, Lord McFadzean, Sir Stephen Brown, Sir Michael Clapham

As Chancellor of Glasgow Caledonian University conferring an Honorary degree on President Mandela in the gardens of Buckingham Palace on 10 July 1996

The guests for dinner at Gogar Bank House before taking the salute at Edinburgh Tattoo on 6 August 1997

Investiture at Buckingham Palace with my mother and Louise in November 1981

Investiture at Buckingham Palace with Louise, Felicity and Lucy in October 1987

The three girls in hats at Tigh-na-Fraoch in 1994

The three girls at our Golden Wedding at the River House in October 2002

1 January 1994 at Renagour with Sophie, Louise, Nutkin, Harriet, Felicity and Emily after New Year's Honours list announcing my Peerage

My introduction to the House of Lords with my supporters, Robin Leigh Pemberton (Lord Kingsdown) and Norman Macfarlane (Lord Macfarlane of Bearsden)

The family Millennium photograph taken at Renagour with all my parents' children, grandchildren and great grandchildren

Back row L to R: James Cox, eldest son of Charlie and Belinda Cox (b. 18/6/83); Iona Campell, eldest daughter of Melfort and Lucy Campbell (b. 3/4/86); Emily Lewis, eldest daughter of Jamie and Felicity Lewis (b. 5/2/84); Arabella Cox, daughter of Charlie and Belinda Cox (b. 30/10/80); William Shirley, eldest son of Robert and Susannah Tamworth (b. 10/12/84); Hermione Shirley, daughter of Robert and Susannah Tamworth (b. 11/12/82); Sophie Lewis, 2nd daughter of Jamie and Felicity Lewis (b. 14/2/86); Geordie Cox, 2nd son of Charlie and Belinda Cox (b. 20/7/86)

2nd row L to R: Rosemary Campbell, 3rd daughter of David and Louise Nickson (b. 11/2/63); Alastair Campbell, eldest son of Bob and Norma Campbell of Altries (b. 21/8/52); Alexander Campbell (Beetle), eldest son of Alastair and Rosemary Campbell (b. 19/12/95); Lucy Campbell, 2nd daughter of Louise and David Nickson (b. 8/7/59); Melfort Campbell, youngest son of Bob and Norma Campbell of Altries (b. 6/6/56); Susannah Tamworth (Viscountess Tamworth), 2nd daughter of Charlie and Mary Sheepshanks (b. 1/11/59); Robert Tamworth (Viscount Tamworth) – ill with Flu! Eldest son of Robin (Earl) and Annabel Ferrers (b. 5/11/62); Alice Sheepshanks, daughter of Struan and Gabrielle Robertson (b. 12/8/64)

Seated L to R: Charlie Cox, eldest son of Geordie and Mary Cox of Gourdie (b. 14/9/51); Belinda Cox, eldest daughter of Charlie and Mary Sheepshanks (b. 12/5/55); David Nickson (Lord Nickson of Renagour, Life Peer), son of Geoffrey and Janet Nickson (b. 27/11/29); Mary Sheepshanks, daughter of Geoffrey and Janet Nickson (b. 5/7/31); Louise Nickson (Lady Nickson), only daughter of Louis (Beetle) and Jane Cockcraft (b. 7/8/30); James Campbell, youngest son of Alastair and Rosie Campbell (b. 14/1/99); Felicity Lewis, eldest daughter of David and Louise Nickson (b. 3/11/55); James Lewis, eldest son of Jimmy and Celia Lewis (b. 19/8/54)

Front row: Charles Sheepshanks, son of William and Alice Sheepshanks (b. 11/5/96); Octavia Sheepshanks, daughter of William and Alice Sheepshanks (b. 31/12/93); Harriet Lewis, youngest daughter of Jamie and Felicity Lewis (b. 28/1/89); Araminta Campbell, 2nd daughter of Melfort and Lucy Campbell (b. 22/5/88); Freddie Shirley, youngest son of Robert and Susannah Tamworth (b. 1/6/90); Alice Campbell, youngest daughter of Melfort and Lucy Campbell (b. 23/6/90); Andrew Petronanos, son of Rosie Campbell and George Petronanos (b. 11/2/88) committing themselves to the major investment required. This was the topical news story of the moment and a great blow for Scottish jobs. We found no difficulty in agreeing that our Trade Unions were still one of the greatest barriers to British productivity and competitiveness.

She knew of my conversation with Robin Butler earlier in the day, and expressed her satisfaction that I was accepting the Chair of the Top Salary Review Body. Fortunately for me she kept off the more delicate subjects – of the high level of sterling against the Deutschmark, and CBI criticisms of the Government's handling of electricity privatisation, resulting in greatly increased costs for industry. She did not refer to the ticking off in front of other guests in the long room at Chequers before Sunday lunch only a few weeks before.

We then rushed off to change; all clothes laid out and baths run, lady's maid on hand to do up the buttons on Louise's dress. We had had the fear of God put into us over the speed with which the Queen changed, and were told we had to be back in the drawing room before she was. In the event, we did a quick turn round and were back within a quarter of an hour; the Household gave us a good mark for being first back in the drawing room. Not so the diplomats, who had to be fetched from their bedrooms. Louise wore her long black dress with the pearl and diamond choker which I gave her early in the summer to coincide with my KBE. She looked splendid. We did not have very long in the Red Drawing Room before we went in to dinner.

We sat down twenty-eight for dinner. The Ambassador sat on the right of the Queen, and on her left was the High Commissioner. Louise was beyond the High Commissioner with William Heseltine on her left. The Prime Minister sat on Prince Philip's right. Paul Greening told me that when the Queen and he were discussing the table plan, it had been suggested that they had seen quite a lot of the Prime Minister lately; and that perhaps she might be placed elsewhere. However, Prince Philip said, 'No, No! There is something I want a word with her about.' So she duly sat next to him. I wish I had known what it was!

There must have been nearly twenty footmen, butlers and servants round the table, all in the Windsor uniform designed by George III. Dinner was delicious. We ate the first course off silver plates and the rest off beautiful porcelain, which we could not identify. For the whole of the first half of the meal the Queen spoke to her right hand neighbour, and accordingly, Mrs Gibbs, the High Commissioner's wife on my left spoke to me; and so on round the table so that Louise spent the first half talking to the High Commissioner. At the end of the first course the

Queen changed and spoke to her left. I noticed Paul Greening next to me watching anxiously for this signal so that he could ensure that everyone else changed partners at the same time! Louise then talked to William Heseltine. Word had evidently got around that she had been brought up in the Castle and that her father had been a Military Knight. He said to her, 'My goodness, I hear your father fought in the Boer War.' This was true. Beetle had been commissioned from Woolwich aged eighteen and sent straight out to South Africa. Throughout the evening others mentioned her participation in the Princesses' Christmas panto-mimes and her other Windsor connections. So she had a delightfully nostalgic evening.

I had an interesting chat with Paul Greening about the Royal Yacht *Britannia*. It was used for Overseas Trade Promotions as well as for Royal Visits. He was the Captain before becoming the Master of the Household. He hoped that the potential for overseas earnings would justify the building of a new yacht when the present vessel came to the end of its useful life. In the event of course we know that despite strong lobbying this did not happen. (A few years later I was having lunch at No. 10 with John Major on the very day that a ministerial statement was being made in the Commons to this effect.) I asked Paul Greening how the invitation lists for occasions such as this were drawn up. He said that a number of lists were prepared each year of likely people with widely differing interests. He went through them with the Queen who made the final choice.

After dinner we repaired to the Red Drawing Room for a short while before setting out on a tour of the State Apartments and the Royal Library. Over coffee in the Drawing Room the Queen talked to Louise. They discussed families and grandchildren. The Queen said she had four and a quarter grandchildren. Louise was able to cap this by saying she had four and three quarters! They both agreed that modern mothers knew far too much and 'far more fuss is made about having babies than there used to be'. Those were the Queen's words, not Louise's! They also spoke of the awful accident a few weeks before when Prince Charles had so nearly been killed by the avalanche in which his friend Hugh Lindsay, a former equerry, had died. The Queen also said that they were going to have to rewire the Castle. The wiring was going to be ring-circuited under the floor because 'I certainly don't want to have to put new silk onto these walls too often.' She was wearing a daffodil yellow dress with a lovely diamond necklace, bracelet and earrings; though not a crown, to the great disappointment of Emily when she enquired of Louise the next day!

We then set out on our tour. This was one of the highlights of the evening. We started at about eleven p.m. and did not return until one o'clock. We began in the Royal Chapel. This housed among other things glass cases containing the Orders belonging to various members of the Royal Family – wonderful diamond Garters, Stars and Georges. Then on, through the State Apartments, through St George's Hall (where Ted Hughes gave me some useful tips for my forthcoming St George's Day speech in the Mansion House), through the Queen's Guard Chamber, the Presence Chamber, the Audience Chamber to the Ballroom. Everywhere there were fabulous portraits, tapestries and furniture. All of course are open to the public at normal times. The Van Dyck triple portrait of Charles I, the portrait of Elizabeth I by an unknown artist and a Rubens self-portrait stand out particularly in the memory.

In the Royal Library the special exhibits were laid out for each guest. Ted Hughes and I were shown our table. At one end was an essay by Edward VII when he was a boy dated about 1850. It described how gas was made following a visit he had paid to a gasworks. Its relevance to my career in industry escaped me for a moment, but it was clearly as close as the Royal Archives could come to the Confederation of British Industry. Ted Hughes' offering at the other end was much more obvious: William Wordsworth's letter of acceptance on being offered the post of Poet Laureate. The two items in the centre recognised our joint interest in fishing and were fascinating.

The first was an invoice dated 1855 for supplying a fishing tackle outfit for the Prince of Wales in the sum of £13.18s.6d. from a firm called Chevalier Bowness. The second was a letter written by Sir Henry Ponsonby, Queen Victoria's Private Secretary, from Balmoral to his wife, dated 6 June 1873. I scribbled down one paragraph in my diary. My transcript may not be quite accurate but it read roughly as follows:

> Here they talk of nothing but fish, and as they catch none it seems to me that they might well find some other subject. As no one catches anything the Queen spoke to me upon the subject and observed 'Something should be done'. This remark I reported to Robertson [Dr Robertson was the Factor]. He boiled up of course. He was out fishing for three or four hours with the rest two days ago and laid down at last, wearied with seeing nothing, when suddenly a fish was seen. He jumped up, ran with his rod like a boy for fear that Ripon would be there first, and plunged into the water above his knees for half an hour – but in vain. Then down home all wet for he had not boots – and next day wondered what gave him a cold. He is seventy-three or four. All right in the evening and most keen at billiards!

(Dr Robertson sounds a man after my own heart, and at precisely the same age I can see myself behaving in exactly the same way. Salmon do not seem to have been any more plentiful at Balmoral in June, a hundred and thirty years ago, than they are today!)

There were some amazing exhibits on display. I remember especially the shirt worn by Charles I at his execution, with ribbons on the sleeves and dark specks of blood down the front. This was the shirt that was sufficiently thick so that he should not be observed to shiver on the scaffold. At one point the Queen turned to me and said, 'If you look over there in that case you will see the Act of Union which will interest you.' There was one of the two Scottish copies of the Act with the seals and signatures of the twelve or so nobles who had signed it in 1707, including as I remember Montrose, Wemyss, Stair and Mar. She also pointed out to me the essay she herself had written as a girl on her parents' Coronation; and the handwritten order issued by Winston Churchill in August 1942 to Alexander instructing him to clear out the German and Italian troops from Africa. Alexander's cable in reply the following April, also handwritten, said that he had complied with the Prime Minister's orders and awaited further instructions. The Queen said, 'My father was very good at picking up this sort of thing. He just asked people for letters that interested him.'

She showed Louise Lawrence Whistler's beautiful design presented to her when she opened one of the Heathrow Terminals. It was a small concave glass exhibit, beautifully lit, giving an aerial view of the Castle with the airport in the background, very similar to the view one so often sees coming in to land from the shuttle from Scotland. I remember a marvellous edition of Audubon's birds measuring about 3 ft by 4 ft. I was frightened to turn over the pages lest I tear them. It was the biggest book I have ever seen.

Louise pointed out to me the little alcove where she remembered Owen Morshead telling her that they watched for the messenger from the battle of Blenheim, where now the current Duke of Marlborough brings the rent flags every year. She also showed me the magnificent Tudor fireplace against which Beetle was photographed. That is the photo we have of him in the drawing room at the River House.

These recollections of the Library don't do justice to a wonderful hour spent wandering round in conversation with other guests and looking at these priceless and historic treasures. Louise recalls one case on our way back to the State Apartments, not in the Library, full of exhibits from the Tippu Sultan, with a particularly magnificent bird, gold, encrusted with diamonds and other precious stones, so pricelessly valuable that it is never normally on display except for these private occasions.

We returned through the Waterloo Chamber and the King's Chamber, down the great staircase where there was a massive suit of armour made for Henry VIII. It was at this point that I was talking to the Duke of Edinburgh. He said, 'Yes. It is full of things. Over there are Nell Gwyn's bellows.' I must have looked incredulous or expostulated in some way for he said. 'Don't you believe me? Do you think I'm pulling your leg? I'll show you.' This he did. Next he took me to look at a case in which lay the musket ball that had killed Nelson at Trafalgar with a bit of gold epaulette still attached to it; this was dug out of the wound after he was dead. In describing this Prince Philip lost the word for 'epaulette' and patted himself on the shoulder with that sense of irritation we all have when a very familiar word eludes our brains. Close by was Napoleon's dressing case. In the King's Dining Room we saw the fine Grinling Gibbons carvings introduced during Charles II's restoration of the Castle.

Finally we returned to the Drawing Room for a nightcap. A vivid memory was to see the Queen and the Prime Minister, the two greatest women in the world, sitting together on the sofa while they chatted in front of the fire. The Queen and the Duke left and we went back along the Green corridor to our rooms, surrounded by yet more wonderful portraits. Outside our room was a portrait by Hoppner of Charles Manners-Sutton, Dean of Windsor and later Archbishop of Canterbury, Louise's great-great-grandfather. The silver entrée dishes which we have belonged to him and George III gave him the gold snuffbox.

In our bedroom were pictures by Canaletto, Landseer (of Queen Victoria on a horse), Hayter and Paul Sandby. And so to bed by 1.15 a.m.

Next morning we were called at 7 a.m. and had breakfast in our room at 7.30 as I had to catch the nine o'clock shuttle back to Edinburgh.

The visitors' book was brought to us over breakfast. It was started in 1984 and only used for the Windsor parties at Christmas, Easter, the Windsor Horse Show and Ascot. Most of the signatures were of Royal Family parties, but we noticed that at the previous Easter party guests included Nigel Lawson, David Attenborough, George Jefferson, Kit McMahon, Nicholas Goodison, David Sheppard, Simon Hornby and John Harvey Jones.

Our room was about to be made up for the family's arrival for Easter, but we did not know who was to use it after us – though the Princess Royal usually occupies it, so Louise's maid informed her.

Thus ended a fairytale evening; over far too quickly like a beautiful dream.

CHAPTER 10

Hambros, General Accident, Clydesdale, Scottish Enterprise 1989–1998

As MY TWO YEARS at the CBI drew to an end I began to receive a number of approaches for further employment. So far as I had any plans, these were to return to Scotland, complete my term of office as Chairman of Scottish and Newcastle and continue with the non-executive directorships I already held with General Accident, Edinburgh Investment Trust and the Clydesdale Bank; they had by then indicated that they wished me to return to their Board after my resignation during the Australian takeover bid for S&N. It had not occurred to me that I might be a candidate as Chairman of other large companies based in the south, but this seemed to be the case. I had one or two preliminary conversations before deciding firmly that I did not wish to prolong my stay in London. I was then asked to take over the Chairmanship of the Scottish Development Agency. This clinched it; I wanted to return to a base in Scotland. I was sixty and was looking forward to spending more time at home, while continuing to work three or four days a week.

Charlie Hambro was one of those who came to see me. He asked if I would like 'a desk' at Hambros, i.e. a London base with all office facilities and a salary in their smart merchant banking headquarters at Tower Hill. I turned down this generous approach but did agree to become a non-executive director of their plc. They were invariably charming and hospitable but I never felt particularly at home there. The freewheeling, individual and sometimes buccaneering management style may have created the success and reputation on which old-fashioned merchant venturers, like Hambros, had based their reputation. But it was a far cry from my own business experience. The somewhat uneasy duopoly between two powerful and able Chief Executives, Chips Keswick and Christopher Sporborg, each with their separate agendas pursued with equal panache, made neither for a clear corporate strategy nor effective board control. I do not think I was of much use to them or to Charlie except as a convenient 'No-man', as chairman of the remuneration

121

committee in turning down again and again the repeated requests from their senior executives for what seemed to me excessive bonuses based on too little evidence of corresponding results! The culture that seemed to me to be based for some individuals on personal greed rather than on very much loyalty to company or colleagues may be common enough in the financial world post 1990s but it is not one that greatly appeals to me. Eventually the margins on Hambros' traditional businesses became too tight and like so many other distinguished household names in the City they fell on their sword at the feet of a foreign competitor.

One of my non-executive colleagues at Hambros, after three years or so, was Robin Leigh-Pemberton, by then Lord Kingsdown, who had completed his distinguished term as Governor of the Bank of England. In October 1989 he had invited me to lunch with him at the Bank and asked me if I would become a member of their Court. This was a very great honour, and not one to be turned down lightly. But it would have involved weekly meetings of the Court every Thursday in London; the invitation came at a moment when I was once again becoming more and more involved with commitments in Scotland. Reluctantly I declined. Robin was most understanding but I could not help speculating how often, if ever, such a distinguished opportunity was turned down.

By 1991 I had enjoyed over twenty years on the board of what had formerly been the General Accident Fire and Life Insurance Company, GA for short. This was based in Perth. It had a fine reputation both in the abstruse world of insurance and underwriting and as one of Scotland's proudest financial companies. It is no exaggeration to say that the economy and employment of Perth depended to a large extent on the fortunes of General Accident and Dewar's whisky. I had served under four chairmen, Harry Polwarth, Harvey Stuart-Black, Gordon Simpson and now David Airlie. Each in their own way had presided over a most prestigious board, Chief General Managers of common skills but very differing styles and, despite the roller-coaster nature of the insurance cycle, many years of sound performance.

When I first joined the board in 1971 I was aged forty and by several years the youngest director. The tradition was that the newest member proposed a toast to the city of Perth at the banquet following the AGM. The entire establishment including the Lord Lieutenant, the Provost and other bigwigs attended. The planning of the menu, the seating arrangements and the elaborate place cards was one of the Company Secretary's most arduous annual tasks. Agents and representatives of overseas subsidiary boards were flown in from all over the world.

Shareholders were noticeable by their absence. They might have asked what the whole junket cost! I prepared a short speech based on a quotation from Sir Walter Scott: 'If an intelligent stranger were asked to chose the most varied and most beautiful area of Scotland, assuredly he would name the City and County of Perth.' I was quite nervous but very pleased with myself at having found this gem. The evening before at dinner the most senior Director, Lord Sinclair, a splendid little man who had been Chairman of Imperial Tobacco, seriously wounded in the 1914–18 war, and by then aged over eighty (no question of non-executives being expected to retire at seventy in those days) said to me, 'Well, my boy, I hear you are to make the speech tomorrow. Don't make the same mistake as I did by quoting that old saw from Walter Scott. Sir John Ure Primrose, the Provost at the time, said that he was surprised at me; the quotation was so well worn it was positively threadbare.' That did wonders for my confidence!

Unlike most companies GA were keen to involve wives in corporate occasions. Louise must have attended endless dinners at Gleneagles over the years. Never one to be overly enthusiastic about business occasions, she came to enjoy the General Accident dinners and found many highly congenial kindred spirits among the wives. In 1988 we went out with the entire board to join in the celebrations for the centenary of the United States Company in Philadelphia. We had a splendid time and afterwards visited Jamestown, Yorktown and Williamsburg, thus improving our knowledge of American history enormously.

But by the last decade of the century global markets and much larger global companies were dominating the insurance industry. In an effort to expand strategically we ran into some rough water especially as a result of the banking crisis in New Zealand and Australia. None of the five large British composites could compete for size with European and American rivals. Various strategies for merger were considered. All involved giving up a degree of independence and with it our unique position in Scotland. This weighed very heavily with the board, but ultimately we all had to recognise that fewer than ten per cent of our shareholders were based in Scotland to share any nationalistic pride we might have. We looked closely at merger with the Guardian Royal Exchange, the weakest of the five composites, in a marriage in which we would have been dominant; but this fell down on personalities. We would have had the Chief Executive, but their Chairman, as it happened Charlie Hambro, proved unacceptable to our board. Then Royal Insurance bid for Sun Alliance. Our Executive and our advisers put up a

strong case for us to intervene with a counter bid. We had a fraught
board meeting with the Executive eager to have a go. There were not
many non-executives present as the meeting was necessarily called at very
short notice. We would have had to bid at a very full price with no
latitude to increase our offer at a later stage without diluting our share
price. I pressed our advisers as to our chances of success and they,
reluctantly it seemed to me, admitted that these were no better than 50
per cent. The non-executive directors present rejected the plan by the
narrowest of votes. If either of these initiatives had gone ahead the shape
of the British Insurance market would be very different.

We finally concluded an agreed merger with the largest of the five
composites, the Commercial Union, under the title Commercial General
Union, but this was a short lived marriage before the new combined
board concluded a further alliance with Norwich Union, under which
brand all UK insurance now comes, though under the peculiarly
infelicitous umbrella of Aviva plc. Like so many others I abhor the
modern corporate craze for meaningless new titles when perfectly sound
long established and respected household names are available. What was
wrong with CGNU to describe the marriages of three famous companies, Commercial Union, General Accident and Norwich Union?

I was Deputy Chairman of GA from 1993 to 1998 during this period
and closely involved with David Airlie in finding his successor. We
wanted the best man for the job of course, but how much better if he
were also a Scot to lead a Scottish company! We both thought that Alick
Rankin, having given up the chair of S&N, would be the perfect choice,
but both agreed that in the modern environment of politically correct
corporate governance we needed a completely independent professional
search of international candidates, both male and female, with no
accusations of 'cronyism'. What a perfectly ghastly word! However I
cannot pretend that we were anything other than delighted when, after
some months, they came up with our original choice. So Alick became
chairman in succession to David and it was Alick and myself for GA, who
concluded the headings of agreement with Nicholas Baring, the retiring
Chairman of the CU and the Chairman designate of the new combined
company, Pehr Gyllenhammar. This meeting took place one Sunday
morning in the CU's private flat in South Audley Street. So secret did
we consider it to be that Alick and I left our GA car and driver at the
Park Lane entrance of Grosvenor House, and walked through the hotel
and on into South Audley Street. We were all pleased that, in these days
when the Press seem to know what is going to happen long before

employees or shareholders, there were no leaks and no advance speculation. Bob Scott, the outstanding GA chief executive, got the top job and continued to hold it after the subsequent merger with the Norwich Union. But most of us who knew the old GA find it sad now, when we drive past the old Headquarters in Perth, that yet another famous Scottish company is just a memory.

In my Collins days we had banked with both the Royal Bank of Scotland and the Clydesdale. There was no doubt which was the most understanding and helpful when we ran into trouble in the nineteen seventies. I used to go to see Robert Fairbairn, the Chief General Manager of the Clydesdale, or later his successor Alick Macmillan. There was no question of being fobbed off with a relatively junior branch manager, as was the case with the Royal, where all decisions had to be referred upwards for approval. The Clydesdale appeared to appreciate our difficulties and were highly supportive when we achieved the objectives we had promised. So it was no great surprise to me when I was invited to join the Clydesdale Board a few years later in 1981. I joined on the same day as two others who became close friends and colleagues in various enterprises, Norman Macfarlane and Douglas Hardie.

The Clydesdale's strongholds were the west of Scotland and the North-East as a result of the acquisition of the old Northern Bank long before the war. It was a wholly owned subsidiary of the Midland Bank but was allowed to operate with a remarkable degree of independence. It was in many ways delightfully old fashioned. There was a large board of Scottish establishment figures, whose main function was to add lustre and prestige rather than to take any active interest in banking operations. Indeed Robert Fairburn, by then the Chairman, appeared actively to discourage this. His sole injunction to new directors was to be on time for board meetings and not to ask questions.

One splendid anachronism was the role of a duty director to supervise the ritual burning of old bank notes on board meeting days. Accompanied by two assistant General Managers and two bank stewards one descended through a series of locked doors to the security rooms in the bowels of the building. Here there was a furnace lit by a steward with the aid of much newspaper and a flare. Before the notes were consigned to hell fire the duty director was supposed to carry out a random check to see that each bundle contained the correct number and designation of notes; then all present signed a leather bound ledger certifying the amount destroyed. It was a considerable novelty to burn several million pounds of cash in this way! Finally there was a splendid *Whoosh* and a cloud of black smoke belched out of the chimney to pollute the citizens of Glasgow. Not for long did this practice survive the attentions of modern bureaucracy in the form of the Health and Safety directorate. If the assembled cast had been attired in Yeomen of the Guard uniforms it would have rivalled the ceremony of the Keys at the Tower of London as a piece of theatre!

In 1987, shortly before I resigned from the board as a result of the conflict of interest during the Scottish and Newcastle takeover battle, the National Australia Bank acquired the Clydesdale. Eric Yarrow was Chairman at the time and a splendidly colourful and stylish anglophile, Rupert Clarke, who had served as a young man in the Irish Guards on Field Marshal Alexander's staff in the war, was Chairman of NAB. For a time all went well but the writing was on the wall and the days of any pretence that the Clydesdale was anything other than a wholly owned subsidiary were over. Eric very generously invited me back onto the board and then in 1991 to succeed him as Chairman. Rupert Clarke asked me to join the board of National Australia in Melbourne.

Richard Cole-Hamilton had followed Alick Macmillan as Chief General Manager. He retired soon after my appointment and we appointed the first outsider in Charles Love from the Trustee Savings Bank. Within a year he was dead as a result of a heart attack while on a skiing holiday in Switzerland. It was New Year's Day 1994 and Louise and I were taking assorted grandchildren to the *Singing Kettle* in the Scottish Exhibition Centre in Glasgow. I had just been elevated to the House of Lords in the New Year's Honours list so we were in celebratory mood. My heart sank when I was summoned over the loudspeaker to be told the news. Later I gave the address at Charles's Thanksgiving service in St Giles' Cathedral.

From that point on the Clydesdale's reputation and independence began to wane. An Australian was appointed to run the bank and the drive to rationalise and achieve the economies from global synergy was on. I was required to reduce the number of non-executive directors from ten to three or four, not an enjoyable or popular process. Gradually the discretion to take executive decisions in a Scottish context was eroded. Meantime our competitors were free to expand without these constraints and in the case of the Royal Bank did so with quite spectacular success under the leadership of George Younger.

There was one golden interlude when Fred Goodwin was appointed as Chief Executive of the Clydesdale. He had established his reputation as a brilliant young accountant in charge of the BICC liquidation and

had been cleverly approached by Don Argus, the CEO of National
Australia. Fred made an immediate impact and who knows what might
have happened if he had stayed and gone on to run the Australian Bank,
a job he was offered as Don's successor. I greatly enjoyed working with
him during our short period of office together. But the Clydesdale was
too small for his talents and he did not wish to move his home to
Melbourne. George Mathewson of the Royal approached him and
despite my best endeavours he left to become within a few short years
the most successful and best-known businessman in Scotland running the
UK's largest bank.

I cannot say that my term of office at the Bank from 1991 to1998 was
the most enjoyable part of my business career. I suspect that my successor
Russell Sanderson would say exactly the same about his six years up to
2004. But there were great compensations. However tiresome some of
the Australian Executives proved, our colleagues on the National
Australian Bank board were most distinguished and all delightful. I may
have been unlucky in my experience of Canadian businessmen, whom I
have generally found to be unexciting and over earnest. (I had turned
down an invitation a year or so earlier to join the board of the Canadian
Bank of Commerce.) No one could ever call the Australians dull! They
were larger than life, full of enthusiasm, warm and most hospitable.
Rupert Clarke and his amazingly colourful wife Cath, and his successor
as Chairman Bill Irvine and his wife Sue were kindness itself to Louise
and me on our various trips. We flew out together in great comfort on
British Airways or Qantas once a year in January for the AGM in
Melbourne. At least a thousand shareholders attended the meeting in the
giant conference centre. I thought I had had my hands full taking Annual
General Meetings of argumentative shareholders at Scottish and Newcastle but they did not hold a candle to those of the National Australia.

We usually managed to have a few days' holiday in Victoria or
Tasmania afterwards. Bill Irvine shared my passion for trout fishing and
we were their guests on two occasions. We greatly enjoyed the
enormous variety of colourful Australian birds. We had been introduced
to these by Ken Wilder, the Managing Director of Collins in Sydney in
my Collins days in the seventies. I had enjoyed Sydney as a vibrant and
exciting city. Now we came to appreciate the different charms and grace
of Melbourne and the surrounding countryside of Victoria. Charles Allen
and his wife kindly arranged a trip round the huge sewage farm outside
the city with its bewildering variety of waders and waterfowl. In between
times we watched the Australian Tennis Championships, cricket at the

MCG and the never to be forgotten final of Australian Rules football at which Bill Irvine had been no mean performer in his youth. I had to make several trips by myself for Board meetings, often flying out from London on a Monday arriving Wednesday morning for a Thursday meeting and back home by Friday! Not to be recommended; and the older one grew the longer it seemed to take to recover from the jetlag.

Another delight was to renew an old friendship from my Eton days. Ralph Assheton and I had been in Pop together. After a distinguished career in RTZ and as a non-executive of other large international companies, now Lord Clitheroe, he had become Chairman of the Yorkshire Bank, a sister of the Clydesdale, also owned by the NAB.

Apart from his keen mind Ralph combines a delightfully patrician courtesy with a wonderfully dry wit. His family have lived in the same house in Lancashire for many centuries. When his eldest son, young Ralph, went off to fight in the first Gulf War Ralph remarked that it was the first time an Assheton had born arms for his country since the battle of Agincourt. The Australians thought he was priceless but they most certainly respected his wisdom and authority. We had a number of happy trips with Ralph and Juliet. He and I combined forces on a number of issues where we felt our colleagues from down under failed to appreciate local sensitivities. I am bound to say we did not often win. Quite one of the nicest by-products of my banking period was the renewed friendship with the Clitheroes.

Elsewhere I have referred to my good fortune in being served by a succession of superbly competent personal assistants. Ellison Simpson at the Bank was one of the very best, quiet, unassuming, unruffled, liked by all. She not only coped with the Bank business but also became expert in dealing with all my personal and family affairs and even the esoteric jargon connected with fishing politics. I also had a driver covering my work at the Bank and Scottish Enterprise, Lance Macrobert; fiercely independent of mind, a passionate Rangers supporter, intolerant of others to a fault, he kept me constantly amused and never once in several years was he at the wrong place or at the wrong time.

One evening when I was sitting late in my office in Glasgow the telephone rang. It was Reo Stakis. He had come to Scotland from his native Cyprus as a boy aged sixteen after the Great War to support his mother and her large family by selling lace. He had prospered by hard work and business acumen to build a large business empire, the Stakis Group, owning hotels and casinos in Scotland and London. He was widely liked and respected and had recently been knighted. He also owned a private property company called Ravenstone. I had got to know him through his trading links with Scottish and Newcastle and also in the shooting field. He was a fanatical shot and a most generous shooting host.

He asked if he could come round to see me at once on a matter of extreme urgency. He explained that his property company had run into difficulties and he had been advised that unless the banks were prepared to delay calling in their loans he would have to declare his company insolvent and himself bankrupt by the next morning. The Clydesdale's interests were relatively modest and I had no difficulty in persuading my executive colleagues to stay their hand. The problem lay with the other two Scottish Banks, who were both taking a hard line. I managed to speak to George Younger, the Chairman of the Royal Bank of Scotland, that evening and later to Peter Burt, at that time Chief Executive of the Bank of Scotland. They both saw the point, as I put it to them, that to ruin such a well-known and well-liked Scottish businessman on the eve of the 1992 General Election would do the reputation of Scottish Banks no good at all. A meeting was called for the next morning, the crisis averted and Reo's reputation saved. His gratitude was touching. He gave Louise one of the priceless original lace tablecloths he had brought from Cyprus all those years before and myself a dozen lovely white silk handkerchiefs, not to mention numerous subsequent invitations to shoot at Glassingall and Rossie. He was a lovely man. A few years later I attended his funeral in the Greek Orthodox Cathedral in Glasgow. It was a remarkable occasion; the church was packed, there were no fewer than three separate orations, and the service, entirely in Greek, lasted three hours.

When I retired from the Bank they commissioned a portrait. I chose Anne Mackintosh as the painter. She lived in Killearn, which was handy. Apart from producing a portrait in the uniform of an officer in the Archers of which both my family and the Bank seemed to approve she was the most delightful company. I looked forward keenly to my sittings. Unfortunately the reproduction copy for us to keep, not in any way the fault of Anne, was not a success. My face was bright red (not unusual) but the uniform seemed to be blue. The other time I had my portrait painted was by another Scottish painter, Leonard Boden, for Scottish and Newcastle. Whether this still hangs in their boardroom I do not know. I knew Louise would not like it when she came to see it in the artist's studio, though I thought it was not bad. She was tact personified. She said, 'I think it's a wonderful portrait. It isn't the man I married but I would have liked to be married to that man,' thus successfully conveying the fact that it was altogether too flattering to achieve a good likeness!

In 1988, at much the same time as others were beating a path to my door with offers of further employment, I was offered two Public Sector jobs. The first came through the Cabinet Office, in other words with the approval of the Prime Minister. This was as Chairman of the Senior Salaries Review Body, then called the Top Salaries Review Body. This is the subject of a later chapter. I had accepted this unpaid part-time appointment in March. Soon afterwards came the invitation to become the next Chairman of the Scottish Development Agency. This was supposed to be a two or three day a week job. The opportunity to do another Public Sector job based in Scotland, and to try to put something back into the place I had worked for most of my business life seemed most attractive. The offices were in Glasgow and I liked the idea of working there again. It was far more convenient for Aberfoyle than Edinburgh. The office was in Bothwell Street. This was to prove even more convenient later on for it was only five minutes stroll down the hill to St Vincent Place to my office at the Clydesdale. So after three years mainly working in London I decided without any reluctance to turn my back on any further major opportunities in the south and to return home.

The SDA had been set up by the Labour Government in 1976 to try to regenerate the Scottish economy. It had three main roles. The first was business development; including the power to invest in Scottish companies, supposedly, but by no means always, as the investor of last resort. The second was infrastructure renewal, trying to bring derelict and degraded sites up to a standard where the Private Sector would find it economic to develop them. It had a virtual monopoly in owning by far the largest estate of industrial property to let, inherited from the old Scottish Industrial Estates. Finally it was responsible for attracting inward investment from overseas. When the Conservatives came to power in 1979 there was intense speculation as to the future of the SDA. The much larger and more interventionist National Enterprise Board in England was quickly axed. But the Agency was perceived in Scotland by Scottish business and Local Authorities as having done a fine job especially in Glasgow and the West of Scotland, where the bulk of its resources had been deployed. As the new Chairman of the CBI in Scotland at the time, I had consulted my council as to what changes we wished the new government to make. The answer was pretty much 'steady as she goes'. George Younger well understood and was sympathetic to the need for partnership in Scotland between the Scottish Office,

Local Authorities and the Private sector in the interests of employment and the economy. He was in no hurry to unscramble for ideological reasons something that was popular and working well. The Chairman and Chief Executive were both replaced and the balance of the Board changed. Otherwise both funding levels and powers remained largely as before.

But matters were very different by 1988. The SDA had become a victim of its own success and I am bound to say had started to act as if it was totally independent of Government, and as if the source of its funding had little to do with the taxpayer. George Mathewson, who later became Chief Executive of the Royal Bank and went on to succeed George Younger as Chairman, had recently retired. He had driven the Agency forward with dynamic flair. Robin Duthie was the equally outspoken and independently minded Chairman. He sometimes gave the impression that the Agency was his personal fiefdom. The Secretary of State and Ministers at the Scottish office resented the fact that they were given no credit for the Agency's achievements. There was no political mileage in it for them at all. Indeed many of the Agency's officials were suspected of being actively hostile to the Conservatives. It did not help that in the Agency's latest annual report there were no fewer than seventeen photographs of the SDA Chairman and not one of the Secretary of State! I made sure there were no photographs of me in my first report.

Furthermore some of the Scottish Conservatives' harder nosed colleagues at Westminster were jealous of Scotland's slice of inward investment and perceived unfair advantages. They were not slow to taunt their Scottish colleagues that the Thatcher revolution had not been implemented in Scotland and the SDA was the last bastion of interventionist socialism. Scotland in those pre-devolution days had gradually won autonomy over many areas that had previously come under the DTI. Needless to say the Prime Minister was not unaware of these criticisms nor did she consider the Secretary of State, by then Malcolm Rifkind, as among the 'driest' members of her cabinet.

This was the background when, shortly after taking over, I received, one Saturday morning, a telephone call from James Scott, the senior civil servant responsible for industry at St Andrew's House, asking me if I had read the *Scotsman* that morning. The newspaper forecast the end of the Agency. Bill Hughes, a Falkirk businessman and current Chairman of the CBI in Scotland, had written direct to Margaret Thatcher, bypassing all the usual channels, suggesting that all the powers and functions of the

Agency should be delegated to local businessmen and that they should also assume responsibility for training and skills in Scotland from the Sheffield based Training Agency. He had received an immediate favourable response and had issued a press release. The Scottish Office was taken completely by surprise, as was I. The Prime Minister had convened an all day Saturday conference at Chequers for early September. My presence was required. I did not think it wise to say that I was actually supposed to be shooting driven grouse in Yorkshire that day!

I knew Bill Hughes well enough. He was the current Chairman of the CBI in Scotland. We met at Gleneagles on 10 August, three weeks before the Chequers meeting. He had picked up his idea from a successful experiment in the New England States in the USA. He wanted to build on the several embryonic Enterprise Trusts that were springing up in Scotland on the initiative of the private sector. His idea was little more than a concept and 'back of the envelope stuff'. He had not developed it in any detail. He envisaged up to fifty such private sector bodies to deliver public sector money for training and business development. This is what had caught the Prime Minister's imagination. I could see the Treasury and Civil servants being pretty cautious in buying into such a scheme for transferring taxpayers' money into the private sector without the strictest of controls, and so it proved. But the Agency, under its new Chief Executive Iain Robertson, was already working on plans for far greater local delivery and less centralisation. The idea of say ten or a dozen local areas with greater involvement from businessmen was not unattractive. The possibility of gaining responsibility for Training and Skills in Scotland at the same time was a highly desirable prize.

I managed one day's shooting as a guest of Derek Palmer of Bass at their moor in North Yorkshire. I see from my shooting diary that we got 73 brace in a gale of wind and I was disgruntled at missing the second day, which was supposed to be even better. I used the Scottish and Newcastle plane to fly down from Teesside Airport early the next morning on the justification that it is not every day that one is summoned to Chequers on a Saturday. On arrival I found the Prime Minister with only one or two officials. It was clearly to be a political meeting before it became Government business. Those present included Malcolm Rifkind; Norman Fowler, Secretary of State for Employment; Hector Laing, Treasurer of the Party and a friend and valued adviser on Scottish issues to Margaret; Jim Goold, who had followed me as Chairman of the CBI in Scotland (another person whose opinions she respected, Jim was now treasurer of the Party in Scotland); Bill Hughes; and myself.

The Prime Minister was in fine form. She clearly relished the prospect of making radical change, which might have political advantages in Scotland. She needed the agreement in principle of Malcolm and Norman, who as Secretary of State for Employment, would be required to give up responsibility for delivery, though not of policy, for training in Scotland. Everyone had their say. I was not opposed to the idea in principle provided that the key powers, policy objectives and funding levels of the SDA remained intact.

We broke for a buffet lunch. We discussed the prospects for the current harvest. Margaret said she always listened to the BBC farming programme at 6 o'clock every Saturday morning. Dennis joined us. He knew about the ongoing takeover bid by Elder's for S&N. He told me John Elliot was not a bad chap. Elliot had always boasted that he had pretty direct access to the Prime Minister's ear, which is why he was so gobsmacked when the Monopolies Commission blocked his bid. Dennis told me Elliot had asked him to become a non-executive director of Elders but he had had to refuse. This of course was very interesting information to me at that time!

After lunch the senior civil servants were asked to join the meeting, Russell Hillhouse and Gavin Macrone from the Scottish Office and Geoffrey Holland and others from Employment. It was agreed in principle that officials should work up a proposal for Cabinet approval and that responsibility for delivery of training and skills in Scotland should be transferred from the Department of Employment to the Scottish office. But as Gavin remarked to me afterwards, the key point as to whether the £300 million training budget would be automatically transferred from one department to another was never addressed.

The meeting had taken all afternoon. By six o'clock there was some consternation among the Scottish contingent about whether they could catch the last plane home. I offered to give them a lift in the S&N plane. We just managed to accommodate five people. 'There,' said Margaret in high good humour. 'Now you see the advantages of the Private Sector!'

On 31 August the following year Malcolm convened a conference at Dunblane Hydro to launch his green paper on Scottish Enterprise, challenging Scottish businessmen to respond to his challenge. I had been slightly involved in the interim but had not seen the final proposals. It was a consultation document. I was sitting next to Ian Wood, chairman of the Aberdeen based John Wood Group. Ten years earlier I had stood outside his insalubrious offices on the quay at the harbour amidst the stink of fish, attempting to persuade him to become CBI spokesman for the North East. Now we knew each other well. As Malcolm finished I said to him, 'Well, Ian, he's certainly let the enterprise genie out of the bottle now!' During the subsequent discussions Ian got up and used my phrase, which clearly delighted the Secretary of State. Afterwards I pulled Ian's leg about stealing my words and it became a standing joke between us, so much so that when four years later Ian Lang gave a reception in my honour on my retiral as the first Chairman of Scottish Enterprise in the Great Hall in Edinburgh Castle, Ian Wood, on behalf of all Local Enterprise Company Chairmen, presented me with a copy of *Aladdin and his Magic Lamp* signed by them all for my grandchildren. I still have it. He of course went on to become Chairman of Scottish Enterprise himself a few years later.

Thus was Scottish Enterprise conceived and born. The next year was a difficult one. The outcome of the Elder's takeover was not settled until the spring. I was retiring as Chairman of S&N at the age of sixty in November. I was due to take on at the Clydesdale Bank and only just starting to get to grips with the complex issues at the Top Salaries review Body. My life was certainly not dull; but it was pretty busy!

For those in the SDA it was a time of great uncertainty. They had no idea what the new organisation would be like or whether they would have a job; and if they were offered employment would it be at the centre in Glasgow or with one of the new Local Enterprise Companies or LECs as they soon became known. Meantime the old SDA had to keep running. Economic development is contra cyclical. That is to say that at times of recession when the maximum creation of new projects is most needed they are in fact scarce because no private sector partnership money is available. Indeed it is sometimes hard to spend the public money available. Exactly the reverse is true following periods of high growth. This is what happened following the so-called Lawson boom and the 1987 election. The SDA was inundated with new projects. Its finances were seriously stretched. It had to cancel or delay many projects to the intense annoyance of business partners, local authorities and politicians and to the anxiety of the Minister of State, Ian Lang.

At this moment Iain Robertson the Chief Executive left for the Royal Bank. I did not blame him. He had been told that he would have to apply for a new job with Scottish Enterprise just like everyone else. If he put in for the new CEO's job and did not get it the implication would be that he had failed at the SDA. This was certainly not the case but it was a risk that in career terms he did not wish to take. Other senior members of staff started to vote with their feet. So I was left with no CEO for the

SDA and no CEO for the embryonic Scottish Enterprise, nor were we in a position to start the recruiting process until the Act of Parliament establishing it had been passed. In effect I had to act as Chief Executive for both organisations for several months. Those senior staff that chose to stay were absolutely magnificent. They worked themselves to death (all too literally in one case) and gave me first class advice and support for very little thanks.

I heard that James Scott, the Secretary for Industry at the Scottish Office, was due to retire in two years and might not be averse to a change of scene. I sounded him out and armed with a favourable response went to see Malcolm Rifkind. He readily agreed. James was a diplomat by upbringing and a most unlikely civil servant to find in the Scottish Office. He did a fine job in keeping the SDA functioning and eventually completing the obsequies over the next two years. He was succeeded by Peter MacKay, another first class man whom I liked and trusted. James was a superb draughtstsman of letters. He liked to say that one of his greatest pleasures on arrival at the Agency was replying to tough inquisitory Scottish Office letters that he himself had written to the SDA only weeks before.

I had no idea whether or not I would be required as the first Chairman of Scottish Enterprise. Everyone seemed to assume so but the civil servants were extremely coy about it. It was not until I became a member of the National Training Task Force, at the moment when the 'kitemark' Investors in People was introduced, that Geoffrey Holland, the Permanent Secretary at the Department of Employment, told me that I was definitely to be offered the job. The Scottish Office officials were too hidebound by the protocol that the Act of Parliament had to be passed first, to even give me a steer. I often found that senior civil servants in Whitehall departments were far more approachable and less cagey than officials at the Scottish Office. Perhaps they were more confident.

Anyway I got on with the task of setting up Scottish Enterprise. First came the interviews with prospective groups of local businessmen volunteering to run the LECs. No one knew what the response would be to the Secretary of State's challenge. In fact it was superb right across Scotland including the Highlands. Here my opposite number in the old Highlands and Islands Development Board, a delightful man called Bob Cowan, was seriously ill, so I found myself assisting the civil servants in conducting the interviews in the Highland Region as well. It was exciting and rather fun. The most difficult moment came with Perthshire and Angus who refused to speak to each other and bitterly resisted the proposition that they should come together under the title of Tayside

Enterprise. I was much helped by the persuasive powers of Anne Gloag, Peter Lederer and the chairman designate Bill Lowe.

One of the more amusing episodes was with Moray, Badenoch and Strathspey. Their area crossed the boundary between Highlands and Lowlands. They were far too small to fit into the pattern for the twelve large groupings planned for the Lowlands, but they were fiercely determined not to be split with part going to Grampian Enterprise and part to the Highlands. They arrived for the interview with hampers of mouth watering Speyside produce: malt whisky by the barrel; Walker's shortbread; Baxter's products; and knitwear from Johnson's of Elgin. The civil servants persuaded them with some difficulty that it might be misinterpreted if they were allowed to distribute this largesse among the interviewing panel. They then proceeded to argue their case with such passion that we felt we were indeed seeing the flame of enterprise burning brightly. Far be it for us to put it out by following the laws of logic or the local authority boundaries. So they won the day!

Eventually and not without some pretty intense local rivalry the provisional LEC Chairmen and boards were appointed. The next stage was for them to put forward their business plans for funding. We had the tricky task of allocating the total budgets available for both training and development across competing local areas. There was a strong tide of opinion running that the West of Scotland had enjoyed more than its fair share of SDA funding over the years. But some formidable personalities were lined up to defend the status quo, such as my old friend Norman Macfarlane from Glasgow and Ian Livingstone from Lanarkshire. The big debate was what powers and what funding should remain at the centre. The LECs naturally wanted everything to be allocated out for local control. Fierce arguments took place involving the new Scottish Enterprise Board, the Scottish Office and LEC chairmen. Ian Wood became a self-appointed shop steward for the chairmen. We all used to meet monthly in my office in Bothwell Street, and with goodwill and good sense resolved most of the difficulties.

I lost two arguments that I regretted. In neither case were ministers robust enough in my opinion. The first concerned the titles of the LECs. I wanted a common umbrella and a common logo and house style so that 'Scottish Enterprise' might become a widely known and respected brand as successor to the internationally known SDA. There had been a passionate last-ditch attempt to retain the SDA's logo. Alf Young of the *Glasgow Herald* led a crusading campaign for the status quo and a number of former SDA luminaries were not slow to board his bandwagon. I wanted all the local companies to trade under the same umbrella, as in Dunbartonshire Enterprise, or Forth Valley Enterprise, or Grampian Enterprise to give three examples; but the West of Scotland moguls wanted their independence and the surviving reputation of the SDA so their companies became The Glasgow Development Agency, and The Lanarkshire Development Agency. I could not get the Scottish Office to take a firm line. I believe that this error has now been recognised and subsequently changed.

The second point was far more significant. I wanted Scottish Enterprise to retain the power and resources centrally to be able to manage large projects of national significance rather than to farm these out to LECs who could not have the experience or calibre of staff to handle them. I believe that one or two well-publicised and costly mistakes in subsequent years might have been avoided if this advice had been taken, in particular the Science Museum and Loch Lomond Shore projects.

Eventually we were able to recruit the first Chief Executive. The outstanding candidate and the one preferred by the new Secretary of State, Ian Lang, was Crawford Beveridge. He was a Scot who had worked for a number of American companies and was now right hand man to Scott McNeilly of Sun Microsystems in California. We had appointed Douglas Kinnaird to do the recruitment. Crawford was earning over ten times the figure of some £80,000 per annum, which was then the maximum we could offer. (By now I knew a good bit about Public Sector pay through the Top Salaries Review Body!) But Crawford wanted to return to Scotland to 'put something back into his own country' in return for all the opportunity it had given him. He had a fantastic Californian wife and two lovely children. It was a huge decision for him. The evening after the final interview, and the day before he flew home, I had dinner with him alone in a Glasgow hotel. I rang Peter MacKay in the Scottish Office the next day to say that I was still hopeful, but put the odds against his accepting at worse than evens. Once he returned to the Californian sunshine, his family and Scott Mcneilly's persuasions I felt his passion for a Glasgow job would wane. I was right; he declined.

There was no other candidate strong enough, so having lost three months we decided that we had to advertise again. Douglas Kinnaird rang Crawford's home a week or so later on the pretext that he had promised to let him know what had happened. He spoke to Pegs Beveridge. She told him that she had never known Crawford so uncertain. Douglas somehow persuaded him to come back at our expense for one more dinner with me. 'This is a job to do your bit for Scotland that comes once in a lifetime. It's a unique opportunity. If you turn it down again and come back with your family after they are through high school you will be just one more "expat" Scot who has come home too rich and too late.' It was a good bit of headhunting. Crawford became the first Chief Executive and Douglas Kinnaird fully earned his fee.

There are two others I should particularly mention who were a constant support to me throughout this time. Douglas Hardie was the Deputy Chairman and Sandra Pollock my Personal Assistant. Each in their separate role was invaluable. Once Scottish Enterprise was fully up and running I asked for my term of office to come to an end after four years in 1993. The renowned Scottish economist Donald MacKay succeeded me. Although Scottish Enterprise was the brainchild of others and was implemented by a Conservative administration, it is a source of pride and satisfaction to me that an undertaking which seemed so perilous at the outset has survived robustly, and almost unchanged in structure, for over ten years, through many vicissitudes, a change of Government and through Scottish Devolution. The bricks with which some of us built the foundations must have been placed on firmer rock than we suspected at the time.

Chapter 11

Senior Salaries Review Body
1989–1995

NIGEL LAWSON first indicated to me that I might be invited to become Chairman of the Top Salaries Review Body when I saw him about the time of his controversial 1988 budget. He urged me to take the job. Shortly afterwards Robin Butler sent for me in the Cabinet Office to tell me that the Prime Minister wished me to take over from Lord Plowden. Edwin was a man of huge distinction, who had risen to prominence in the aircraft industry in the war as a young civil servant, and had been involved in one way or another in a wide variety of public appointments ever since. He had been a member of the Body since 1977 and Chairman since 1981. He was a man of small stature but immense wisdom and reputation; by then aged eighty-one, he was due for a rest.

I went to see him in his London flat to ask his advice. He started by telling me encouragingly that this job was 'the ultimate poison pill'! There was no way you could win. If the Government accepted your advice you had recommended far too little for the Senior Public Servants and those of them, if any, who remained your friends would tell you so in no uncertain terms. If the Government rejected your advice you had got it wrong anyway by recommending too much, and they would get nothing.

Edward Heath had established the Review Body in 1971, along with those for the Armed Forces and the Doctors and Dentists. The Nurses followed in 1983 and the Teachers in 1991. The task of the TSRB remained much as it had been when it was set up, namely to advise the Prime Minister on the remuneration of senior civil servants, senior military officers from the rank of two star upwards and senior members of the judiciary. In total the constituents numbered about two thousand with over half of them in the judiciary. The problem was that there was never a right moment for senior people to receive a pay rise; meanwhile the pay pressures built up from below and, since the end of the thirteen years of pay freeze policies under successive Governments, the lid had finally blown off the kettle in the private sector. The differential between Private and Public pay at senior levels was widening all the time.

Edwin told me that Margaret Thatcher was particularly sensitive to the issue because of the mauling she had had from her own backbenchers, nearly leading to a Government defeat in 1985. The TSRB had carried out a fundamental review and recommended significant pay rises in an attempt to play catch-up with the marketplace. The Cabinet had accepted this, but the decision had still to be announced when the Prime Minister went to address the 1922 Committee. She never mentioned it. Conservative MPs came out into the corridors to find the news on the wires and in the evening papers. All hell broke loose. So the TSRB had been marking time a bit in recent reports while the pay pressures continued to build up. That would be my problem.

The other piece of advice Edwin gave me was very valuable and I made use of it often. He told me that it was important to keep a private dialogue going with the Prime Minister, either directly or through the Cabinet Secretary. Frequently the Review Body would get the bit between its teeth and set off on a course that could never be acceptable to the Government. Although it was by its very nature an independent Review Body, indeed that was its justification and function, there was little merit in continuing to make proposals that the Government could never accept. The trick was to keep the Prime Minister up to date with the Review Body's thinking so that she was not taken by surprise, and at the same time temper the Review Body's ardour towards a solution that might prove acceptable. Sometimes it was not wise to let the members know that these quiet soundings were taking place; on others it was useful to give them an unofficial Government steer. The Prime Minister wanted a safe pair of hands. I was supposed to be it!

The workload was not as great as that of some of the other Review Bodies; for example the Armed Forces Pay Review Body took evidence throughout the year and travelled to wherever British troops were serving. We normally convened for the first time in July, met monthly and reported to the Prime Minister in December for a Government decision in February. The Office of Manpower Economics, OME for short, a separate department of the Department of Employment provided the secretariat; and extremely professional and dedicated they were too. Mike Horsman was in charge through most of my term of office. I came to respect his shrewd advice and calm detachment. The offices were in Sardinia Sreet off Kingsway for a while, and later in Oxford Street. It was of course an unpaid honorary appointment.

Anyway I decided that the time commitment would not be too arduous even if the responsibility were somewhat daunting; and that I could arrange the timing of meetings to coincide with other board meetings in London. I had long ago made up my mind that it is vital to be Chairman of any organisation in which you are involved. In the first place it is more fun, but most importantly one can arrange all the meetings a year ahead to suit one's own plans, particularly in my case holiday and fishing plans! Another of my immutable rules was never to allow one's secretary, however competent, to control one's diary. Either one should be able to accept a date or invitation or not. I would never allow provisional dates to be held against the convenience of other people! I enjoy chairing meetings. The key to it is to decide what outcome you want to achieve in advance for each agenda item. Work out a strict timetable with the secretary or chief executive so that you finish on time. Make certain that everyone at least has an opportunity to have their say, going round the table if necessary, so that no member feels excluded or ignored. Then, unless there is a clear majority in the opposite direction, sum up succinctly with the answer you had decided upon in advance. In this way it is easy for the secretary to write a clear minute that you won't have to spend hours revising later!

On 29 March I went to see Robin Butler in the Cabinet Office to accept. That evening Louise and I were due to 'Dine and Sleep' as guests of the Queen at Windsor. Robin told me that the Prime Minister was also going to be there so he would see that she knew of my decision that afternoon. Elsewhere I describe this memorable visit and the fact that later that evening she seemed pleased that I had accepted the job.

For a year I sat under Edwin Plowden's chairmanship before taking over in 1989 for my first report on Top Salaries, but the thirteenth of the TSRB, 'Presented to Parliament by the Prime Minister by Command of Her Majesty' in February 1990. When I finally retired after six years in 1995 the members of the TSRB presented me with a leather-bound copy of all the reports. I treasure this as a record; but it scarcely makes light bedtime reading, nor would it give much enjoyment to any reader of this book. So I will merely recount one or two of the more significant or amusing moments.

I inherited an experienced and distinguished collection of members. It was a delight to link up with Terry Beckett again, always a source of sound advice, though sadly we found ourselves in disagreement over the 1992 recommendations and he felt obliged to resign. But even then I was grateful to him because he could have decided, instead, to put in a minority report, which would have damaged our credibility.

Peter Cazalet was an ex officio member as the new Chairman of the AFPRB. This was a most helpful arrangement because his mandate stopped at the Captain RN, Brigadier and Group Captain level while mine began at Rear Admiral, Major General and Air Vice-Marshal. The differentials between these ranks were being constantly eroded. No sooner had a reasonable gap been established, say 10 per cent, before the Government would approve a much bigger award to the forces than they would to senior officers. In two or three years of this we were back to square one. It was aggravated for the Royal Navy by an increment for serving in submarines, so that a submariner might get the good news that he had been promoted to Rear Admiral and simultaneously get a cut in his pay! The Treasury were always against any automatic escalating link to preserve the differential once it was correctly established. At my first meeting with the Ministry of Defence and the Chief of the Defence Staff under Lord Plowden's chairmanship, he asked Sir John Fieldhouse at the outset what was the most important point he wished to raise. Unhesitatingly the Admiral of the Fleet said, 'The differential between one- and two-star officers.' An hour or went by while we ranged over a variety of evidence. Summing up, Edwin asked if there was anything else Sir John wished to say. Fixing him with an intense gaze from steely blue eyes accustomed to look across the high seas from the bridge of his ship, Sir John merely repeated with heavy emphasis the same eight words: 'The differential between one and two star officers.' The message sank home but it was not until 1 April 1994 that I was finally able to persuade John Major of the problem by dint of using the ash trays on the Cabinet Room table as visual aids! A permanent minimum differential of 10 per cent was agreed. Whether this decision has survived the intervening ten years I do not know. Anyway on this and many other matters concerning forces' pay Peter Cazalet was invariably constructive and helpful.

Roger Chorley and Anthony Wilson were both eminent accountants. Roger had invented the so-called 'Chorley formula' for the endowment required before properties could be accepted by the National Trust. Anthony among other roles had been head of the Government's Accountancy service. There was a judicial sub-committee to help us with the arcane subject of structure and remuneration for lawyers and judges. A splendid man called Sir Cecil Clothier ('Spike' to his friends) chaired it, ably assisted by two others. One kindred spirit from the brewing industry was Jeremy Pope, who took meticulous and detailed notes during meetings, sometimes of inestimable value when we were trying to recall who said what, though it must be said that the Secretariat seldom put a foot wrong. The other was another lawyer, a partner from Clifford Chance, Hugh Piggott. Last but by no means least came Louise Botting, at the time the only woman member but happily joined by three others later on, Rosemary Day, Yve Newbold and Patricia Mann. Louise had made her name as a broadcaster on the BBC 'Money Box' programme and her fortune as the founder of her own financial services company. She was an expert on pensions and a wonderful and invariably helpful contributor on all other subjects. I was fortunate in being able to attract her later on to become the first woman member of the Board of General Accident. These were the people who constituted the membership when I first took over. Subsequent retrials brought changes in membership and apart from the three women already mentioned, George Bain, Gordon Hourston, Sydney Lipworth, Mark Sheldon and my successor Michael Perry had all joined by the time I stood down in 1995.

It is easy to forget nowadays that inflation was in double figures for nearly ten years from the early seventies to the early eighties with huge pressure on earnings. For much of this time under both Conservative and Labour administrations various forms of pay policies were operating. All had one thing in common: the severest restraints fell on those with the highest salaries. Throughout the eighties inflation reverted to around five per cent, until for two years at the end of the decade, after excessive growth rates of nearly four per cent in 1986–8 it threatened to breach double figures again in 1990. Market forces fuelled by the increasingly global nature of big business and the boom in the City of London had inevitably sparked a huge game of catch-up for top earners in the Private Sector. But the lid had, despite the Thatcher pay awards of 1985, stayed firmly on top Public Sector pay.

It is difficult but not impossible to make comparison between the importance and responsibility of very senior jobs in the Public and Private Sectors. Two of our remit groups, the Civil Service and the Military, were career vocations, immune to some extent from the market place. The third, the Judiciary, was most assuredly not. Recruitment for High Court Judges for example was primarily from the ranks of the ablest and therefore the most successful Queen's Counsel. Their earnings pre-appointment were often five times or more their subsequent salaries on the bench. It was never seriously disputed that the elements of security of employment, the interest of the job, and the personal choice of a vocational career in the service of the nation, for Senior Civil Servants and Military Officers implied some 'discount' in remuneration compared with similar jobs in the Private Sector. But what logic related the pay of the Lord Chief Justice for example to that of the Secretary to the Cabinet and Head of the Civil Service?

We had to consider the three 'R's: not only the appropriate levels of Reward, but also the issues of Retention and Recruitment. Was there a problem in retaining people at these salary levels or were a significant number leaving? Was there a problem in recruiting new entrants on the terms on offer? Seldom was there any evidence that senior Civil Servants, Generals or Judges were leaving or seeking early retirement. Nor was it seriously suggested that there were recruitment difficulties in numbers or quality for the Civil Service or the Military at the stage when new entrants were starting their careers. But if over time those at the top end gradually lost some motivation by falling further and further behind the Private Sector marketplace, there could certainly be long-term implications. It was a different matter for the Judiciary. Although the Lord Chancellor's Department always maintained that there had never been a case of anyone refusing an invitation to become a High Court Judge, we had anecdotal evidence that it was becoming increasingly common. The invitation was apparently never formally issued until discreet preliminary soundings had made sure it would be accepted! There were real difficulties on occasions too in filling all the vacancies for Circuit Court Judges.

By 1991 the 'discount' for working in the Public Sector for a grade 1 Permanent Secretary had grown to nearly two thirds of his Private Sector equivalent. In other words the Chief Executive of a large company might then have been earning £300,000 (and how modest this seems by today's standards!) against the Permanent Secretary, Admiral or senior Judge on £100,000. But even more unfair was the fact that the earnings of every other group of employees in the country had exceeded inflation by a mile since 1985. GB average earnings had gone up by 22 per cent in real terms. Senior Private Sector earnings had risen by 41 per cent. The earnings of the most senior Public servants had actually fallen by 3 per cent.

This was the background at the time of my third report, number fifteen in the sequence of TSRB reports on pay in 1991. We were due to submit the report to the Prime Minister as usual at the end of the year. We had carried out a so-called 'fundamental' review; that is, we had taken far more evidence than normal and addressed the key issues of policy. It was essential as we saw it that the Government implemented our recommendations in full rather than rejecting them or 'staging' them. 'Staging' was a favourite Treasury device for postponing the cost impacts by accepting the recommendations of Review Bodies in principle but delaying the implementation for one year or more. It was particularly unfair on those who were due to retire in the interim and who thus would be entitled to a smaller pension.

However there was one occasion when I took advantage of the device to achieve over time the 1992 recommendations for the judges that the Government had rejected. By 1994 the judicial sub-committee were hell bent on a full frontal attack to put them forward once again as a single proposal. Their view was that if the Government wanted to stage them that was their affair. Our job was to recommend what was right. My view was different. I thought that if we again recommended them in full there was every chance that they would be rejected again, but that if we aimed to achieve them over five years there was every chance that they would be accepted. The issue was unresolved when the Lord Chief Justice, Peter Taylor, came to give evidence to us. (It was so sad that he became ill relatively soon afterwards and died of cancer. He was such a nice man.) I took a chance and asked him, without any warning to my colleagues, whether, given the choice, he would prefer us to try again to achieve the salary levels for judges that everyone agreed were desirable, and risk rejection, or go for the long view and ask for them to be implemented by 1999. 'I would greatly prefer the longer view,' was his instant response. That settled the matter for us; that is what we recommended and was in due course achieved.

The usual pattern was for the Review Body to request written evidence from all interested parties in the spring each year. We then took oral evidence at a series of meetings through September and October and considered our conclusions. The first drafts of our report started to appear on the agenda for November and December. At the first meeting we heard the Government evidence. The Secretary to the Cabinet, Robin Butler throughout my time, and the Permanent Secretary at the Treasury, Peter Middleton to start with and then Terry Burns, always opened the batting. We then saw the Lord Chancellor himself, James MacKay, and the Permanent Secretary of his Department, Tom Legg. The Lord Chief Justice usually came on his own; in my time this was firstly Lord Lane and then Lord Taylor of Gosforth, as Peter Taylor subsequently became. Representatives of the Judges followed the Lord Chief Justice. A separate meeting took place in Edinburgh for the Scottish judiciary where the issues were similar but the structure even more arcane. It was a vexed question as to where Sheriffs should rank in relation to Circuit Court Judges in England and what the differential should be between the Lord President of the Court of Session and the Lord Justice Clerk. I could not resist sitting in on the judicial committee when they took evidence in Scotland on one or two occasions. I enjoyed being a fly on the wall when the great legal luminaries represented their own requirements for pay and rations!

For the Civil Service Robin Butler came in to bat again, this time as Head of the Civil Service, followed by the Civil Service Commissioners and then the General Secretary of the First Division Association. She was a very bright, attractive and highly articulate lady called Liz Symons. She is now Baroness Symons of Vernham Dean speaking equally eloquently from the Government's front bench in the Lord's. The Permanent Secretary, Michael Quinlan, and the Chief of the Defence Staff represented the Ministry of Defence. After John Fieldhouse as CDS came Air Chief Marshal Sir David Craig, now Convenor of the Crossbench Peers in the Lords, followed by two Field Marshals, Sir Richard Vincent and Sir Peter Inge, who wrote me a charming letter of appreciation on my retiral in 1995. Various other Permanent Secretaries gave evidence for their own departments and from time to time others came to give evidence on particular aspects of our work.

It was one of the great fascinations and attractions of the job that the subject of pay always focuses people's minds. If I was out at a dinner party and some eminent judge was present I could be fairly sure that, if someone let slip my particular role, he would sidle up to me for a chat over the port! We could more or less invite anyone we wished to appear to give evidence before us and almost without exception they were always keen to come. So that during my time at the TSRB I had the great privilege of becoming acquainted with all these great men, the most senior and distinguished public servants in the kingdom, who were collectively running the country under our elected politicians. However serious our subject might be I was anxious not to create too formal an atmosphere and the discussions were always relaxed, friendly and frequently humorous.

By the autumn of 1991 it was clear that inflation was at a high level, the economy was not flourishing and the Government was in trouble following Maggie Thatcher's departure. It seemed inevitable that the new Prime Minister, John Major, would call an election in the spring. It would have been hard to conceive a worse moment for us to submit a major report on Senior Public Sector pay or a less likely moment for any Government to implement our recommendations. So I wrote to the Prime Minister suggesting that it would be in everybody's interests for us to delay our report until the following summer. I asked his permission to report in July rather than January. We hoped this would take some of the politics out of the situation and that whichever party was elected it might be easier for a new Government to accept our proposals in the wake of a success at the polls.

My request was accepted but the *Times* leader of 24 September, headed REWARD WITHOUT RISK, thundered its disapproval. 'The Prime Minister was ill advised,' it said.

> Postponement makes Mr Major seem to be hiding something from the electorate, aided and abetted by the Tory appointed Chairman of the Review Body, Sir David Nickson, who first suggested the delay.
>
> The indications are that the Boards research into comparability between the public and private sectors was throwing up such a scale of discrepancies that only a pay rise of between fifty and one hundred per cent would enable the public sector to catch up. Postponement can only reinforce such suspicions.

The Times was right about the scale of the discrepancies but completely wrong about our motivation or the size of our intended recommendations.

In the event the Conservatives were re-elected, but neither the political nor the economic climate turned out to be any more favourable for bold decisions on Senior Public Sector pay. Our report was duly delivered on time. In it we said:

> The recommendations we make in this report have little to do with the short term and everything to do with the long term quality and effectiveness of the public sector. The United Kingdom has had an enviable record of exceptionally able people at the most senior levels in the judiciary, in the armed forces and in the civil service. They are motivated by a sense of public duty and vocation, and sustained by the interest they take in their work and the prestige of their roles. But pay must play a part. If those at the top were to become less than fully motivated, and recruitment of those of the necessary calibre became difficult once again as we move out of recession, then it would take years to recover the position. At a time when the civil service, the armed forces and the judiciary are all undergoing great change it is essential not to undermine the commitment of those at the top of these services.

At this stage I had only met John Major once or twice. Going to see him was always much more formal, but far less daunting than going to see Margaret Thatcher. The first time I called to discuss matters with him was a year or so earlier when he was Chancellor. Unlike my informal calls to see Nigel at No. 11 I was summoned to the Treasury. The review body were contemplating an increase that I felt would be unacceptable to the Government and I took advantage of Edwin Plowden's advice to try to get a steer. I thought I might get a better indication from the Chancellor than from the Prime Minister at that stage. I told John Major what we had in mind and suggested that we did not want to surprise him. He had a stinking cold and seemed as a result to be in a poor mood. 'I'm not only surprised, I am completely shocked" was his response. I left pretty quickly but as a result of the meeting was subsequently able to persuade my colleagues on that occasion that we would be wise to temper our recommendations a little.

So important did we consider our 1992 report that I took the unusual step of asking for an opportunity to present our findings to the Prime Minister in person. I had of course discussed this with Robin Butler first. Robin was always accessible and I saw him in the Cabinet Office off Whitehall on numerous occasions. He was invariably charming, wise and constructive in all our dealings. On this occasion he indicated that although I could bring one or two members of the SSRB (one of our recommendations was that the title should be changed from 'Top' people's pay to 'Senior', hence SSRB instead of TSRB). He indicated that the PM would probably have one or two members of the Cabinet with him and as a full Cabinet meeting was to follow on the subject we had exactly one hour to make our case. The Government were anxious that the meeting should be kept secret and that the press should not be aware of it. No one wished to be 'door-stepped' on the issue. So our entry to No. 10 was to be through the Whitehall entrance to the Cabinet Office.

I had decided to take with me two members. One was Spike Clothier, who as chairman of the judicial sub-committee was best qualified to answer any questions on the legal front; the other was Louise Botting, who would add both style and expertise to any meeting. The date was 3 July 1992. The first snag was that Spike, a keen rowing man, said that it was the Friday of Henley Royal Regatta and he needed to be drinking his customary glass of champagne on the lawn before lunch by 1 o'clock at the latest. He could only come if a Government car was available to take him there. Robin Butler took this in his stride.

It was a drenchingly wet day. We entered through the Cabinet Office and were led through the tortuous route through to No. 10, so familiar to aficionados of *Yes, Prime Minister* and 'Sir Humphrey'. John Major greeted us courteously at the entrance to the Cabinet Room and we took our places on one side of the famous table while he sat in his customary place on the other flanked by some of his colleagues. I cannot remember everyone who was there and from our point of view there was no record of the proceedings. I do recall that William Waldegrave appeared particularly sceptical about our arguments and Norman Lamont, by then Chancellor after Nigel Lawson's resignation in 1991, arrived late, was clearly preoccupied with some papers in front of him on which he continued to work, and appeared to pay no attention to what we had to say. We put our case as well as we could and answered the questions we were asked. These lasted longer than expected so that when we came out the rest of the Cabinet were hanging about outside waiting to go in. We exchanged pleasantries with one or two before being ushered back to the green baize door. Here our guide became nonplussed. His security pass would not work to get us back out of No. 10. No one else could help. Robin Butler appeared. I suggested that perhaps we could leave through the front door. No, the press would see us. What about going out through No. 11? No, for the same reason. So we hung about for some time chatting to members of the Cabinet still waiting to go in. We all wondered what those inside were saying about our report. We were not optimistic. The impasse was resolved by the discovery that the security locking system had run out of the paper roll which recorded who had passed through the door. It was farcical with a script straight out of *Yes, Prime Minister*!

We were escorted out onto Whitehall. There was Spike's Government car, as arranged, to take him to Henley. Louise Botting caught a convenient taxi. There was no sign of my car. The rain poured down. I had neither coat nor umbrella. The security door had closed behind me. Eventually I walked along to the gates outside Downing Street and asked a policeman if he had seen a black Ford Granada. 'Yes Sir,' came the response. 'Your driver said you were in at No. 10 so we have sent him in.' So there I was, by now soaked, outside the gates while Dudley Knight, my delightful driver for so many years in London, was sitting outside the door of No. 10 from whence I had been forbidden to emerge.

The Government duly rejected our recommendations, making a much smaller settlement, though I think from what John Major said privately afterwards, they probably thought it sensible but politically impossible to implement at that time. There is never a right moment to award big pay increases to senior people however justified they may be. At our next SSRB meeting I arranged with officials that we would install a large TV set in our conference room. I explained that as we clearly had got it wrong we had better have a video presentation on how to do better next time. There were some puzzled faces. We then showed the two *Yes,*

Prime Minister episodes, one where Sir Humphrey and his opposite number in the Treasury are fixing their own pay, and the other when Sir Humphrey got stuck outside the green baize door. That was the best SSRB meeting we ever had!

John Major was always courteous and considerate in all my dealings with him and wrote me a charming letter in April 1995 in which he said, 'I know that as Chairman the burden on you has been particularly heavy and your efforts have been paramount in enabling the SSRB to tackle expeditiously and with sensitivity the important issues it has faced. Your service on the Review Body over a busy and sometimes difficult period has been *extremely helpful* and I am most grateful for it.'

CHAPTER 12

Fishing

I HAVE BEEN extremely fortunate to enjoy so much superb sport all my life. Indeed as I look through the pages of my fishing and shooting diaries it is hard to believe that I ever had time to do any work. Fishing, shooting and deer stalking have taken me to many beautiful places; introduced me to many fine people, ghillies, keepers, stalkers as well as all my other friends and companions on the river or on the hill; provided constant exercise and countless golden memories. I have been spoilt by the most generous hospitality from many kind friends. At the age of seventy-five I am still enjoying all three sports to the full and have even more time to indulge myself. By the end of May this year I had fished for salmon on no fewer than twenty-eight days without landing a single fish! Not a statistic of which I am in the least proud, but perhaps it does give an indication of both my obsession with the sport and my success in achieving total retirement at long last; and the scarcity of spring salmon nowadays coupled with my own lack of skill.

Earlier in these pages I have described the dedication with which both sides of my family have pursued similar pursuits for several generations. Whether one's hobbies are deeply imbedded in one's genes, or whether it is all a question of the environment in which one was brought up, I leave wiser men to judge. Certainly as a small boy before the war I can never remember a moment when fishing was not a top priority whenever my father was free to take me.

Near our family home in Caernarvonshire ran a small tributary of the River Conwy called the Afon Roe. This joined the tidal reaches of the main river at Caerhun, an estate that later belonged to my uncle and then to me. The Afon Roe was no more than a fair sized burn in Scottish terms. Here my uncle and my father as small boys had learned to fish, and here I followed in their footsteps. It was a good school because the banks were wild and well protected by trees. Woe betide you if did not rapidly learn to cast underhand with either hand to circumvent the overhanging branches. Little success would come your way fishing downstream and across. You would be seen by the trout, which though small and unsophisticated, were by no means easy to catch. No, you had to crawl as close to the little pools as you could and fish the wet fly upstream. And you had to strike like lightning at the merest hint of an underwater rise or the least detectable twitch to the cast. To this day I still tend to strike too quickly on the chalk streams of the south country for much larger and more leisurely fish as a result of this early upbringing. I developed a quite vicious and instinctive reaction, which projected the little trout out of the water in a thrilling parabola over my head. Many were the disasters with broken casts once I graduated from this idyllic kindergarten to more serious fisheries and more ponderous quarry.

We measured our fish not in ounces yet alone in pounds, but in inches. A six-incher was a fair fish and should have gone back, for the size limit was seven, but often it did not. An eight-incher was serious. A nine-incher was a leviathan, much to be desired and the cause of great rejoicings, occurring perhaps once a holidays. A ten-incher, which might perhaps weigh six ounces, was the stuff of legends, never achieved by me but reputedly occasionally by my uncle as a boy. I could quote many of Patrick Chalmers' poems by heart, learnt from my father, in particular his ode to small trout and small streams, entitled:

ON LITTLE FISH BEING SWEET

Not at once of Test and Itchen,
  Sing I nor of Kennet's state . . .

. . . First I'll sing of little rivers
  And of very little trout.

Little trout whose claims do beckon
  So insistently and sound,
Little trout whose bulk we reckon
  Six or seven to the pound –
These I sing, to these beholden,
  These long since a song did earn,
Crimson spotted, plump and golden,
  Flung a-kicking from the burn.

Leaping down the brown hill's shoulder,
  Trailed of birk and mountain ash,
Bent upon by granite boulder,
  Little waters hop and splash;
Pied by snows of last December,
  Bens above the May days flout –
Ah, that's how you'll best remember
  Little rivers, little trout!'

Grease your brogues with dreamland tallow,
    Forth with me and fish like kings,
And by pot and swirling shallow,
    Fill a creel with fingerlings.
Where our noses first got blistered,
    Where our greenhearts first went swish,
Where the paws of boyhood glistered
    With the scales of little fish.

. . . and so on and so on for verse after verse.

Our favourite fly was the ubiquitous Greenwell's Glory tied exquisite-ly by my father, who was a masterly tier of all trout flies. Its inventor, the eponymous Canon Greenwell, was in his nineties when my father was a small boy. My Great-uncle George was at the time Bishop of Jarrow and knew the Canon who was at Durham. He wrote to him asking him if he would write a letter to his two small nephews, who were starting to fish. The Canon duly wrote an encouraging letter enclosing a cast of three Greenwell's Glories of his own tying. This became a treasured possession. Some seventy years later on my last visit to see my father, who was dying, he said to me that he was worried as to what to do with the Canon's letter and the flies. Clearly his thoughts had returned to his boyhood and for some reason this was preying on his mind. I asked if he would like me to present them to the Flyfishers Club in London of which we were both members. A look of great relief came over his face. He said in a very weak voice, 'Yes, David, that would be wonderful. That is exactly what I would like.' Those were the last words I heard him speak. This year the Flyfishers Club have paid me the great compliment of inviting me to be the guest of honour at their annual dinner at the Savoy. What great pleasure that would have given my father.

In the more innocent days before and during the war I was allowed to depart for hours on my own without a thought for safety, and often my sister would accompany me, though it meant braving the barks and sometimes the nips from some pretty mean Welsh sheepdogs in the farmyard through which we had to walk to reach the stream. Sometimes there were expeditions by car, and then when petrol rationing arrived with the war, on bicycles to one of the lakes in the hills. Later we went further afield to the Conwy above Llanrwst to try for sea trout at night.

Back at Eton before my father became a housemaster we lived at Baldwin's End Cottage, a short walk across Fellows Eyot from the Thames and from the stream, which divided it from Luxmoore's Garden. Here the fishing was of a very different sort. To start with the quarry were minnows to be caught in a glass bottle with the end knocked out. Then I sat for hours watching a float and hoping for bleak or dace, or perhaps with great good fortune a roach or a chub. Once, when fishing for minnows with bread paste, a small pike took the minnow. Great was the excitement.

There was talk of trout in the Thames. Once I did catch a small one on a fly in the Luxmoore's stream, proving that they must have occasionally spawned there before it became polluted. But it was not until I was a boy at Eton that any success came my way. I had sprained my ankle badly in the April holidays while fishing a hill loch (or llyn I should say as it was in Wales) and was not allowed to play cricket for several weeks. So I obtained permission somehow to fish for trout from the Windsor water-works. Eventually I did catch a trout on a spinner of two pounds six ounces, large by my standards but puny as Thames trout go. I bore it back through School Yard in triumph to show my father. It transpired that some Old Etonian, Luard by name, had just written to the Headmaster offering a prize to the boy who caught the largest Thames trout in the year. As it happened mine was the only trout. This was also the only prize I ever won at Eton. It was worth three guineas, and, with that princely sum I bought my first Fishing Diary, which lasted me for fifty years until the Atlantic Salmon Trust kindly presented me with a much grander volume on my retirement as Chairman in 1994.

My father was first and foremost a trout fisherman. As an impecunious schoolmaster he was dependent on his elder brother for any salmon fishing invitations in the school holidays. He had been introduced to the chalk streams of Hampshire by his uncle George, who when bishop of Bristol fished the Test at Leckford, and the Frome. Numerous branches of the Wills family lived around Bristol and I have no doubt were generous to their local bishop with fishing invitations. There were several pupils of my father's whose parents or relations also had trout fishing. His fishing diary shows that he was often able to escape from Eton for a day or even just for an evening rise, which for an eighty mile round trip in a small car on the winding roads of the 1930s and an early school to take at 7.30 the next morning, displayed a certain keenness. So he became an ardent disciple of Skues and Halford, an expert on the entomology of the trout's diet, which he imitated with such skill, and a capable practitioner on the riverbank. What better instructor could a boy possibly have had?

So in due course I was able to accompany him to Longparish or Mottisfont on the Test, to the Kennet at Kintbury, and to its own lesser known tributary the Lambourne. Another favourite place was the river

Gade in Hertfordshire near Tring. Whether it still exists as a trout stream or has been swallowed up by pollution and developments I do not know. I caught my first Test trout at Wherwell on a carrier called the Dublin stream in August 1945. For some reason old Colonel Jenkins had given my father a week there. He rode down on a grey pony to see how we were doing. The war had only been over for a few weeks. All the trout were wild in those days, hard to catch and even harder to land. I can remember disaster after disaster as our fine and no doubt poor quality wartime casts were snapped in the weeds.

Later that year I made my first of countless fishing trips to Sutherland. The excitement of boarding the night sleeper on my own, leaning out of the window at first light with the sparks and smuts from the engine blowing back onto my face, to see the endless expanse of heather as we struggled up the incline towards Dalwhinnie, with place names to conjure with such as Dalnamein, Dalnacardoch, Drumochter and Ben Alder on either side. Little did I imagine that I would be fortunate enough to enjoy such wonderful shooting and stalking there in years to come. Eventually we reached Inverness and I changed trains for Lairg. The richness of the East Ross-shire countryside after the bleak grandeur of the Monadhliaths surprised me. A lot of my fishing life has been spent in Easter Ross so it is more familiar now. In Lairg I caught an ancient brown bus along the north shore of Loch Shin to Overscaig. Among my fellow passengers were some noisy hens in a wire cage. At last I arrived at Fiag Lodge to be met by the Craigmyle family. There over the next fortnight, and again the following year, we caught numerous small trout in the hill lochs, pursued a few grouse over an idiosyncratic Gordon setter with a mouth like a rat trap, and I missed my first stag. Scotland, I decided, was the place to live. How right I was!

Fishing holidays at Ballynahinch in Connemara and in Skye followed before schooldays were over and army life began. We caught a few sea trout but nothing large. In Ireland there was a pretty waitress at the Castle and for the first time I realised there might be other things in life but fishing. But I was far too shy to even talk to her.

Every summer holidays we fished the Conwy for sea trout too. It was one of the most celebrated of Welsh sea trout rivers with fish into double figures caught every year. But you had to fish all night in the dark to achieve success and I doubt if we ever stayed much after midnight. My uncle had a salmon trap in the tideway at Caerhun. There had been a trap there since the Romans had their camp of Canovium close by. It was thrilling for a boy to climb down the ladder into the trap at low tide to scoop around with a net among the mud and rocks for a monster sea trout. Every year the size of the largest sea trout caught in the trap exceeded the weight of the largest salmon; but the largest sea trout I ever caught on a rod on the Conwy only weighed five pounds. The cost of repairing and maintaining the trap against the vicious surge of the tides became prohibitive, and anyway we have all become far more conserva-tion minded as fish stocks have declined, so eventually I gave the right to fish the trap to the River Board for conservation purposes before I sold Caerhun estate. Other fishing holidays for sea trout with my father and our family took place later on at Camasunarie in Skye and at Lochboisdale in South Uist.

One night on Loch Coruisk I arranged to be landed on a small island while Alan Johnson, acting as the ghillie, rowed my father and Graham Mackrill up the loch. The jagged outline of the Cuillins towered above us as the light faded. I caught one or two small finnock but was cold and bored before I heard the boat returning after midnight. Loud voices carried across the loch. 'It must have been a huge fish – six or seven pounds at least?'; 'Oh yes, probably more, the largest I have ever hooked. It went off like a train.' Graham had hooked and been broken by a monster sea trout in the dark. He and my father continued to speculate about its weight far into the night over the whisky. Four months later I handed a postcard from Alan Johnson to Graham when I went down to shoot with him in Yorkshire. The postcard came with a broken cast with a Peter Ross on the tail fly and a Black Pennell on the dropper. 'I think this may be your friend's property,' it said. 'It was found in the mouth of a sea trout we caught a few weeks later. It weighed one pound thirteen ounces!'

Apart from a few stock fish on the Test, and a monster of 6½ lbs in Iceland this summer, the largest wild brown trout I ever caught were on two business trips to New Zealand. In 1967 Louise and I went on an exhausting round the world trip for Collins for seven weeks. In the South Island I had a fishing interlude and caught two brown trout over four pounds at Lake Te Anau. In those days the State Tourist hotels were pretty basic. There was nowhere to put the fish, which I wanted to take back to Auckland for an office party. I put them in our bath. We were unceremoniously asked to leave by an irate manager. We flew back from Christchurch with a trout stuffed down each leg of my waders. The temperature was in the nineties. The 'trout-en-croute' at the White Heron hotel in Auckland that evening was not a success!

In 1982 we had a farewell trip from Collins. We escaped the business hospitality briefly for a visit to a lake near Lake Taupo called Lake

Otamangakau, much more beautiful with the heather and Toi-Toi grass and the snow on the volcanic top of Mount Rupehu than the translation of the Maori name meaning 'foul smelling swamp'. Here in the early morning I caught a wild rainbow trout of nine pounds twelve ounces. Our bearded guide was so delighted that he flung his arms round Louise and, rather to her surprise, embraced her. I was glad he chose her and not me!

A couple of fishing trips in Tasmania with Bill Irvine, the Chairman of the National Australia Bank, between board meetings in Melbourne, also produced spectacular trout fishing on a lake called Little Pine. I also had the luck to see a Tasmanian devil, an echidna, a wombat and a duck-billed platypus!

Over the last fifty years I have had the very occasional day on the southern trout streams thanks to the generosity of friends; on the Driffield beck in Yorkshire, as an annual pilgrimage to the delights of Elmswell and of much generous hospitality from Graham and Pam Mackrill; on the Wissey in Norfolk with Michael and April Falcon, and very occasionally on the Test or Itchen with Robin Napier. I adore trout fishing, and still regard dry fly fishing as far more skilful than salmon fishing. The mental image of a lemon-brown shape, every spot clearly visible, poised on the fin in gin-clear water in the 'window' between banks of emerald green water-weed, swinging to and fro in the current as it sucks down the hatching duns, medium olives, iron blue or pale-watery, is as vivid and compelling as the day I first saw it.

But it has been to the salmon and especially to the salmon of Scotland that my loyalties and attention have turned since the 1950s. I caught my first salmon on 17 April 1945 when I was fifteen on the Welsh Dee in the Fir pool at Manley. It was the very first entry in my newly acquired fishing diary. I have entered every other fish meticulously ever since and now, sixty years later, I am rapidly approaching my thousandth salmon, caught on thirty-six different rivers in Scotland, England, Ireland and Wales as well as in Norway and Iceland.

The Glazebrooks have been family friends for four generations. Rim Glazebrook farmed near Erbistock and had asked my father to bring me over to try for a salmon with his son John who was my contemporary. This first fish took a No. 6 Silver Doctor and weighed 8 lbs. Immediately afterwards I caught another on a prawn of the same size. It is many years since I fished with a prawn, now banned as too effective on most rivers, but in those days the logical next resort after a fly as a matter of course. How times change! My father gaffed both fish. Nowadays the use of a gaff is considered rightly as quite unnecessary and rather barbaric.

Salmon fishing opportunities were few and far between. The two largest salmon I have ever caught were both landed on the same day at Brockhampton on the River Wye on 29 March 1950. They weighed twenty-five and a half, and twenty-four and a half pounds. I was a guest of Claude Kirby, a sort of honorary Godfather, who later left me all his fishing tackle. That evening I left by train to go back to Windsor to take Louise to the Beagle Ball at Sandhurst. The river was in perfect order after a week of floods. 'Why,' he said, 'you want to go off poodle-faking instead of catching more fish I can't imagine.' Stung by this remark, but laden down with both fish, which he had generously given me, I set off by train from Hereford for my parents' house at Eton. Here both fish were proudly displayed on the drawing room carpet as Louise arrived for the dance. We danced till dawn; I dropped her back at Windsor Castle, caught the five o'clock milk train via Reading back to Hereford and caught two more twenty-pounders in the afternoon. Those were the days!

Odd days leave permitted me to join my father and uncle on the River Slaney in County Wexford occasionally over the next ten years or so. We stayed with the Skrine family in a typically decadent Irish household of much charm and disrepair. I recognised the same cobwebs above my bed from earlier years and usually managed to survive one or two days before picking up the inevitable flea from the numerous dogs. The Slaney was a gorgeous river and then full of spring salmon. I once attempted to gaff a fish of nearly twenty pounds with an old Irish gaff with an open bend and a blunt point. The fish was not ready but I was over eager. Disaster followed as I backed up a high bank. The fish fell off the gaff, back into the river with a great splash, breaking the cast in the process. I still have an old black and white photograph of the episode taken by my father from the opposite bank at what he thought was my moment of triumph.

Fishing disasters are notoriously more memorable than successes.

Since then most of my salmon fishing has been in Scotland. I have been lucky enough to fish most of Scotland's famous rivers: the big four, Dee, Spey, Tweed and Tay, and many of the medium sized ones such as the Findhorn, the Oykel, the Shin, the Ewe, the Deveron, the Awe, the Nith and once the Helmsdale. But for my taste two stand out above all others.

The Almighty certainly must have had the salmon fisher in mind when he designed them. They are the Naver and the Laxford. Both are the perfect size: not too large to be daunting like the Tay, yet sufficiently big to pose a challenge to the caster in high water or a wind; not too small to create the impression of an overgrown burn, more suitable for a trout rod. Both are a desirable length. The Laxford, which I have only fished once but which my Dobie relations fished regularly for many years, can be covered from its source in Loch Stack to the sea in a day, and that is what I did with two fish to show for it by evening and two others lost. The Naver can be fished from Beat one to Beat six, all fifteen miles of it in a week, with endless variety and hardly time to cover each pool more than once a day when it is in good order. Through kind friends I have enjoyed many fish and many happy times there.

But the two rivers I have fished most regularly are those nearest our homes, the Teith, which flows through Doune, and the Conon in Ross-shire. Nowadays I can walk through our garden gate at the River House to the Castle pool on the Teith with salmon rod in hand. The Teith is a charming and beautiful river that used to have a reputation as one of the best spring rivers in the second division, but now the run is mainly confined to the autumn. I can fish it as a member of the Doune Anglers, our local angling club, or one day a week as a tenant of Moray Estates or with our great friends and neighbours Colin and Caroline Stroyan as tenants of Cambusmore. One or two fish a year is all I catch but I have done that with enormous pleasure since I first fished Blairdrummond as a guest of John Muir forty years ago.

But it is of course to the River Conon that I owe my first allegiance and two thirds of the salmon I have caught in my life. In 1976 I was able to consider for the first time to realise an ambition to own my own salmon beat and to reinvest some of the money I had inherited from my uncle. I had no difficulty in deciding that he would have approved! At first I bid for the Craig fishings on the River Orchy in Argyll. Providentially my offer was refused. It would have been a disaster. Then I started to look at what else was on the market with Jimmy Priestley, a kind and generous family friend. We looked at a beat on the Oykel but then discovered that Roderick Stirling was selling the Upper Fairburn fishing on the Conon. It had certain advantages in that as a Hydro river it offered a guaranteed water supply with none of the dangers and disappointments anglers find in dry summers on natural rivers; it had an impressive record of grilse catches for twenty years. But there were serious disadvantages too. The opposite bank was owned by the Hydro board and leased out as day ticket water with little control over fishing methods or angling pressure. There were major impending oil related developments in the Cromarty Firth. There was no house or accommodation. But as a result it was not as expensive as more fashionable beats on more famous rivers. Also interest rates and inflation were in double figures. It was a good time to buy if not to sell. Jimmy decided that he would prefer to look elsewhere. I could not go it alone. Another friend and neighbour, Douglas Prior, was attracted to the idea and to the river. We found a third partner in John Fielden from Shropshire and our offer was accepted.

Thus began the happiest of chapters for the three of us and for our families. We have had many years of superb fishing in the summer for grilse. All our children and most of our grandchildren have caught their first salmon there. My father came every year until his death in 1983 and caught his last twenty fish there. I still use a rod and a wading staff I gave him for his eightieth birthday.

In 1988 we bought Tigh-na-Fraoch, the small farmhouse on top of a hill, which I have already described. Here our family and friends come to stay and fish with us for several weeks each year.

The Conon is now all in private hands and has changed from a relatively unknown river to one with a high reputation among anglers and for its management. I succeeded Peter Whitfield, who had done so much for the river after purchasing the Brahan fishings in 1984, as Chairman of the Conon District Fishery Board ten years ago and have had great fun, interest and satisfaction as a result. At the same time another group of friends purchased the opposite bank to us called the Coul Fishings, so we have been able to manage the two together to our mutual benefit and without the acrimony that can arise when the ownership of two banks is split. It has all been the happiest and most successful of ventures. Another great comfort is that all our children know each other and are friends, so there is every chance that it may continue for at least another generation.

Three fishing holidays in Norway on the rivers Rauma, Laerdal and Aa, and five more in the last five years to the Hofsa in Iceland, conclude my salmon fishing Odyssey. On the Rauma in 1967 my tackle was inadequate for the stupendous power of the river and the Norwegian salmon. I hooked ten fish and was broken by five of them. Louise, who came for the holiday rather than the fishing, claims that it was the only time she has seen me weep. We went to the Laerdal with the Priestleys and the Jardines. My father came too. He hooked a fish in the middle of the light Norwegian night that took off downstream. He was the same age as I now am and had had a bit of heart trouble. I seized the rod and pursued the salmon over rocks and undergrowth and a barbed wire fence for several hundred yards, my line and backing screaming from my reel.

At last I caught up with it in a pool appropriately named the School pool, and was in the process of subduing it, all thought of my father forgotten, when a voice at my elbow said, 'David, I rather think that is my fish. Could I have my rod back, please?' He had followed me all the way down that rugged bank. He duly landed the fish and we both sat down for a rest.

I went to Norway again, to the River Aa, in 1991 with another party of friends, Alick and Suzetta Rankin, Colin and Caroline Stroyan and Robin and Jenni Napier. We had a lovely holiday in a comfortable lodge with fine scenery but the fishing was very disappointing.

Alick Rankin so sadly died in 1999. As a direct result of giving the address at his funeral I was invited by his great friend Loudie Constantine to join his annual party to the Hofsa in Iceland. I had always longed to go there. For the last four years Louise and Colin Stroyan have been unselfish enough to allow Caroline and me to share a rod for a week in August. The Hofsa is about the same size as the Naver and just about as desirable. There are seven beats and you change each day. There is a comfortable lodge. The party is always quite delightful (Loudie chooses his companions with care) and he and Elizabeth are the kindest and most charming of hosts. The Icelandic scenery is dramatic, wild and awesome; the birds are wonderful: ptarmigan, golden plover, whimbrel, dunlin, merlin, Arctic terns and skuas, black-tailed godwit and harlequin duck abound and are all remarkably confidential. I have yet to see a red-necked phalarope but the first year Loudie and Elizabeth generously took time off from their fishing to drive us to see some gyr falcons along the coast. The fishing is sensational. To see a fresh eighteen pound salmon come right out of the water at one's feet savagely to seize one's 'hitched' or 'dibbled' fly is an unforgettable experience. We have had some wonderful adventures there and hope to have more.

Casting a salmon fly with a big rod is an art in itself. It is almost a sport in itself especially when as so often there is little prospect of a fish. Great satisfaction may be obtained by fishing down a long pool casting regularly and meticulously so that not an inch of likely water is uncovered. Modern carbon fibre rods have revolutionised the power and distance that can now be obtained for relatively little effort compared with the heavy cane or greenheart rods of my youth. My uncle was a fine and stylish overhead caster off either shoulder. In those days I knew nothing of the Scottish syles of Spey casting, single or double. Nowadays I never fish any other way and would never teach a beginner anything else. They are more versatile, avoid any contact between fly and rocks or bushes, and are much safer in any wind and just as effective as any overhead cast. My father was not a particularly good caster of a salmon fly but was a thoughtful and successful fisher by dint of always thinking how to present his fly to the salmon in the most natural manner. In my fishing diary I have a page written by my uncle for my benefit and I reproduce it for any grandchildren who may one day read this.

> When you have fished out your cast move forward three or four paces according to taste leaving your fly at the dangle. Strip in as much line as is convenient according to the bank, or whether you are wading. Raise the rod to about eighty degrees so as to take more line off the water, but bearing in mind that you must have enough weight of line to make the rod work. Make a powerful back cast so that the line will travel fast. Because the line is travelling fast there need be no pause, as soon as you have launched the back cast press thumb of your leading hand on the cork, which will cause the tip of the rod to come into action and propel the line forward at the moment of time when there is no weight on it. Aim at about eye level above the water. There should be no effort about the forward cast. This can be demonstrated by the fact that the moment you have 'pressed the trigger' you can remove the leading hand. I am sceptical about the theory of the height of the back cast, except in so far as it is necessary to clear the bushes behind. Normally the line should be brought back well below the rod tip at about waist level.

In retirement my father compiled an anthology drawn from the best of all the great fishing writers. He included one or two excerpts of his own. It was illustrated by Tim Havers and published by Antony Atha, another fishing friend of mine, as a beautiful limited edition. I have a copy beside me as I write today. It is titled *A Portrait of Salmon Fishing*. It is a fitting epitaph. I owe so much to my father and my uncle. Their fishing example, enthusiasm and wisdom have given me a lifetime of happiness and excitement.

This year I set myself two objectives. The first was to finish writing this book. The second to catch my thousandth salmon. I am very happy to have achieved both.

CHAPTER 13

Shooting

O CCASIONALLY IN THE school holidays my uncle would invite my
father to shoot at Gloddaeth, the pheasant shoot he ran in North
Wales in the thirties. My first shooting recollection is standing with my
father on Boxing Day 1938, the last season before the war, at a stand
called the Kennel Walls. Thereafter I replied, whenever I was asked what
I wanted as a present, that I wanted a gun. My mother was opposed to
this. She took the view that there was no point in teaching me to shoot
since I would never be able to afford it. It would be far wiser to stick to
fishing. There was an old hammer four-ten with thirty inch barrels
among the guns in the gun cabinet in my grandparents' house at Cefn
with which both my uncle and my father had learned to shoot. I eyed it
covetously. I do not know what happened to all the twelve-bores. My
recollection is that they were supposed to be handed in for the war effort
to be used by the Home Guard, but certainly when my uncle's pair of
Purdeys, with which I have now shot for nearly forty years, reappeared
in 1945 they were still in pristine condition. But by August 1940 the
four-ten was the only weapon left. My father could resist my entreaties
no longer and my shooting career began at the age of ten.

Archie Hill was the Head keeper at Gloddaeth. He used to come over
with his ferrets and my initiation began. Rabbits were our only quarry
apart from the occasional wood pigeon coming to feed on the oat stooks.
At harvest time we stood outside every field as the tractor towing the
reaper and binder went round in ever decreasing circles. At last the
rabbits bolted as their sanctuary diminished. I seldom hit one. I was far
too over excited. A year or so later I was allowed to bicycle the seven
miles over to Gloddaeth in the Christmas holidays with the four-ten on
my back in a canvas sleeve. I would return frozen but content with a
couple of rabbits slung over the handlebars, a most welcome bonus for
our wartime rations. I learnt the art of ferreting and how to paunch and
skin a rabbit. Often the ferrets 'stuck' down the burrows defended by
large Welsh boulders. We had to put the polecat ferret down on a line,
and if that failed to take to our spades and dig. Eventually I was allowed
my own ferrets and to go off by myself with my gun. One Christmas my

163

pet ferret, known as 'pinny bach', disappeared down a hole on the last afternoon of the holidays. I had to leave her as we went back to Eton by train the next day. I was distraught.

One day I wounded a rabbit that crawled into an impenetrable hedge of brambles. I unloaded my gun and, taking it by the barrels and lying on my stomach, attempted to administer the *coup de grâce* with the butt. The stock broke at the wrist. This was a serious lesson to me: never mishandle a shotgun. Archie then produced a lovely little four-ten that he had taken off a poacher, though the barrels were pitted inside, and gave it to me. Lucy now has this and uses it for vermin. It is likely that Rosie's sons will learn to shoot with it by and by.

The entries in my first shooting diary give a flavour of those early beginnings:

> *September 1940.* Ferreted Fridd-y-bont wood and a few burrows in the field. Enjoyed myself very much. Got 7 rabbits. Ferret got 3.
> Walked up fields in line. Got my first proper crossing shot and another not quite so good.
> *January 16th 1941.* Snowed. Ferreted Crogwyn and the Sycamore. Saw a snipe. Shot badly. Got stuck all afternoon . . . [and so on and so on].

At Eton my father and Denys Wilkinson had the shooting on North Field and at Boveney. In those days there were plenty of grey partridges. There was a splendidly reprobate farmer called Tarrant who used to take me out, thus:

> *Dec 23rd 1941.* Flighted duck at Mr Tarrant's farm, close to the suage [sic] farm. He got a teal. It was my first time flighting. I enjoyed myself enormously.
> *Dec 22nd 1943.* Went out by myself onto North Field for an hour. Two coveys of partridges in the kale. Got one out of each of them.

One of them, I remember, towered far out into head–high kale. I could not find it, so in despair I crawled up and down the rows of kale on my hands and knees, until eventually, to my great delight, I came upon it, stone dead and lying on its back as towered birds always do. It was an old cock and I can vividly recall the strong chestnut horseshoe on its breast.

Later on my father organised partridge drives for his shooting friends among the masters and used willing young Etonians like me as beaters. Apart from Denys Wilkinson I can remember Fred Coleridge and Cyrus Kerry as other shooting housemasters, and on occasions the Headmaster

himself, Claude Elliot came out. But at Arthington where the Sheepshanks assembled an Eton house party every August for the grouse, he was
well described by Leslie, the keeper, as 'Yon mon who couldn't 'it 'em'.

In Wales my father had the shooting over several farms on the rough
hillsides, small woods and fridds. Archie Hill had been keeper at Caerhun
before going to Gloddaeth so knew the ground and the farmers
intimately. This was vital to my being allowed so much latitude to
wander around by myself with a gun at such an early age. The main
quarry were rabbits and the occasional woodcock, with pigeons and the
odd partridge in September. One September my father and I walked
from the house the long climb to a mountain called Druim where there
was the very occasional grouse; and here on 4 September 1942 I shot my
first grouse at the age of twelve; also, so my diary records, a blue hare
and an adder.

As I look back on these innocent early days with rod and gun I think
how lucky I was, and by contrast, how difficult it now is for small boys
to start to learn to fish and shoot. Opportunities for humble rough
shooting are scarce. Regulations and safety concerns are many. Everything is geared to organised pheasant shooting. The young are either
unable to enjoy it or in some cases spoiled by having too much
opportunity too early. Similarly with fishing: the chances of a boy living
near enough to burns or hill lochs where small wild trout still exist, or
to rivers or ponds where early experience with chub, or dace, or roach
can be had for the asking, are few and far between. Fishing and shooting
as sports depend on a thriving young entry and woe betide the future if
regulation and lack of opportunity make this impossible.

As with the beginnings to my fishing career little did I dream that I
would have so much superb shooting over so many years. It was a gradual
process. In Wales my uncle bought Caerhun in 1953. There were some
coverts, and he and my father started a modest pheasant shoot. Below the
isolated little thirteenth century church of St Mary's and the site of the
Roman camp lay a salt marsh on the Conwy estuary. Here one could
hear the wigeon whistle during sermons; and keenly anticipate the cold
slog through the mud in thigh boots, to be in position by dawn the next
morning as the wigeon flighted in from the sea to feed on the salt grass.
It was rare for conditions to be right. A combination of a low tide and
a low river upstream were essential in order to be able to reach the stone
butt set out in the mud. A cloudy night with no moon helped. The duck
stayed to feed all night under a full moon. Finally you needed a strong
south wind to keep them low enough to shoot if they decided to bypass

the butt and head on to the marsh up river. Only rarely each Christmas holidays were all conditions suitable.

In Anglesey we went to walk snipe and flight duck with Rim Glazebrook and then more grandly to visit Brynbella with his elder brother, Reg, whose own son Bill was an Eton contemporary of mine, captain of my father's house, and a lifelong fishing and shooting friend. Charles Wynne-Finch used to invite me to his homes at Voelas in Denbighshire or Cefn Amwlch in the Lleyn peninsula to walk after grouse or to shoot woodcock or teal. Then my uncle, Dominick Browne and Rim Glazebrook took Ruabon Mountain, to which I have referred in an earlier chapter, and grouse driving was added to our Welsh shooting repertoire.

In Scotland opportunities and invitations grew steadily as we got to know more people. Our first venture into renting shooting was at Loch Dochart near Crianlarich, which I shared with two friends for three years. Here we learnt to stalk on a DIY basis, to drag beasts off the hill by ourselves and to mount family picnic expeditions when we walked after grouse or ptarmigan. Here Felicity caught her first trout unaided. I bought a pony from Jock Stewart of Ardvorlich but, as our activities were strictly confined to weekends, not surprisingly it refused to be caught. We sold it on to James McNab. Then we had an aluminium stag-barrow made by the Killin blacksmith. This worked better until I loaded it with two hinds in the snow and it collapsed into a burn on top of me.

For a year or so I had a gun with Derick Forbes at Callander House near Falkirk. But the big breakthrough came when Peter Joynson and Andrew Stainton asked me to join them for the grouse at Doune in 1963. Here we averaged over five hundred brace a year for fifteen years, walking up in August and driving every Saturday until November. From this came more and more local invitations to shoot grouse. They were plentiful then. I thought nothing of having a dozen or fifteen driven grouse days in a season; and those were just the ones I was able to accept in a busy working life! Every year, at least once, we visited my sister and brother-in-law at Arthington to shoot grouse on his moor at Pockstones in West Yorkshire. Every year until his death in 1969 my uncle gave me days at Ruabon where there were then plenty of grouse. Many more lovely days came in Scotland with Eira Drysdale at Ralia and Drumochter, with Jimmy Priestley at Invergeldie, and with other friends elsewhere.

An early example of my father's caricatures in the manner of H.E. Bateman which delighted generations of his pupils at Eton shows the vital importance of taking driven grouse well out in front of the butt!

Hazards of the Shooting School

Left: The world's largest heap of used cartridges.

Below: '. . . grouse coming low and straight for the butt present difficulties to many shooters. They should be taken well out in front. A visit to us will cure you of taking these oncoming birds too late. Confidence is everything.'

Pheasant shooting too grew in frequency and quality. For a couple of years I had a gun at Blairdrummond with the Muirs, then for several years with the Joynsons at the Glassert, until Peter gave that up to concentrate on the pheasants at Doune, as the grouse by then were becoming scarce. He himself gave up running the shoot owing to a period of ill health in 1994. Since then, although everyone concerned has greatly missed his inimitable company, I have had enormous satisfaction, interest and enjoyment in running the shoot there; and continuing to share the costs with two other great friends, Gordon Simpson and Mark Sherriff, while Peter and Kate continue to join us from time to time to help 'pick up' with their spaniel Tore.

The world of so-called 'corporate shooting' began in the seventies. By the time I became a brewer it was well under way and the brewing industry were not backwards in entertaining each other in this way! I benefited accordingly. As Suzetta Rankin so charmingly put it, 'How you and Alick can justify whoring your way around the country with your guns, at your shareholders' expense, beats me.' Some of the best and most enjoyable days were with the Bulmers of cider fame at Drumlanrig. I have been fortunate to continue to shoot there with a non-corporate friend, Simon Dunning, for many years since. He has provided everything one could wish for, marvellous shooting, generous hospitality and superb company.

When I was at the Countryside Commission a series of faxes started to arrive inviting me to shoot with Joe Nickerson, the legendary shot, celebrated businessman and Lincolnshire farmer, who had achieved the record bag of wild grey partridges at his home at Rothwell in the sixties. I had never met him so I refused, saying rather pompously to Louise that I did not want to shoot with strangers; though I did wonder why he wanted to meet me! Eventually I discovered that he had also invited my old friend William Wilkinson, Chairman of the Nature Conservancy Council. Under the quite mistaken impression that I had anything to do with heather management in Scotland, he wished to talk to us about the establishment of the Heather Trust. My interest easily overcame my principles. Thus I arrived at Rothwell in late January in a snowstorm to be greeted by the great man sitting behind his desk already attired in a dinner jacket. 'Ah,' he said, 'you've come. My man will take your guns.' I had to confess that I had only brought one gun. 'You have only brought one gun to shoot at Rothwell!' he exploded. I felt like the little man who always got it wrong in H.M. Bateman's cartoons, nearly sinking through the floor.

He sent me down to his gunroom to choose a pair to my gun. The room was stuffed with Purdeys and Woodwards. 'I only collect two things, best guns and original Thorburns.' I verified this in the capacious downstairs loo the next morning. There were thirty-nine small original Thorburns on the walls.

The next day it was still snowing. William and I stood outside after breakfast waiting for the other guns to arrive. None appeared. 'We are only shooting three guns,' said Joe. 'You two draw for numbers one and two, and I'll stand behind you.' This he did with his pair of twenty-eight bores. We shot over four hundred good pheasants, cocks only at some stands. I doubt if William and I between us contributed more than half the bag. Joe hardly missed all day. I shot with him once more at Rothwell, when Sam Vestey was the other lucky gun, and once for grouse at Wemmergill. Joe made some superbly empirical remarks from time to time:

'If it was not for me there would not have been a European grain mountain,' referring to his seed business.

'If you want to shoot grouse you need to own at least four grouse moors. In a good season you can let them. In a bad one you will always have grouse on one of them.'

'I never bother with my pheasants until after Christmas. I shoot grouse until the end of October, partridges in Spain in November and December, and come to Rothwell for January.'

'If you see a cock pheasant with a white ring round its neck at Rothwell it has come at least fifteen miles. I can't abide them.'

He was the best shot I have ever seen; a real Edwardian character in his perfectly cut suits and his white spats. He was generous to me but I had no way of repaying his hospitality.

Few people would disagree that driven grouse are the *crème de la crème* of all shooting. The wildness and beauty of the surroundings, the sheer speed of the grouse, the uncertainty of a totally natural quarry, and of wind and weather, all combine to put driven grouse shooting in a class of its own. I have quoted Patrick Chalmers on fishing already so I will do so again with a verse or two from his poem 'The Big Pack'. My daughters will remember me reciting the whole poem to them as we crouched together in my butt waiting for the first covey to appear on the skyline:

Where high the hills of heather
　　Heave to the skyline's rim,
Mountains and peaks together
　　The great cloud shadows skim.
But faster than the rack flies,
　　Or e'er the shadows ran,
The pack, the wild grouse pack flies.
　　Take toll of it who can.

Proud August's past her blooming
　　In gulleys and in cuts,
Down the big winds go booming
　　Upon the waiting butts,
Where talented and 'tenty
　　Sit men whose custom is
To pick up five and twenty
　　For thirty cartridges.

Nay here's no necromancy
　　No mountains moved on words
That blur of blotted pansy
　　That's birds, that's birds, that's birds,
That's grouse, the gale for drover,
　　A headlong cloud go they.
They're up, they're on, they're over.
　　Take toll of them who may!

Twenty-five grouse for thirty cartridges for driven grouse in October is stretching poetic licence to the limit! Anything better than one in three would be good going. I must confess to a secret vice in that I have been an inveterate cartridge counter my entire shooting career. I always take a bag, or bags, of fifty or a hundred and count the residue on my return. Over a season I know exactly how I have fared. The ratio varies very little nowadays from year to year, and so far I am not getting worse. But I am under no illusions about my abilities. A really good shot will beat one in two over a season quite comfortably. Drewitt Chaytor, a friend of my father's and one of the two little boys celebrated in that classic fishing book *Letters to a Salmon Fisher's Sons*, regularly used to do three in five at driven grouse in Yorkshire. There are plenty of good average shots, but the number of those with whom I have shot whom I would rank as really first class are very very few. Joe Nickerson for one, John Muir another, and from Jimmy Priestley's October team at Invergeldie, himself and Edward Douglas-Home, and perhaps at grouse, though not at pheasants, Billy Jepson-Turner. The Joyce brothers at Dumfries

House, where I occasionally shot with Jan Collins, were in a class by themselves. Archie Edmonstone is very good. Finally it would be hard to find a better grouse shot than my nephew William Sheepshanks. Of course one hears or reads of many others in the shooting press and by hearsay, but these few stand out from those that I myself have seen.

What factors combine to make a good shooting day? There are many but assuredly the size of the bag is the least important. If fishing is in the main a solitary sport, game shooting is essentially a team game. The company of friends, companionship, cheerful banter, and conviviality over lunch are everything. To shoot with strangers in a competitive environment is to me the antithesis of sporting enjoyment.

The weather and scenery go together. It is hard not to be disappointed in thick mist on a grouse moor or in drenching rain beside a pheasant cover. Wind and weather play a vital role in all field sports. Some wind hopefully in the desired direction is an essential for a good day's shooting.

On the other hand views of sunlit heather in August or golden woods in November can live in one's mind's eye long after the season is ended.

The sight of other wild life is certainly an ingredient: geese on their way back for the winter from their breeding grounds in the far north; the unusual sighting of bird or animal, peregrine or eagle; a huge flock of siskins wheeling off the alders in the sunlight; a fox or roe deer cantering across a stubble. These too stick in the memory adding to the day's enjoyment.

The camaraderie of keepers, beaters and pickers-up is vital. Shooting is a classless sport, thank goodness, and without an easy rapport of good-humoured banter between guns and beaters half the fun for me would go.

Picking-up with their dogs for many is more fun and more important than the shooting itself. Over the years I have only had seven Labradors. Each one has been a close member of our household as well as my constant companion in the shooting field. Shooting without a dog for me would be a pale shadow of the fun and joy I get from watching my own and other people's dogs share our enjoyment.

The size of the bag is entirely relative. If you set out on a rough day's walking hoping to get twenty head comprising two or three varieties, say pheasants with a woodcock and a pigeon thrown in, but return in the evening with forty head including partridges, snipe and duck, you have had a red letter day. If you hope for a day of a hundred pheasants and only get sixty, you have had, from a host's viewpoint if not a guest's, a considerable disappointment. Big days are of course exciting in prospect but quality is always more important than quantity. I have seldom found that I have enjoyed the occasional really big day as much as the one where I can remember most, if not all, the birds I have shot when lying in a hot bath afterwards. There are very few really high pheasant shoots in Scotland. Personally I am against those specialist stands or shoots which boast an average of six or seven birds per cartridge even for competent shots. I think too many birds get pricked and it does nothing for my personal enjoyment to be quite so humiliated! But equally there is nothing worse or more artificial than a stream of low pheasants. As with all things in life it is a matter of achieving the right balance.

And so one is back to marksmanship and one's personal performance against one's own standards; and here I have to admit that I am cross with myself if I have shot really badly on any day, but quietly pleased on those occasional days when things go better than expected. So this is also a factor in the overall cocktail of ingredients that go to make up the enjoyment of a shooting day.

All my life I have kept a shooting diary recording every single day but as I read the volumes again I must confess that I find the endless statistics rather meaningless. It is the occasional comment on wind, weather, or the behaviour of fellow guns or dogs that provide the vivid flash of memory. I rather wish that I had written more and recorded all the figures rather less diligently.

I have left stalking to the last and have included it in the same chapter as shooting, partly because it has much in common, but partly because I have never owned or organised my own stalking. I have been very much the occasional lucky guest enjoying the hospitality of others. To truly understand deer stalking I think you have to have acted as your own stalker or for other people, over many seasons in many places. I have only had this chance on one or two occasions and have been conspicuously unsuccessful, through not understanding the ground or the wind or both, but basically because I am by nature far too impatient and impetuous. Nevertheless I have had many wonderful days in the wildest scenery Scotland can offer in every sort of weather, from golden days when you can rejoice all day in spectacular views of deer, hill, sky and water, to others of such cold wet misery that you vow never to venture to the hill again!

For the charm of stalking lies for me not so much m the excitement of the stalk, or the relief and satisfaction of a good clean shot, though both are important, but in the joy of being on the hill in all weathers, always in superb scenery, often with the prospect of seeing an eagle or a peregrine, usually in the company of knowledgeable and delightful companions, taciturn for the most part but who suddenly become loquacious once the business is done and the white ponies can be spied on the path far below as the pony boy leads them up to the stag. Those are the moments to savour once eyes and wind make it impossible to take to the hill again. And I think for me at the age of seventy-five that moment has probably come. As usual my sister encapsulates my feeling for the hill far better than dull words of mine:

> Oh wind in the heather you sing me a song
>   Of mountain and moorland, where freedom blows strong;
> Where mist round the fir trees drape curtains of sleep,
>   And tear-stained with water the rock faces weep.
>
> Oh breeze in the bracken you murmur a rhyme
>   Of city-free spaces, eternal as time,
> Where chimes of the hairless the honey-bees ring,
>   And crooning and droning, a cradle song sing.
>
> The pipits are piping they sing me a chant
>   Of cloud patterned hill tops, and sunlight aslant
> The weathered grey boulders, where lichens have grown
>   A rusty green tracery printed on stone.
>
> The wind and the wildness both tell me a tale
>   To heal me and help me when friendship is frail.
> Oh blessing of beauty my heart must belong
>   Where the wind through the heather can sing me a song.

My main stalking experiences have been in three places. One was Ben Alder lodge near Dalwhinnie where Philip Byam-Cook was so kind to me over twenty years or so. He was a London lawyer credited with saving the finances of the Grenadiers after the war who also looked after the affairs of the Sheepshanks family to their great advantage. That is how I came to know him. He was a passionate if not to say single-minded stalking enthusiast with no other topic of conversation, who could never understand that fishing was my first love. I went to Ben Alder every year for a couple of days and shot many stags there.

Once, coming off the hill with the Head Stalker, Geordie Oswald, a small man but a fine character, I asked if deer ever suffered from liver fluke. He nodded towards the stag we were dragging down to the loch and said, 'The only fluke that stag suffered from was made of lead'!

For the last ten years I have taken a week's stalking at Strathconon. Previously this had belonged to the Macdonald-Buchanan family, who became friends when we bought our fishing lower down the glen. It was without doubt one of the finest deer forests in Scotland. It now belongs to a Danish family and I fear is being steadily ruined by a misguided management policy of overculling. But we continue to have enormous fun there every year largely due to the two incomparable stalkers whose company on the hill is a delight to all of us: Angus Cameron, the best stalker I have ever known, and Murdoch Maclean. Felicity, Lucy and Rosie all shot their first stags there, as did Jamie; Alastair and Melfort have added many more to those that they have shot elsewhere. We are able to stay at Tigh-na-fraoch as Strathconon is only half an hour up the glen, and we make sure we also have the fishing that week so those not on the hill can go to the river.

But by far my favourite and most special stalking enjoyment has come at Pait Lodge as a guest of Colin and Caroline Stroyan. Colin bought Pait and Monar forests off the Stirling family ten years or so before we bought our fishing on the Conon. Like the Conon, Loch Monar had been flooded to make way for Hydropower and two of the three Stirling lodges disappeared below the surface. But Pait survived. It is the most romantic and remote place I know, reachable only by boat, up the loch from Monar, after twenty-five miles of the beautiful but twisty single track road up Strathfarrer. Many have been my dramatic arrivals after stormy voyages up the loch, always to be greeted by Caroline and the dogs waiting on the windswept shore, and by Col with a large whisky before the blazing sitting room fire. They have been so clever in eschewing the installation of electricity or telephones. The lodge is lit by the original Victorian oil lamps. So that it is the one place I know where you can feel truly remote from the pressures of the modern world. I first went there in 1982 and have been lucky enough, despite a number of appalling gaffes, to be asked back there ever since. I have killed many stags and had great happiness and many adventures on the hills of Monar and Pait. Colin and Caroline have also been my companions on countless days shooting and fishing too, and are our closest friends and neighbours at Doune. So perhaps that makes a good point at which to conclude this chapter.

CHAPTER 14

A visit to Balmoral
10–13 September 1992

A MYSTERIOUS telephone call from Blair Stewart-Wilson to our housekeeper at Renagour, Jean Sykes, first alerted us. 'Is Lady Nickson known by her first name, Helen, or as Louise?' A week later in early June came a further call to Louise at home asking if 'David still shot?' And if so the Queen would very much like us to stay at Balmoral for two days shooting – 'single guns' – and three nights, to coincide with the Prime Minister's annual visit to Balmoral. Blair went on to say, 'We have all been thinking whom we could ask to stay to talk to the Prime Minister about Scotland and we immediately thought of David.' Louise left a note on the kitchen table for me, saying 'Phew! We are asked to Balmoral, but fortunately I have looked in your diary and see you are in Australia; so we can't go." In fact I was not due to depart for Australia until the Sunday evening so it was possible. A further call and subsequent letter from Blair confirmed it all. The Queen's response in agreeing to the suggestion had been, 'Oh well, I know *her* much better than *him*.'

We lived in some apprehension in the ensuing weeks. One night, as at Windsor four years earlier, seemed a wonderful prospect, but three might be a bit of a strain at that moment with all the endless tabloid press publicity about Di and Fergie. We had been due for our last week's fishing on the Conon so had to put off Norman and Tessa Arthur, and change the dates for Michael and Sally Livesay. They both seemed to think we had a pretty good excuse.

Packing was a daunting prospect. What did we need to take, and our suitcases were very shabby! We were warned that at least one night would be a barbecue, but we would need to change into a suit for tea after shooting every day, and Louise would require at least one evening dress for formal dinner. So she rushed ahead with the outfit that she was having made for our Ruby Wedding in October. Then we had to take guns and shooting kit, none of which I needed on the Conon, plus all our fishing gear for the week beforehand, not to mention a suitcase for my trip to Australia; I had changed my flights to leave from Aberdeen airport directly from Balmoral. All very complicated. The Conon District

Fishery Board triennial elections were due to be held in Inverness on the Friday; so Lucy and Melfort nobly volunteered to drive up from Glasgow after the CBI dinner, at which John Major, en route to Balmoral, was to be the main speaker, in order to represent me.

Thursday 10 September

We duly said goodbye to our Conon guests at Tigh-na-Fraoch. Michael Livesay had caught two good fish the day before, while Gordon Simpson had one that morning from the Old Gauge pool, to make six for his visit. We had plenty of time to load the car with all our luggage, managing not to leave anything behind. Lance, my Bank driver, appeared with all my business papers for Australia, and kindly found time to wash the car for me. We wrote endless notes of instruction and advice for Lucy who was arriving that evening. A quick photograph of Louise, looking very smart in her red suit, for my Conon photograph album, doubtless to be captioned 'Setting off for Balmoral', and we were away.

We had been told to arrive between 6.30 and 7 p.m. Of course we were far too early. So we stopped in a lay-by on the hill road at Invercauld before dropping down to the Dee; little did we know that we would be driven up and down that same road twice in the next two days with the Queen and Prince Philip at the wheel. While we waited a red squirrel ran across the road, a good omen we thought. We dropped down the hill, swung onto the Deeside road and, still too early, took a trip down the Dee. I recalled catching salmon in the Crathie Manse Pool, Anne Foul, The Telegraph and Fir Park in the 1960s when we used to fish Lower Invercauld with my parents, my uncle Jack, Antony Atha, Peter and Kate Joynson, and Will and Lillian Collins. We all used to stay at the Ballater Arms.

We retraced our steps across the Crathie bridge and right past the policeman (Metropolitan not local) at the gate. On we went up the drive and there, suddenly, was the Castle ahead. There was a moment of doubt as to whether to proceed to the Tower at the far end, but the presence of a footman standing outside soon resolved our uncertainty. There inside the door to welcome us were Blair and Susan Hussey. We walked straight in, no question of unloading the car; no time even to collect anything from it. We never saw it again until our departure. Nor did I see my gun until it was laid out on my butt at the first drive the next morning!

The Hall was full of the usual clutter of country house sporting kit – fishing rods, maps, charts of stags shot and grouse bags over the years, butt sticks with orange tips on the table, a rack of very smart Royal rugs neatly folded and two china jerries filled with water for the Corgis and Dorgis. After shooting there are seven dog bowls with goodies and biscuits and a silver knife and fork for making the dinners, which HM likes to do herself when possible.

And so through the hall we went, and into the main passage – staircase on right, morning room on left, and sitting room beyond, not very large, comfy and not over smart. There was the Queen coming to greet us and to introduce us to our fellow guests, Matthew and Anne Ridley and Barry and Diana Farnham. Prince Edward was also there. Shortly afterwards Princess Alexandra and Angus Ogilvy arrived with a tartan doggie bag full of odd bits of cake and snacks for the corgis – very popular with HM who immediately unpacked it and distributed its contents. (She fed all her dogs compulsively throughout our visit, including her Labradors and a rather wild black and white spaniel at the shooting lunches.) Our side of Conon smoked salmon, carefully gift-wrapped by Louise, was borne in by a footman and graciously received. This led to a question from the Queen as to whether one could taste the difference between wild and farmed salmon. She expressed her disgust when they found they could not get the Royal Yacht into Laxford Bay because of the fish cages – 'The Laxford of all places!' said she. They had put into Erribol and seen the small fish – 'What are they called?' – being fed with a horrible mechanical machine. This of course produced a long broadcast from me on the Laxford, on the problems of farmed salmon etc., etc. When her eyes started to glaze over we switched to stalking.

'Oh,' she said, 'Melfort was stalking here last week and he wrote such a good thank-you letter about the stag he shot with the branch of a tree stuck in its horns. I laughed out loud.' She then recounted the tale of Melfort's stalk in detail. It had lost nothing in the telling since I had heard the story at first hand from him a few days before! Then we got into grouse shooting and I told her about the *antis* who had disrupted Will Sheepshanks' first day on the moor at Pockstones. She was appalled and rushed off to tell Prince Philip about it, who had just entered the room in pullover and open necked shirt. It seemed to me that we had had an animated conversation for about ten minutes, but I suspect that I had broadcast far too much, in my usual boring way so familiar to my friends and family; and I think she fairly seriously avoided giving me further opportunities to monopolise her over the next three days.

Matthew Ridley was just back from Siberia where he had been stalking a very large species of roe, twice as large as our British deer. He was a quite charming and much quieter version of his younger brother Nick. His wife Anne, daughter of a previous Lord Chamberlain, was delightful too. So were the Farnhams. We had met them once before shooting in Norfolk with Roddy Ralli at Barwick. The other person present was James Patrick, a charming young Irish Guards officer, who was just starting a three-year stint as Equerry.

At seven thirty the Queen led us off to our rooms with Susan Hussey and Blair in attendance. We were down a corridor on the ground floor at the front of the Castle. We passed and were next to the rooms where the Majors were to sleep on Saturday night. We were met by a lady's maid, Karen, and a valet, Christian, both from Buckingham Palace. They were unpacking our suitcases. Our rooms were adjacent and there was no question that we should not sleep together, or the necessity to streak naked down the passage as described by Melfort's cousin Francis Stafford! A few moments later the Queen wandered back and, seeing a pile of coats and boots outside our door, pointed out that there were perfectly good hooks available in the passage alcove for our shooting kit. It was all very relaxing and no different from any normal hostess showing one to one's room. She was wearing a tartan skirt and a yellow jumper.

We changed into pullovers and corduroys, no tie and reassembled in the sitting room at 8 p.m. Three Range Rovers at the door, with HM driving the first, set off for Inchnabobbett, a bothy on the bank of the river Muick about five miles away. Susan Hussey drove Louise. I was in the third vehicle driven by Blair with Angus Ogilvy. He was staying till Monday before moving on to Birkhall. It was to be his sixty-fourth birthday and he wanted to try for a Macnab – salmon, grouse and stag on the same day. 'I am sure that would be acceptable. I will ask the Queen.' A few months later I met Angus elsewhere and he told me he had indeed achieved his Macnab.

The bothy was all done up in pine with nice pictures and candle shades hand painted by Rodger Macphail, a gift from Prince Andrew and Fergie. We had drinks. There was no sign of Prince Philip. Suddenly a waiter appeared with grilled starters. It was Prince Edward in a white T-shirt with *Tango in the Night* across his chest. Then Prince Philip appeared in an apron and a white chef's hat, having gone out an hour ahead to barbecue the meal. It was all very informal with no sign of security or staff anywhere, though I suspect they were not far behind the scenes. We sat down to dinner. I was next to the Queen again. We had delicious venison cutlets and plum tart. I tried not to be boring. We talked about her dogs at Hollerwick where they had just been shooting for two days.

Ensign, 3rd Battalion Coldstream Guards

Sandhurst 1948, accompanying the Commandant, General Sir Hugh Stockwell, on the occasion of the visit of King Abdullah of Jordan, grandfather to King Hussein

The Passing Out parade with Field Marshal Viscount Slim and Hughie Stockwell, whose advice prompted the title of this book

Trooping the Colour 1950 – the dress rehearsal when I carried the King's Colour

1st Guards Brigade Headquarters in the Suez Canal Zone 1953. I was Staff Captain standing next to a wonderful RC Chaplain, Father Dan Kellaher. Front row: Jack Stack, David Fraser (later General Sir David), Geordie Gordon Lennox (later Lt General Sir George), George Ramsay, DAQMC, with whom I shared an office, and Peter Hills

Collins Board at 144 Cathedral Street, Glasgow in 1977
<u>From L to R:</u> *George Craig, Paul Rowlands, Craig Fyfe, Jan Collins, Ian Chapman, Self, Mark Collins, Charles Allen*

The CBI's twenty-first birthday at Centre Point in 1986 with Sir Terence Beckett, the Director General and HRH Prince Philip, Duke of Edinburgh

With Sir Alec Douglas Home and David Dunglass (now the Earl of Home) at an Economic Forestry Group lunch in 1985

With Margaret Thatcher and Sir Reo Stakis at a reception in Scotland about 1984

President of the CBI speaking at the Annual Dinner of the Prudential in 1988

With Donald Dewar, Secretary of State for Scotland, and Sir Fred Goodwin, at that time the Chief Executive of the Clydesdale, at the opening of the new Edinburgh offices

Chairman of the Clydesdale Bank with Ian Lang (now Lord Lang of Monkton) the Secretary of State for Scotland, at the unveiling of the portrait of the Founder of the Bank

Chairman of Scottish Enterprise with the United States Ambassador Raymond Seitz in 1992

Toasting the Premier of China, Zhao Ziyang, on his State Visit in 1985 at a lunch in Scotland

One of the Labradors she was handling belonged to Prince Charles. 'Overtrained,' was her comment. 'I have to have it here as Diana does not like dogs. There are no grouse here this year.' She explained that we would be shooting at Delnadamph. 'There are dreadful roadworks at the hump-backed bridge over the river Gairn. Coaches hold up all the traffic so we are kept waiting and all the tourists come and gawp at us.' She then gave a good imitation of a tourist saying, 'Look there's the Queen.' She said it was all very boring when she was on holiday. Louise sat between Prince Philip and Matthew Ridley.

We drove back through the heather, seeing lots of deer in the headlights, for a final nightcap. Anne Ridley nearly put her bag down on Queen Victoria's chair – the ultimate faux pas, not to be touched under any circumstances. Prince Edward took me through to see a relief map of the estate and explained it all. The whole of the lower floor was swathed in tartan except for the sitting room and morning room, 'because my grandmother couldn't bear it so she stripped it all off.' The Queen spoke about 'Mummy having a cold and coughing, but being her she just won't take any notice.' Then the Royals just slipped away – no goodnights – and we all went to bed.

Friday 11 September

We were called at 7.30 with a tray of tea; torrential rain and high winds outside. Louise breakfasted in bed. I repaired to the dining room by 8.30. The Queen and Prince Philip did not appear at breakfast but Prince Edward did. He was clad in a yellow sweater, riding breeches and boots. I wondered momentarily if this was his wet weather shooting gear, but in fact he was going riding with the Queen. He told me modestly that he had given up shooting because the grouse avoided his efforts to shoot them. He had taken to picking up; this he did to good effect dressed in very conventional tweeds later in the day. We had a sumptuous breakfast though the bacon was tough.

Our departure for the hill was delayed until 10 o'clock by which time we had hung around in the hall and the weather had improved a little. Prince Philip drove a long-wheelbase Land Rover with the back converted to hold two rows of seats facing each other. The five resident guns piled in, not a policeman in sight, and off we went the sixteen miles to Corgarff where Philip Astor was to join us. There was no sign of our guns and cartridge bags. Eventually to my relief I found them laid out on my butt for the first drive. Mine were colour coded blue with adhesive tape. I kept this on my gun sleeve for several seasons, so when friends asked its significance I was able to show off and explain! The Queen bought the moor at Delnadamph from the Stockdale family in about 1980, as there were few grouse at Abergeldie, Balmoral or the Spittal, and Alwyn Farquharson will not give them a long lease on Invercauld, 'though he has twenty-six days driving there'!

I had incorrectly assumed that the tabloid papers with all their sensational Royal gossip would be conspicuous by their absence at the Balmoral breakfast table, but that the paparazzi would be crowded round the gates outside. Not a bit of it; all the tabloids with the exception of the *Sun* were laid out with headlines such as 'Fergie to lose Title'. It was noticeable that members of the Household showed no reticence in reading them. I never saw a reporter or photographer the whole time we were there.

On arrival we were introduced to the Head keeper, Sandy Masson. He had been at Dougarie with Jim Boscawen when we stayed there once and we had seen him last at Diana Boscawen's wedding. All the beaters were Scots Guardsmen on Balmoral Guard duty. I've never seen a better disciplined line of beaters in a long shooting career! We had two low-ground downwind drives above Corgarff Castle before lunch. Prince Philip placed all the guns. We did not draw. He always took the outside butt himself. He missed very little but when he did his imprecations were clearly audible at the far end of the line. Angus Ogilvy also shot well. I did not.

I missed my precious Labrador, Siskin. To my huge disappointment she was just coming into season so we had to leave her behind. Although it would have been fun to have her out it would have been a huge anxiety as the kennels were hundreds of yards from the castle. There would have been no question of popping out to give her a quick run after dinner! Anyway Louise said that HM's shooting dogs smelt strongly of kennels.

Susan Hussey rang Louise at 10 o'clock to ask if she would like to go round the Castle, and if so to be in the drawing room by 10.15. None of the other guests had been round Balmoral before. They went round the house − silver pantry, china cupboards, ballroom (famous for the ghillies' balls; they also have film shows there on occasions and it was laid out accordingly). One of the Royal Worcester turquoise dessert services was decorated by Landseer. On one plate there was a red squirrel. Louise coveted it madly. Susan said that the Household had tried to get a service decorated for the Queen depicting her corgis, but it was very difficult to get this type of work done nowadays. Many of the sporting pictures were by Landseer, others of Queen Victoria were by Winterhalter. Tartan was in profusion. Louise felt that Queen Victoria might appear round the corner at any moment such was the atmosphere. There were stags' heads everywhere. The best were in the hall, declining in quality to the most dreadful switches in the back passages. Almost all had been shot by members of the Royal family – many of the best by the Queen herself when she was Princess Elizabeth, or by King George VI or by Prince Albert. They returned to the drawing room for coffee, where Princess Alexandra and Blair joined them. She had been pinching windfall plums from the garden.

At twelve o'clock everyone gathered up their wet weather clothes and assembled in the hall. The Queen arrived back from her ride apologising for being late. Everyone climbed into Range Rovers, Louise in the second one driven by James Patrick. They sped off, led by HM driving fast – 'I wasn't a FANY for nothing,' she said to Louise. (Note: FANYs were the women army drivers in the 1939–45 War.) HM was furious at meeting two coaches on the hump-backed bridge to which she had referred in conversation the previous evening. They duly arrived at the lunch cabin, a mile beyond Corgarff Castle.

Lunch had been delivered in advance; but under the Queen's instructions guests laid out the tables just as one would do anywhere. It was the same relaxed and informal party as for the previous evening's barbecue. Louise had the opportunity to say how very sorry everyone was for the family over all the horrid publicity over Fergie. This seemed to be well received.

We all came down off the hill for lunch. The weather was still damp and windy. After lunch Princess Alexandra, Susan, Louise and James Patrick walked down to the main road and on to the knitwear shop which we often pass on the road to Tomintoul. Then they drove back to Balmoral, where they went round the gardens and glasshouses with a spectacular display of begonias and other exotic pot plants. They met the head gardener, Mr Young. The lawn in front of the Castle is seriously large, perhaps five or six acres. In the middle is a little stone to mark the spot where the front door of the previous castle was positioned. This was demolished in 1855.

They walked on past the nine-hole golf course, which is used a lot by the staff, to the Factor's house, where they met Catriona Leslie. The Leslies are great friends of Rod and Penny Stirling. She was very friendly and highly complimentary about our daughter Lucy. The Queen drove past from the hill where she had been picking up; and on seeing the walkers joked that she was very impressed that they had walked the full sixteen miles from Corgarff.

During the afternoon we had two drives. I was next to Prince Philip. On the upwind drive he got a right and left out of one covey, reloaded and got a third. Then came two more coveys to his left, missed, furious swearing. Then he got a very, very long curling crosser going back on the wind. It fell out of sight far down the hill. After the drive there was more language for the benefit of his dog which would not go back far enough to pick the grouse. I only had one shot at this drive. But the downwind return was different. He got several and wiped my eye comprehensively. I longed for Siskin to pretend to look for grouse behind my butt that I had not really shot in order to conceal my lack of success.

HM did not come into the butts. She picked up well behind the line. She was hard to identify, well wrapped-up in Barbour, hood, mackintosh trousers against the weather. This meant that one had to be very careful to see the coast was clear before spending a penny! Her spaniel chased hares enthusiastically, belying the myth that all Royal shooting dogs are perfect. Her dog trainer (was he a third generation of Meldrums?) had a pack of handsome black Labradors, impeccably behaved, who hoovered up everything after each drive not already picked by others. Philip Astor was the only gun with a dog, a little cocker. As we stopped for lunch there was a terrific thunderstorm. The door of the Land Rover was open and we all got wet. The cocker was missing so poor Philip Astor stood out in the downpour getting soaked to the skin. Eventually it appeared. He seized it by its rump, hurling it bodily into the vehicle, to cheers from us all, and vastly to the amusement of Prince Philip. The bag for the day was thirty-one brace.

We got back in time for a quick bath and change before tea. This was a splendid spread – scones, sandwiches, shortbread, jams and cakes galore. The Queen sat at the head of the table, behind a colossal silver hot water jug, pouring out the tea into pretty cups with a tartan border. I am always an enthusiastic tea drinker especially after shooting and Louise claims she heard me say, 'Would it stretch to another cup of tea, Ma'am, please.' We went into the drawing room afterwards, sat round the fire and attempted *The Times* crossword.

We changed for formal dinner at 8.15. Louise looked stunning in her new Ruby outfit. The Queen was wearing a multi-coloured rainbow dress and said to Louise, 'This is the first time I've put on a long dress this holidays.' The men were mostly in kilts. The dining room table looked magnificent with food and wine to match. Louise sat next to Prince Philip for the second evening running and as she is not the most enthusiastic shooter found conversation a little harder. Matthew Ridley on her other side inadvertently referred to conditions underfoot on the hill as distinctly 'squidgy', a word we had all decided was best avoided following the recent leaking of the Diana tapes!

After dinner I had a long chat with Prince Philip on a variety of topics: John Major, the economy, the political scene in Scotland, Senior Public Sector salaries (at that time Buckingham Palace were using our top salary scales as a reference point for salaries in the Household), the press and the question of the royal finances and income tax. This was of course before the days when it was agreed that HM should pay tax. Louise had brought some old Sea Ranger photographs from the wartime days when they were all together in the Windsor troop. The Queen then produced her own albums covering the same period including the Christmas pantomimes with several photos of Louise in them. She took Louise and Matthew Ridley upstairs to see her Edward Seago pictures of the South Atlantic and the Falkland Islands. The sitting room was a gloriously homely room with seven large dog snoofs for the Corgis. On the table were family photographs and the famous red boxes. Prince Philip's sitting room next door was much tidier with several of his own paintings on the walls.

In the hall downstairs there is a marble life-sized statue of Prince Albert designed to swivel to watch Queen Victoria going upstairs. This apparently is frequently played with by the grandchildren and once was found covered in lipstick – 'Very difficult to get off.' In conversation with Prince Edward I mentioned Namibia where Rosie and Al are about to be stationed. He told me that on the Royal visit there one radio announcer had greeted them as 'Queen Elizabeth the Eleventh of England and the Duck of Edinburgh.'

There are other memories or remarks which I would like to include in this account. But I have attempted to exclude anything which might be remotely confidential and to try to give the entirely accurate impression of a happy family house party, albeit on a rather grander scale to anything to which we are normally accustomed!

Saturday 12 September

In contrast to yesterday we woke to a lovely day with a stiff south-west wind and set off for Delnadamph as before. This time we were on the high ground known as 'the back of the brown cow'. The views were spectacular, as I looked out towards those famous grouse moors Allarge and Edinglassie. The girls went round the gardens in the morning and did a more extensive tour of the grounds. Louise sat in the front with HM as she drove at great speed along those twisty roads. There were no accompanying police cars but she was obviously confident that she would have a clear road ahead.

Andrew Lawson Johnston was shooting in place of Philip Astor and Blair was shooting so we were seven guns. All the ladies came out after lunch. It was a stiff climb to the butts; Louise managed well. Prince Philip steamed ahead, obviously very fit. We had two long drives, fine views and rainbows. The Queen and Princess Alexandra said they had once seen a beautiful moonbow and felt like writing to the *Field* about it. The bag was fifty brace.

We hurtled home, not leaving till 5.30, which was pushing it as HM was due to give an audience to the Prime Minister at 6 o'clock. But this did not deter her from stopping the car on the way back because she felt her dogs needed a drink from a burn. The Majors had spent the day with Robert Fellowes, who had succeeded Bill Heseltine as Private Secretary since our Windsor visit four years ago. We had tea as normal and the audience was delayed till we had finished. We met the Majors after tea.

I had met him on a few occasions by then but it was the first time I had met Norma. She was very easy to talk to and told me about the work she is researching on the history of Chequers. Before dinner the Balmoral shop was opened for us. We all spent a lot of money.

In the evening there was another barbecue. The Queen set off first with the Majors. I was asked to drive one of the Range Rovers and Louise came with me. This time we went to the 'Gelder', the Prince Consort's bothy, now converted. It was lit entirely by candles. Prince Philip cooked some superb grouse stuffed with haggis. 'You, you and you,' he said, gesturing to us shooters, 'get a whole grouse. Everyone else including the Prime Minister only gets a half.' Louise was allowed to help lay the tables and hand round the first course. The Queen said, 'Alexandra and I are thinking of starting a catering firm. We shall call it Windsor and Ogilvy.' There was a hole in the rush matting covering the floor. So HM and Princess Alexandra got down on all fours to try to do a temporary repair by the light of a little gas lamp.

John Major said to Louise that he was sorry that 'The Government had had to reject David's recommendations for increases in the pay for senior public servants, particularly as it was a very good report.' This was the report of the SSRB about which I had seen him and other members of the Cabinet at No. 10 in July. To me he said that he would like to take up fishing when he retired and that he was concerned about the level of Sterling within the ERM.

Sunday 13 September

We had a leisurely start. I went round the gardens with Matthew Ridley and Barry Farnham. Then we were taken to the game larders and stables. There were three stags hanging in the larder (and curiously for that time of year one hind!). Little did I think that eleven years later I would be stalking on the Spittal beat myself, at the age of seventy-three, and come back with the Head stalker Ben Fernie with a stag weighing 17 st 2 lbs.

At the stables I could imagine Queen Victoria on her pony with John Brown. I went for a walk up the Dee as I wanted to look at the Balmoral beat.

Then we all assembled for Kirk. The visiting Minister was David Munro from the North Kirk Bearsden. The Royal Daimlers took the Queen, Prince Philip, the Majors and the Ogilvys from the front door while three Range Rovers driven by Blair, James Patrick and myself left from the Tower door and swept past photographers, crowds and police to park behind the church. We sat directly behind the Majors, who were behind the Royal pew. The party from Birkhall arrived with the Queen Mother and her guests. Her Private Secretary Alastair Aird, who was in the same house as I was at Eton, came to sit beside me. There were some good familiar hymns: *At the name of Jesus, All things bright and beautiful, The Lord's my Shepherd* and *Glorious things of Thee are spoken.* The sermon was fair, too long, but avoided the obvious pitfall of mentioning Royal marriages.

The Queen Mother and her party came back to the Castle for drinks after the Service. I talked to her about fishing – of course! The Queen said to her, 'Do you remember Louise from Windsor days? We've just been looking at the old photograph books.' To which she replied, 'Dear old Windsor. We must see the photographs.' So there was Louise, standing between mother and daughter, looking at the albums of the young Princess Elizabeth, Princess Margaret and the Windsor gang. A typical Sunday lunch followed. Louise sat next to the Duke of Edinburgh again! They spoke about Namibia and barn owls.

The Prime Minister was delayed by long telephone calls. He returned in good humour saying that the Germans were going to put up their interest rates in the morning and he was confident that this would avert the Sterling crisis within the ERM. That evening I was due to fly from Aberdeen Airport to Heathrow before catching the overnight flight to Melbourne. I knew that on Wednesday morning I would be asked for my views at the board meeting of the National Australia Bank. I felt confident that I would be able to report favourably and wondered if I would dare to say that I had had it straight from the horse's mouth, the Prime Minister of Great Britain! When I turned on my TV set on arrival in my hotel in Melbourne thirty-six hours later I was totally baffled by the headline news that the Pound had collapsed and we had withdrawn from the ERM. Instead of expounding my confidence in Sterling to my Australian colleagues I had to ask them in some bewilderment what on earth had happened while I was airborne! I have often wondered since what very different scenario there might have been if Nigel Lawson had been able to persuade Margaret Thatcher to join the ERM at the right rate in 1985 instead of in 1990. I felt sorry for the Prime Minister. He must have had such a shock after his apparent confidence in the rarefied postprandial atmosphere at Balmoral.

After lunch we said our goodbyes, signing the Visitors' Book each on a separate page. The Queen marks exactly where she wants each guest to sign with a pencilled cross. She gave Louise her cheek to kiss as she curtsied to say her farewells. They both came out to see us off. The registration number on my car started with the three letters KGB. This brought a final gibe from Prince Philip!

So there we were feeling like Cinderella as the clock struck midnight with our fairytale visit at an end. We drove back to Mains of Altries to a noisy, heart-warming welcome from Lucy, Melfort, Iona, Araminta and Alice.

A couple of postscripts: a couple of weeks later Melfort and Lucy went to the Balmoral Guards' cocktail party. Lucy spoke to HM who said, 'We did so much enjoy having your parents to stay and we actually got your mother up the hill.' A parcel arrived at Renagour containing two grouse; needless to say by force of habit I looked to see if they were young birds. One of them had a ring on its leg. It had been ringed in 1987, five years old, a real Methuselah in grouse terms! I could not resist sending the ring back to the Factor, Martin Leslie, and received a somewhat embarrassed reply.

CHAPTER 15

Last but not least
1979–2004

I T IS OFTEN said that Scotland is a small place. It is certainly true that in
the worlds of business, politics and what may loosely be called Public
Life that everyone in Scotland tends to know everyone else. There is a
period when certain names occur again and again, whenever the search
is on for a new trustee, a new director or a new Chairman for this body
or that. The more exposure an individual gets the more their name
becomes known, and provided they perform with reasonable diligence
and competence the more opportunities come their way. Equally, the
moment they start to retire from appointments, and to take themselves
off the endless circuit of dinners, meetings and conferences, so their
network of contacts dries up relatively quickly, and they are relegated
once again to the peaceful obscurity from whence they came. I have
always been notoriously bad at saying 'no' to new opportunity. I was
always pleased and flattered when I was invited to take on a new role.
As a result when my name did start to feature on various 'wanted lists' I
accepted far too many of them. The title of this book *Two at a Time*
reflects my innate inability to say no. My trouble has been that instead
of having two jobs at a time I have frequently had ten or a dozen! As a
result I have devoted far too little time to doing some of them sufficiently
well.

The last few chapters have described in some detail the major business
appointments that I have been fortunate enough to hold over the past
twenty-five years as well as our family life, sport, and a couple of very
special Royal occasions. In this chapter I hope to describe more briefly
some of the openings in the voluntary field and several delightfully
flattering honorary appointments that have come my way. These have
varied widely from becoming a member, and later an officer, in the
Royal Company of Archers, the Queen's Bodyguard for Scotland; to
being appointed Vice Lieutenant for Stirling and Falkirk; becoming a
trustee of various Royal Trusts and other charitable organisations; being
created an Honorary Doctor of three or four Scottish universities and
eventually Chancellor of Glasgow Caledonian University; various one-

off occasions and finally of course the great honour and unforgettable experience of being created a Peer in the 1994 New Year's Honours List.

I will begin by describing my involvement with the management and politics of the conservation of the Atlantic salmon. I have mentioned throughout this book my lifelong passion for fishing and shooting. Inevitably I became interested in the natural history, management and politics involved in both these field sports. As an inveterate 'joiner' I went to a meeting at the Western Club in Glasgow at which the Atlantic Salmon Trust was conceived in the 1960s. This was organised by Rufus Mackenzie, one of the two splendid 'little' Mackenzie Admirals, who served the Trust as its first two Directors for nearly twenty years. Later I attended as a delegate the first of the five-yearly Symposiums held in Edinburgh. In due course after many years on the Council I succeeded David Clarke as Chairman in 1989, and enjoyed very much being in joint harness with the second of these two senior sailors, John Mackenzie, who served the Trust so well as its Director, before I handed over the Chair to another old friend, Bill Bewsher, in 1996. The Trust is one of the most widely and internationally respected of the numerous organisations involved in Atlantic Salmon Conservation. Its mission is to conserve the wild salmon by funding research and advising on best management practices throughout the UK. It has an international perspective and, as it has no membership to service, it is able to rise above the various factional disputes which inevitably arise from time to time in the management of any popular sport.

The Fishmongers' Company have been hugely generous in their support for the Trust, for the Salmon and Trout Association and more recently in Scotland for the Association of Salmon Fishery Boards. Some of the more congenial occasions at the Trust were the quarterly meetings in London in Fishmongers Hall. It was always a privilege and a delight to sit in the ornate Chair of the Prime Warden in the magnificent Court Room of Fishmongers Hall to conduct AST Council meetings. There was never any risk of over running due to poor chairmanship because at precisely half past twelve the chief steward entered bearing glasses of sherry on a silver salver for all members. This usually brought questions and comment to an abrupt end as everyone looked forward to a congenial lunch.

My predecessor, David Clarke, a Norfolk farmer, had done a splendid job for the Trust by tireless fundraising. Indeed the Trust was his main occupation and he cared passionately about it. I am afraid that I was so occupied in other directions that I gave far less time to it, relying on the admirable competence of John Mackenzie. I took the quarterly Council meetings in London or Scotland, and talked a good deal on the telephone to various people on current issues, but that was about it. I did go to St John's, New Brunswick, to give the opening address to the Fifth Atlantic Salmon Symposium in June 1992. I have always bitterly regretted that I was unable to accept an invitation to fish that most famous of Canadian salmon rivers, the Restigouche, from Wilfred Carter, the Director of our sister organisation in North America, the Atlantic Salmon Federation. The chance to catch a large salmon on a dry fly in that famous river is not one to be turned down lightly. I cannot now remember why I had to return home from Canada so quickly and why I could not cancel my previous diary engagement but with the benefit of twelve years' hindsight it now seems a very bad decision!

Inevitably, after buying a share in a beat on the River Conon in 1977, I sought to become involved in the management of the river becoming a member of the Conon District Fishery Board in 1980. In due course I became Chairman in 1994 and have probably spent more time on this over the last ten years than on any other single organisation. In 1996 I was elected President of the Association of Scottish Fishery boards, an honorary position but one that gives me considerable satisfaction and enables me to re-enter the fray from time to time on issues that I regard as particularly important.

I chose to start the introduction to this book with the funeral of the Queen Mother in April 2002 as a point in history to which my grandchildren could relate. On that morning I was chairing the Annual General Meeting of the Association in Pitlochry. We stood in silence as a mark of respect for this lifelong salmon fisherwoman. Afterwards I wrote to Prince Charles at Birkhall to send a message of sympathy and to say that over forty of Scotland's salmon rivers were represented at the meeting, including the Aberdeenshire Dee and the Thurso on whose banks she had spent so many happy days.

I received the following reply:

Dear David

I was so touched that you should have written as you did about my beloved grandmother. I have dreaded her eventual departure and now she leaves behind an enormous chasm in my life. However she also leaves behind the most wonderful legacy of unbelievably happy memories; of fun, laughter and an atmosphere of constant affection and interest in everything. Such vital and extraordinary spirits are rare and I feel profoundly blessed that the Good Lord allowed me to have such a heavenly grandmother who taught

me so many valuable things in life. Oh how we shall all miss her and
everything she stood for . . .

(and then in his own hand Prince Charles had written)

My grandmother would so have appreciated your wonderful gesture at
your AGM.

Yours very sincerely

Charles

In 1995 a senior Civil Servant in the Scottish Office, David Dickson,
told me that the Secretary of State for Scotland, Michael Forsyth,
intended to set up a task force to 'consider the challenges and
opportunities facing Scottish salmon fisheries with a view to recommending a Strategy for the management, conservation and sustainable
development of the stocks into the next century'. He wanted me to chair
it. This was a fantastic opportunity to try to make a real impact on the
management of my favourite pastime. I accepted with alacrity. Michael
was our local MP for West Stirlingshire. He had had a meteoric rise to
fame as one of Maggie's bright young men since winning the seat in the
1983 General election, first in the Foreign Office and then as Minister
of State in the Scottish Office in the early nineties when I was Chairman
of Scottish Enterprise.

He and his wife Susan were near neighbours and friends of ours at
Aberfoyle, and our paths had crossed on a number of occasions. In 1990
he had had a hiccough as Chairman of the Scottish Conservatives.
Margaret Thatcher to her dismay had been forced to ask him to stand
down as Chairman owing to a certain amount of adverse press comment
and under pressure from the party hierarchy. It so happened that very
evening, 7 September, I was staying with Hector Laing and his wife at
their home at Dunphail in Morayshire in order to meet the Prime
Minister and Dennis Thatcher. This was the last occasion I saw her
before her defeat in the leadership election two months later. I sat next
to her at the informal buffet supper. As usual I must have talked too
much because I remember her saying to me, 'Look here, don't you think
we had better go and get something to eat because otherwise we will be
last.' She was obviously very distressed by her day in attempting to avoid
Michael's departure; he was a great favourite of hers. Later in the evening
I sat up very late with her Private Secretary, Peter Morrison. We both
drank a good deal of whisky. He related the grisly details of the day at
No. 10. At one moment of particular tension a previously scheduled call
for the PM had come through from President Reagan at the White

House. 'Well I can't speak to him now,' came her response. 'I'm dealing with something really important'!

At some stage someone had created an enthusiasm in Michael for salmon fishing, and so when he became Secretary of State in 1995 he resolved to do something about it, hence his invitation to me to chair the Task Force. He and Susan thoroughly deserve the success they have had since they became such keen anglers because he is one of the few politicians who have actually done anything to try to improve the situation. The membership of the Task Force consisted of a mixture of salmon biologists and experienced salmon managers. Scottish office civil servants under the able direction of David Dickson provided the secretariat, while assessors were appointed in the persons of Professors Tony Hawkins of the Marine Laboratory, Michael Usher of Scottish Natural Heritage, and the Inspector of Salmon Fisheries, David Dunkeley. We met mostly in my offices at the Clydesdale Bank throughout 1995 and 1996, delivering our report in early 1997. We received an enormous volume of evidence much of it contradictory and controversial. The fact that we were able to produce a unanimous report and to distil all the arguments in reasonably digestible form, together with our sixty-four specific recommendations, was, I suspect, due more to the skill of the draughtsmen than to any guidance from the chair.

Eight years on, it is a source of some satisfaction to me that so many of the recommendations in the 'Nickson Report', or to give it its proper title *The Report of the Scottish Salmon Strategy Task Force*, have been implemented; and to know that it is still used as a guide and reference by salmon managers, and indeed by the Scottish Executive itself under a very different administration from the one that set it up.

The Fishmongers' Company paid me one of the nicest compliments of my life in 1999 in appointing me an Honorary Freeman. I was given a splendid certificate to this effect. It is especially gratifying because I believe that outside the Royal family there are only three other people living who are in receipt of this honour. Two of them are exceptionally brave Generals, Sir Anthony Farrar-Hockley of Korean War fame as the Glorious Gloucesters, and Sir Peter de la Billiere of the SAS and the first Gulf War. As a result I was entitled to become a Freeman of the City of London and am fortunate to be invited to many of the Fishmongers' annual functions. Everything at Fishmongers' Hall is delightful from the great historical traditions, the superb silver, the wonderful pictures including Annigoni's famous portrait of the young Queen Elizabeth, the delicious food, not forgetting of course the charm and distinction of the members of Court themselves. They have been exceptionally generous and constructive in the cause of salmon management in Scotland, not least in the appointment and funding for the able and effective director of the Association of Scottish Fishery Boards, Andrew Wallace.

Among many other causes supported by Fishmongers' is the famous Norfolk school of Greshams. In 1990 Louise and I had a happy day there presenting prizes at their speech day and the following year I had the same opportunity at two famous Scottish schools, Glenalmond and Morrison's Academy at Crieff.

I wish I could feel that all the time and effort I have devoted to salmon conservation organisations over the past thirty years had done anything to restore this magnificent species to its former abundance. So much has been done, but so many factors seem to remain beyond our control: climate change; increased marine mortality; predation; interceptory netting and the appalling effects of fish farming. This was caused by pollution, the proliferation of diseases and parasites such as sea lice, and the genetic threats posed from the ability of the hundreds of thousands of farm escapees to breed with the wild salmon. These and many other problems mean that the salmon's future survival remains precarious.

My other great love has been the sport of game shooting. I would have liked to be able to try to put more back into that sport too, but there was a limit to the amount of time I could spend away from family and those who were paying my salary! I was a trustee of the Game Conservancy from 1988 to 1991 and a member of the judging panel for the Laurent-Perrier Wild Game conservation awards for a while. Both were full of interest for me but I just could not find time to do them justice and reluctantly decided to give them up. Later I was a director of the Countryside Alliance when it was going through a very difficult time financially in the late nineties. It was important for them to have individuals with a business background and in my case someone who knew absolutely nothing about hunting, but believed passionately in the freedom of individuals to continue to enjoy their own country pursuits free from the interference of the politically motivated urban majority.

The Alliance brought together the organisations responsible for hunting, shooting, fishing and other field sports. Fox hunting has already been abolished in Scotland, under the notoriously ill-conceived Watson Bill, and is fighting for survival in England and Wales. Most people believe that, if hunting goes, shooting and fishing will be the next targets for the anti-blood sports lobby. The various marches and rallies organised by the Alliance, numbering hundreds of thousands, demonstrate the sense of solidarity and outrage felt throughout the countryside.

I have tried to attend most of the debates on this issue in the Lords. On two separate occasions I heard Labour front bench spokesmen, Lord Williams of Mostyn and Lord Whitty, say words to the effect that 'In a democracy we have to be very careful and very cautious before we legislate against pursuits of the minority just because a populist majority driven by press and media is opposed to them.' They were actually speaking in both cases on Bills to legitimise homosexual practices; not fox hunting! But the principles they expressed seemed to me to apply equally as well to the debate on countryside pursuits and I enjoyed making the comparison in one of my rare speeches.

Throughout the nineties I was reasonably active as a Trustee in various other capacities including The Princes Youth Business Trust, The Princess Royal's Trust for Carers and the Imperial Cancer Relief Fund. We held a series of Christmas concerts in Glasgow Cathedral every second year alternating with St Paul's in London for ICRF. It has now completed a successful merger to bring the two largest cancer charities together under the title of Cancer Research. I was very lucky in persuading two outstandingly efficient and charming ladies to run these concerts, first Suzetta Rankin and later Julie Edmonstone.

In the seventies two of my closest friends, Peter Joynson and Gordon Simpson, were kind enough to propose me as a Member of the Royal Company of Archers. I was fortunate to get elected because there is an age limit of fifty. Most Archers enter at a much younger age usually with some previous family connection and certainly with much stronger Scottish qualifications than mine. However I just made the age deadline in 1979 at the age of forty-nine. It was a great thrill to put on the splendid uniform and to go on parade again after an interval of twenty-five years. The Archers, usually referred to as 'The Royal Company,' is the Queen's Bodyguard for Scotland. With four hundred members it is much larger than the other two bodyguards, which operate in England, the Honourable Corps of Gentlemen at Arms and the Queen's Bodyguard of the Yeomen of the Guard. Founded in 1676 it received its first Royal Charter in 1704. It became the Monarch's Scottish Bodyguard in 1822. It was originally formed as an archery club and the longbow is still the principal weapon. Many Archers still shoot on a regular basis and there are a variety of prizes competed for annually, some of them of great historical antiquity. The Musselburgh Arrow for example was first competed for in 1603 and is believed to be the oldest 'active' sporting trophy in the world. Gordon

Simpson is one of the most distinguished Archers and his two sons, Walter and Allan, have continued the tradition, having won the Queen's Prize and other trophies on countless occasions. Gordon tried very hard to encourage me to shoot. I could not have had a better mentor but sadly I failed to make enough time to go through to Edinburgh to attend the weekly shoots on the lawn at Holyrood palace and in the winter in the butts at Archers Hall.

The Royal Company is under command of the Captain General and Gold Stick for Scotland. Other Officers include four Captains, four Lieutenants, four Ensigns and Twelve Brigadiers (historically French NCOs!). In 1990 I was promoted to Brigadier. This was a great surprise as most officers are chosen from one of the great traditional Scottish aristocratic families or from among the many senior military officers. My friends suggested that it must have been thought necessary to have someone from the world of 'trade' for political correctness! Anyway I had thirteen years as a Brigadier before climbing the ladder to Ensign in 2003 and Lieutenant in 2004, as my elders and betters fell off their perches or transferred to the non-active list.

The present uniform dates from 1862 though there were many previous versions. It consists of a dark green tunic and trousers with a stiffened bonnet; a cap badge of crossed arrows on a green and white cockade is worn with a single eagle's feather. Officers wear two eagle's feathers and have gold piping on their tunic and bonnet. They do not carry a bow but have a long ceremonial sword. These are in short supply and I had to order a new one from Wilkinson's, a not inexpensive item! As a new officer you are presented to the Queen at the annual Garden Party at Holyrood along with any newly appointed Lord Lieutenants. In 1979 it was a very windy day. I had failed to secure my feathers in the approved manner side by side. As I left my place to line up for the presentation George Younger kindly pointed out that my windblown feathers were giving quite the wrong signal to Her Majesty. They were undoubtedly giving the proverbial two-fingered 'V' sign.

In a high wind it is possible to imagine what women have to cope with in wide brimmed hats at weddings or Ascot. One feels like a sailing ship in a gale but there is no way to reduce sail! Feathers do sometimes blow off. Prudent officers keep a supply of elastic bands in their pocket to assist Archers under their command who inadvertently become improperly dressed. Once I saw a feather sail over the crowd to land on the roof of the Queen's tea tent just before she emerged. I spied a very tall guest, borrowed a bow from a nearby Archer, and standing on tiptoe the guest was just able to retrieve it for me, much to the relief of its owner standing red-faced to attention some fifty yards away. There are numerous good stories of mishaps and misdemeanours on parade. Admiral Sir Angus Cunninghame-Grahame when inspecting his company before the Tercentenary parade in 1976 is credited with saying:

'You, my dear fellow, are looking like what I believe is known in military parlance as a shit-heap; not that I'm in much better shape myself, since I seem to have put on my dinner jacket trousers by mistake.'

Most duties take place in Edinburgh at Holyrood at the Annual Garden Party or at the Investiture. Every second year or so a new Knight of the Thistle is installed at St Giles' Cathedral where the Royal Company provides the Guard of Honour. In 1982 I was on parade in George Square in Glasgow where the Queen was doing a 'walk-about'. We were assembled in groups of six, told to form a circle and, in a unique manoeuvre, to 'place our bows across our bottoms', forming a sort of mobile sheep pen to prevent the assembled populace from pressing too closely to the Royal Personage. I was taking my responsibilities pretty seriously and when I felt a persistent pressure on my nether regions I resisted robustly, requesting the over eager Glasgow matron as I supposed to 'Stand back Madam'. Whereupon a large security officer with a suspicious bulge under his jacket forced himself past me with the words, 'Stop playing soldiers. Don't be so bloody silly. I *am* the bodyguard.' Twenty years later I was on the steps of Glasgow Cathedral helping to receive guests as they arrived for the Golden Jubilee Thanksgiving Service.

There are two or three dinners each year at Archers Hall in Edinburgh. These are splendid occasions with everyone dressed in the green tailcoats and white ties that form the Mess kit. Like so many traditional and ceremonial occasions and organisations it is easy to poke fun at a lot of old men who enjoy dressing up and reliving their youth on parade. But the Royal Company is entirely self-supporting. It costs the taxpayer nothing and provides a splendidly colourful addition to Scottish Royal occasions. It was sometimes said that the House of Lords was the best club in London. I am not so sure that is any longer true. What is certain is that the Royal Company of Archers is undoubtedly the best club in Scotland and there is not a single member who does not feel privileged and proud to belong.

The next honorary appointment to come my way was to be invited by Freddie Graham, that colourful Argyll general with one half of his moustache black and the other white, to become a Deputy Lieutenant for Stirling and Falkirk. Freddie had masterminded the campaign to 'Save the Argylls' during a round of defence cuts in the seventies. As Lord Lieutenant he had insisted that as many Deputies as possible should acquire uniform in order to take part in the annual service at the Church of the Holyrood in Stirling on Armistice Day, and at the war memorial afterwards. I believe this is quite unusual for lieutenancies in other counties. James Stirling, his successor, has continued the tradition. I became Vice Lieutenant on James's invitation in 1997. Apart from the odd occasion when I have stood in for him when he has been abroad my responsibilities have been light. He and his wife Fiona have been particularly hard working and public spirited in the interests of the local community for over twenty five years.

A few other one-off occasions have been fun. Twice I was asked by the General Officer Commanding Scotland to take the salute at the Edinburgh Royal Tattoo, a delightful evening preceded by dinner at Gogar Bank House and a drive behind a police escort through cleared streets to the Castle esplanade. On the second occasion we had six granddaughters in the audience and Johnnie Hall went out of his way to make them feel part of the show. Several times we dined at Holyrood. The last occasion was for the State banquet for the King and Queen of Norway on 5 July 1994. Once we stayed there as guests of Norman Macfarlane, the Lord High Commissioner in 1992. We were in the Hamilton suite. We had two identical double beds in separate bedrooms forty yards apart. I know, because I paced the distance through the two intervening anterooms. A historical perspective perhaps on the modern catchphrase 'your place or mine?' Louise got lost on her way back after dinner and walked straight into another room where a rather surprised Lord Derby was already in bed.

Towards the end of the eighties there was wide encouragement to the idea that Higher Education in Britain should be much more widely available and that a qualification from any of the excellent polytechnics should be seen as just as deserving as a degree from a university. As a result some 'polys' were invited to apply for university status. A number responded to the challenge with enthusiasm and imagination. In Scotland the number of universities increased to twelve with the addition of Napier, Abertay, Paisley and Glasgow Caledonian by the early nineties. At the time Scottish Enterprise was starting to establish its own identity as it emerged from the shadow of the old Scottish Development Agency. So I suppose it was natural for the new universities to encourage the spirit of enterprise and business qualifications by honouring the Chairman with

Honorary Doctorates. All the same for someone who had never been to university and had no educational or professional qualifications whatsoever it was flattering and gratifying to be recognised in this way. So I added degrees from Napier, Paisley and Glasgow Caledonian to the one I already had from Stirling for services to Aquaculture.

But far more significant and momentarily embarrassing were the simultaneous invitations to become Chancellor of two of them. We had just returned to Renagour from a holiday in Tasmania after the Annual General Meeting of the National Australia Bank in Melbourne. I found messages from two separate Vice Chancellors asking me to meet them. I did so while explaining my dilemma in that I would have to choose between them. In the event it was natural for me to decide on Glasgow Caledonian. Its campus was in Cowcaddens in the heart of Glasgow, not a stone's throw away from Cathedral Street where I had spent the first twenty five years of my business career with William Collins. I had just become Chairman of the Clydesdale Bank with my office in St Vincent Place only five minutes walk away. So I met Hamish Wood, the Chairman of Court, and Stan Mason, the Principal and in due course the New University was inaugurated at splendid ceremonies in Glasgow Cathedral and the City Chambers in 1993.

The birth of a new university is exciting and challenging for all concerned. The management challenges in financial and administrative terms are only equalled by the problems of creating a new culture and identity. Academics are not notoriously malleable or particularly flexible in accepting change. In discussing my role as Chancellor it had been established that my term of office would be for ten years and that I did not in any way wish to become involved in the affairs of the Court or Senate. My position was to be Honorary but I hoped to be kept well informed and to be supportive as required, taking part whenever possible in the six-monthly degree ceremonies that took place in the magnificent new Glasgow Concert Hall just across the road from the campus. Glasgow Caledonian was formed from a merger of the former Glasgow Polytechnic and Queen's Nursing College. It had no difficulty in establishing its credentials for 'inclusivity', that horrible but politically correct term, to describe the admirable objective of attracting undergraduates from homes with no previous experience of Higher Education. The majority of entrants also came from a relatively restricted catchment area in the West of Scotland.

It also set out to be innovative and highly entrepreneurial. And here perhaps lay the downfall of the first Principal who had both these

qualities. He began to behave as if he were the prima donna chief
executive of a major plc with some of the perks and attitudes to match.

I must confess that I found Stan Mason great fun and an invigorating
person with whom to work. It was a considerable shock to learn that he
had transgressed the bounds that were acceptable for anyone charged
with the responsibility for administering public funds. He had also made
the mistake of failing to maintain the support of the Court and many
members of staff were disaffected. The Press had a field day; and the
adverse publicity continued for over two years. The Scottish Higher
Education Funding Council was on the warpath. Stan had to go. It was
a messy business.

I became involved to some extent in the appointment of his successor,
Ian Johnson, an academic but also a career civil servant whom I had met
on the National Training Task Force in the Department of Employment
at the time of the establishment of the kitemark standard 'Investors in
People'. Ian is a brilliant administrator and was exactly the right person
to pick up the pieces, though the task of restoring the University's
reputation taxed even his formidable powers for a while. But now ten
years later it is all forgotten and he has done an outstanding job. He and
his wife Mary became firm friends and we shared common passions for
fishing and bird watching. However we had one nearly fatal disagreement early on. He had poured his energies into getting to the bottom of
all the disciplinary implications of the Stan Mason debacle and was
absolutely convinced that the two Vice-Principals were equally culpable.
They were charged and convicted of gross misconduct under the due
processes of the University's disciplinary procedures. The University
Court upheld this decision. The sentence was instant dismissal and the
loss of all pension rights. The final court of appeal was to the Chancellor
sitting with one internal and one external assessor. So I had to become
personally involved. I found this very difficult because I believed that the
two individuals involved were decent men who had been under the
shadow and influence of a very powerful boss. Undoubtedly they had
transgressed but my view was that their offences had not been as heinous
as was implied by the verdict of gross misconduct. And for them to lose
not only their jobs and reputations but also their pensions seemed to me
unduly draconian. But under the procedures the only way this could be
avoided was to reduce the accusation to one of serious misconduct, a step
that was anathema to those who had been involved in all the heat and
fire of the traumatic events. The members of the appeal panel were split
so I decided that justice and fairness lay in the more lenient sentence. It

was not a popular decision, except I imagine for the two Vice-Chancellors involved whom I have never seen again; Ian was very upset, but I still think my decision was correct. Anyway after that our relationship and that of the University went from strength to strength and it is an association on which I look back with great pleasure.

Graduation ceremonies can be quite exhausting because you are on your feet shaking hands and capping up to six hundred graduates twice a day. But it is an enormous privilege to provide the final acknowledgment to so many young (and sometimes not so young!) people after years of ambition and endeavour. I wished I could have talked to them all for a while but the timing dictated that the production line had to roll at the rate of six a minute. When we started it was customary for the level of degree to be announced so that you could tell who had achieved honours degrees or even better a first. But the Senate decided on grounds of elitism that it was unfair to discriminate in the announcements. I got round this by memorising in advance all those who had achieved firsts from the printed programme so that I could spend just a second or two longer in my congratulations. I may have missed one or two but I don't think I ever made a mistake the wrong way. For a long time it mystified those on the platform who could hear but the mental exercise helped to keep me alert during the long procession of graduates past me. A less laudable mental exercise was to count all those who were chewing gum as they received their degree. My record was twenty-seven including one doctor of philosophy. There was never a single woman among them and women were in general much more polite and appreciative in their response than the men, whose most frequent reply to my attempts to congratulate them was 'cheers'. Quite often when I spied a particularly pretty girl in the queue, the man in front, large, hairy and kilted, and probably hot and nervous too, would leave a generous quantity of sweat in my palm. I never did solve this problem apart from an all too visible wipe on the seat of my pants under my robes.

Nickson's Law is that 'The younger the University (and we were the youngest of all) the more gorgeous the Chancellor's robes.' Mine were magnificent, light blue, scarlet and gold with a soft bonnet in brightest puce with a gold tassel to the hysterical delight of my daughters when they first saw them. I conceived this law when on parade with other Chancellors of more venerable antecedents. Oxford, Cambridge, Glasgow, Edinburgh and St Andrews all looked pretty dull by comparison.

The conferring of Honorary degrees was always a great delight. Usually I felt the recipients were doing *me* an honour by accepting them.

It was so interesting too to meet them and their wives and families over lunch afterwards. I particularly remember Jackie Stewart, Richard Branson and Alec Fergusson but pride of place must go to Nelson Mandela. In July 1996 Mandela paid a State Visit to London. He agreed to accept Honorary Degrees from seven universities including Oxford and Cambridge. Glasgow Caledonian was the only Scottish University. It was obviously impossible for him to fit seven universities into his packed programme so it had been arranged for a composite ceremony to take place on the lawns of Buckingham Palace. The Duke of Edinburgh was Chancellor of Cambridge University. At the time we were on holiday in Ross-shire at our house near Dingwall for a week's fishing. As Louise and I prepared to leave to catch the Inverness plane early that morning Pam Mackrill noticed that I had a large tear in the jacket of my blue suit, the only one I had taken north to wear. A quick repair was made with the black adhesive tape we use for splicing the joints of our fishing rods together. I left feeling inadequately dressed for Buckingham Palace but secure in the hope that my gown would hide the adhesive tape!

A splendid ceremony then took place. The assembled delegations took their seats on the grass in lovely sunshine. President Mandela and Prince Philip took their places on a platform. The Lord Chamberlain, David Airlie, invited us to come up to confer our degrees in turn, Oxford with Roy Jenkins and Cambridge with Prince Philip going first. Their orations were delivered in Latin, making it pretty hard for most of us to follow. After each delegation had completed their speeches and conferred their degree they retired back to their chairs, except for the seven Chancellors who took their place on the platform behind Mandela. When it came to the turn of Warwick University the Chancellor, Sonny Ramphal, a former Secretary General of the United Nations, walked back to his place with his delegation. Everyone including President Mandela and the Duke of Edinburgh realised what had happened and started to laugh. When Sonny Ramphal turned round to see the Duke beckoning vigorously to the platform he too roared with laughter as did Mandela. It was the happiest of errors because of course Sonny Ramphal had been a friend and visitor to Mandela in prison on Robbins Island. Our turn came last by which time everyone was very relaxed. I have a video of the presentation. I was able to have a short chat with the great man when we retired into the Palace afterwards.

We flew back to Inverness that evening feeling we had taken part in an historic ceremony that would never be repeated. On the plane I started to feel increasing discomfort in my right eye. So fussed had I been in the morning over my coat that I had put two contact lenses in the same eye. I am notoriously clumsy at the best of times and particularly ham fisted, as my family would testify, but this was one of my better efforts. I had somehow felt that Mandela looked a little blurred!

The City of Glasgow had long supported Mandela and renamed a street Mandela Place while he was still in prison. Glasgow Caledonian's South African connections were largely based on a programme for medical outreach to remote communities. President Mbeke's father had also had connections with the west of Scotland hence his Christian name Govan. A few years later I conferred an Honorary degree on him too in South Africa House in Trafalgar Square where demonstrations against apartheid had taken place for so many years. On another occasion he visited the University with his wife and named a building for us. They were both delightful to meet. Prince Andrew accompanied them.

I have avoided any attempt here to dwell on the many serious issues facing higher education and the current controversy over top-up fees. The one certainty is that British Universities are under funded and academics under rewarded. We shall suffer nationally in the long term unless we can find an acceptable way of bridging this gap. I enjoyed my time as Chancellor and Glasgow Caledonian were extremely generous in their send-off and clever in the presents they gave us on retrial; not least in that Ian Johnson remembered my story about seeing a snowy owl in Shetland and found a superb Copenhagen china model, which now graces our hall table. Magnus Magnusson was appointed Chancellor as my successor in 2002.

The last voluntary job of any significance to come my way was to serve on the Honours committee that made recommendations to the Prime Minister for Industry, Commerce, the Financial sector, Agriculture etc. It was chaired by a senior permanent secretary and all the permanent secretaries involved attended to speak to their own departmental lists. The Ceremonial Branch of the Cabinet Office provided the secretariat. It had been decided that one or two laymen should be introduced to leaven the Civil Service predominance. For very obvious reasons the membership of these committees was completely secret and it was not until several years after I had finished my term of office that I mentioned it to anyone. We met twice a year, once only for each Honours list, and although the full list was available most time was spent on considering candidates for CBEs and Knighthoods. The honours system is coming in for some criticism in the press at present. All I would say is that in the few years I was on this committee I was deeply impressed by the enormous care that was taken, the level of research and information provided and the scrupulous fairness and objectivity exercised. I never remember feeling that any political pressure was being exerted; nor do I recall finding that the eventual Honours list when announced differed from the names on the list we had put forward. The only regret was that so many wonderful and deserving people whose names came forward failed to make it because there just weren't enough places to go round.

I suppose that in the present climate of envy, of wanting to change all that smacks of the traditional establishment, and of cynicism about so many people's motives, that some radical reform of the system is inevitable at some stage. But why? An Honour still gives enormous pleasure to recipients, family and friends. It rewards excellence and public-spirited voluntary service when material rewards are inappropriate. It may occasionally provide an incentive to take on arduous jobs even if any inference must inevitably always be implicit rather than explicit. But I honestly believe that in the vast majority of cases an honour comes as a delightful surprise; and even if those jobs where some recognition might be anticipated are completed successfully, there is absolutely no certainty that the individual may not lose out to even more worthy candidates with stronger qualifications at the time.

I suppose I would say that, wouldn't I? Having been lucky enough to benefit twice already; and then in 1994 came the final and totally unexpected accolade. A letter from John Major on 16 November 1993 saying: 'I have it in mind on the occasion of the forthcoming list of New Year's Honours to submit your name to the Queen with a recommendation that Her Majesty may be graciously pleased to approve that the dignity of a Barony of the United Kingdom for Life be conferred upon you.'

Louise opened the envelope as I was away from home. I still have it with her handwritten her comment on the outside: 'Golly! Gosh!'

Nowadays the Honours system is no longer a route to a Life Peerage but until a year or two ago a couple of Peerages headed every Honours list. So four or five people became Life Peers by this route each year instead of by the far more common one of political appointment; and because my name began with N and my fellow new boy was Patrick Wright, who had just retired as head of the Foreign Office, my name headed the list by virtue of the alphabet. A week or so after I got the letter we went up to stay with Lucy and Melfort for a pre Christmas visit. They took us to a production of the musical *Me and my Girl* in the Aberdeen theatre. In one hysterically funny scene the new heir to the

Barony of Harefield Hall rehearses his forthcoming introduction to the Lords in his robes. It may have been hilarious but the Campbells may be forgiven for wondering why Louise and I continued to giggle quite so inanely for the rest of the evening.

You are not allowed to use your new title until the Garter Principal King of Arms and in my case, living in Scotland, also the Lord Lyon, have agreed your new style. I went to see Conrad Swann at the College of Arms and corresponded with Malcolm Innes. It was agreed that the Nickson coat of arms taken out by my great-grandfather when my Uncle George was made a Bishop should be 'matriculated' to Scotland and that I should choose the two 'Supporters' to which I was now entitled to be added to it. The Lord Lyon in a letter said, 'I rather think you may wish to have as *nomen dignitatis* BARON NICKSON. I have not heard formally from Dr Swann about this possibility, but I do not think it would cause any great difficulty as the Nicksons are not a particularly numerous or well-organised family or group in Scotland.'

Having dismissed my family in this somewhat cursory manner the matter seemed to be settled to everyone's satisfaction. We flirted briefly with the alternatives of Lord Aberfoyle or even Lord Strathconon but I rightly anticipated that I would be mobbed up by my friends quite enough without going for some even more pompous title; and anyway the Nickson name had served me well enough for sixty-five years and I was the last of our male line, so why change now? In due course the date for my introduction was fixed for 4 May and Sir David I remained until then, which is still the name under which Louise, and a few others, might prefer to know me.

True to form my sister once again came up with an offering to deflate my pomposity:

THE BALLAD OF LORD CLUMSY

Sir Clumsy hasn't fallen in the Conon or the loch
   Or backed his big Isuzu on his gun and bust its stock;
He hasn't spilt his pudding or dropped a glass of beer
   No he's only dropped his knighthood to call himself a peer!

He started in the army but dropped that to pick up books
   (When he wasn't shooting pheasants, grouse or swans or gulls or rooks)
He captained British Industry till he fell for brewing ale
   (All the while pursuing salmon like Sir Parsifal the Grail).

Next he slithered into banking to try to juggle money
  (With his aptitude for slipping this was really pretty funny)
He plays a lot of tennis – so doesn't count his calories;
  Though Lady Thatcher tried to make him count the judges' salaries.

He's very influential on the Atlantic Salmon Trust
  But they don't know the gaff(e)s he's dropped or what a lot he's bust;
Prince Charles might well be nervous to be ghillied in a boat,
  For he'd surely overturn it and leave the Prince to float.

He's a most exciting driver, spotting birds in every tree
  And he knows a lot about them – and indeed he's fathered three.
His relatives are proud of him and think he's simply great
  When he isn't breaking glasses or smashing up a plate.

I could reel off all his virtues like a poetry recital
  But last night he rang and asked me for suggestions for his title;
Since his mother hails from Lockerbie where Nicksons were marauders
  I think he ought to call himself LORD CLUMSY OF THE
    BORDERS.

On 6 January I had a long standing appointment at No. 10 to see John Major about some matters to do with the Senior Salaries Review report which we were just about to submit. He was very kind and generous in adding his congratulations in person. Once again I was overwhelmed with kind letters from far and wide but this time I did have a little more time to write my replies.

I did have a lot of fun with my Armorial Bearings. I wanted two salmon as the supporters, to which I was now entitled, on either side of the Coat of Arms. The powers that be did not think fish would be in the least appropriate. I pointed out that the Glasgow trams and buses used to boast two fish on the City's coat of arms. What was good enough for Glasgow was certainly good enough for me. Eventually it was agreed. The draughtsman produced two heraldic fish looking remarkably like hideous pike. I demurred, saying that I would provide my own design. Robert Adie who had produced an excellent motif for the Atlantic Salmon Trust was commissioned; and so, after long delay and not inconsiderable expense, a pair of nice little Conon grilse support the new Nickson coat of arms.

I also kept our family motto 'Pedem prolatum referro nunquam' which can be freely translated as 'having once made up my mind, I don't change it'. But it is suggested by my family that in my case it could equally mean 'having put my foot in it yet again, I am incapable of withdrawing it'.

Conrad Swann provided excellent advice on the introduction cere-mony. I was told that I could have up to sixteen people for lunch afterwards including himself and my two 'supporters'. These were not fish but two other Peers of my choosing! Robin Leigh-Pemberton, three years my senior at Eton, now Lord Kingsdown and recently retired as Governor of the Bank of England, had become a great friend when I was at the CBI and later at Hambros. We had stayed with him and Rose at their lovely house, Torry Hill, near Sittingbourne to shoot once or twice. He had just become a Knight of the Garter and wore his Garter Collar for the first time at my introduction. Norman MacFarlane was the other. He and I had first met in the 1950s during my early days at Collins when he was starting his stationery business. He had developed this with spectacular success into the MacFarlane Group; going on to a long list of distinguished appointments including the Chair of Guinness, later Diageo. We had been colleagues on the Boards of a number of Scottish companies. He and his wife Greta were also close friends.

Conrad Swann advised me to have my lunch in the Barry room, rather than the Peers dining room: 'They have a much better menu and the wine list is superior.' This got me into trouble with the banqueting manageress, a formidable Scots lady from Blairgowrie called Miss McWilliam.

'I am told.' I said in all innocence, 'that I should have my lunch in the Barry room.'

'Who told you that?' she replied.

'The Garter Principal King of Arms,' said I with confidence.

She left me in no doubt that it was absolutely nothing to do with him and that, not for the first time, he had overstepped the mark. 'It is very unfair on my staff in the Peers' dining room.' So, suitably rebuffed, I booked the table there and very well indeed they looked after us.

I had greatly hoped that my mother aged ninety-one would be able to come. Sadly she was not quite well enough. However on my last visit to see her in the nursing home in Harrogate, a few days before she died, I was able to take the video of the Introduction ceremony and watch it with her. Her younger sister, my Aunt Ruth, was able to come, as was my sister Mary, to join Louise and myself with our three daughters and sons-in-law. Rosie and Al had come all the way from Namibia where Al was stationed at the time, a fantastic effort. Four of our granddaughters were able to watch the ceremony from the gallery and join us for tea afterwards. We stayed at the Ritz and had a splendid family celebration dinner at Boodles.

It goes without saying that it is an enormous privilege to be a member of the House of Lords and thus part of the legislature. There is a clear obligation to attend when it is possible. The Clerk to the Parliaments advised me that it would be most appropriate to sit on the Crossbenches particularly as I was still serving as Chairman of the SSRB and most people appointed through the Honours system followed this route. However as I had been a Conservative voter all my life and undoubtedly owed the fair wind I had enjoyed ever since 1979 to the Government I asked to sit on their benches. For the first three or four years I was in London on business fairly frequently and was able to attend off and on. But by 1998 my visits became less and less frequent and at the age of seventy regular London visits began to pall so I decided to become a Crossbencher after all. If I had lived in the south of England I am sure that I would have relished the opportunity to become more actively involved in the work of the House. I fear I have played but a small part. I still regard it as a huge privilege to be able to attend and occasionally to vote when I am there but nowadays that is not more than a dozen times a year at the most. The House is already a different place from ten years ago, more confrontational, less considerate and if the truth were told, less fun.

I have spoken very seldom. It is frightening how quickly one loses touch with subjects and events on which one would have spoken with authority and confidence until quite recently. I also find that since Scottish Devolution there is very little Scottish business on which I could speak with some knowledge. Too many speeches are made that add little or nothing to debates. My weakness all my life has been talking too much. Perhaps in the Lords at least I am learning the virtue of silence!

My own view is that the Labour Government was right to seek the abolition of the hereditary principle. However experienced and diligent many hereditary Peers were and are, it can not be correct in the twenty-first century to be a member of the legislature of the United Kingdom by accident of birth. Nor could it be acceptable to have a permanent inbuilt majority against the democratically elected Government in the Upper House. But if they had been prepared to consult, to seek common ground and to phase change over several years then I do think consensus might have been possible. As it is they have handled the whole issue of Constitutional Reform in an appallingly hasty, high-handed and badly thought out fashion. As a result they have alienated many who might otherwise have supported them.

I am totally opposed to an elected Upper House. It would become a pale party political mirror image of the Commons filled with second-rate people who could not get elected to the Lower House. Unless of course it was given more powers like the US Senate, which would always be anathema to the Commons! I believe that the Prime Minister is right in seeking an independently appointed membership that broadly reflects the balance in the Commons but still with an independent Crossbench element of at least one third.

I think there should be a retiral age even for Life Peers like myself and at seventy-five I have reached it! But I shall not seek leave of absence until the course of reform is clearer and still hope on occasion to exercise my vote on the Constitutional issues if I can.

A final story: early on I found myself standing in the Gents shoulder to shoulder with Dennis Healey, who I still think wrote the best political autobiography of recent years; though I have equally enjoyed Douglas Hurd's in the past twelve months. He did not know me from Adam but seeing I was new said in avuncular fashion, 'Welcome to the House of the living dead.' Well, that may be the view of distinguished ex-parliamentarians in their gloomier moments but for the non-political animal it is still a huge privilege and an honour to be there.

Envoi

I BEGAN THIS BOOK by writing the two appendices that follow, seeking to record all that we know about our families for the benefit of our grandchildren. But I came to the conclusion that if any non-family readers had travelled with me thus far that I would be imposing on their patience beyond reason by including material that can only be of interest to a few. So read on at your own risk. You have been warned!

Writing a book about oneself is undoubtedly an indulgence. The Memoir Club, who have been so continually supportive and encouraging, state that one of their objectives is for their authors to enjoy the process. I have certainly done so; and in so doing have relived by recollection so much that I had forgotten.

It has brought home to me yet again how extraordinarily fortunate I have been in my inheritance of robust good health, energy, enthusiasm and enjoyment. Luck has gone with me all my life. I have been blessed with wonderful parents, a marvellous wife and children of whom I am so very proud.

There have been no great disasters and no great sadnesses. I envy no man. We have had a host of great friends who have been so very kind to us.

Laughter has seldom been absent from our house for long – and as someone once said, 'Laughter is the oxygen of life.'

Louise's Family

Cockcrafts, Percys and Mathers

NORTH OF THE M62 and west of Halifax and Bradford lies the Yorkshire village of Heptonstall. Nearby is the hamlet of Cockcroft, whence presumably came the origins of the Cockcroft and Cockcraft families. My father-in-law researched his ancestors some fifty years ago and we have various family trees in his hand based partly on records from the parish register and partly on his interpretation of family documents. He shows a Richard de Cockcroft in 1296 but makes no claim to any direct line of descent until Henry Cockcroft born in 1480. From here he records five generations born in 1516, 1550, 1610, 1641 and 1685 before we come to Samuel Cockcraft (the last syllable spelt with an a not an o by now), born in 1730. Various Yorkshire names recur in these sixteenth century references such as 'of Kippenholme', 'of Mayroyd', 'of Burlees'. It is however to Samuel that we must look before we can put any leaves on the bare branches of the tree that Beetle drew.

Somewhere along the route lies another ancestor with the splendid name of Caleb Cockcrofte who was admitted to the freedom of the Skinners Company in London in 1610 and who was clearly a man of some standing for he had several apprentices, and left a will in 1643 with a number of generous bequests to the poor of villages near Heptonstall. Louise has a copy of the parish register between 1593 and 1659 in which details of his will are recorded. There is also a photograph of the very splendid Cockcroft crest either from a gravestone or from the lintel of a farmhouse. A cockerel stands above an elephant 'passant argent on a chief azure three mullets of six points pierced or'. Beetle's own signet ring however bore no cockerel, no elephant, but 'a sun resplendent'.

We don't know a lot about Samuel except that he held a civil appointment in Gibraltar and afterwards in the Tower of London. It seems probable that he was the first Cockcraft to establish a long tradition of Naval or Military service. He married Susanna Macleod, second daughter of Sir John Macleod of Raasay. Her portrait painted by Samuel Shelley (1750–1808) used to hang in the billiard room at Renagour and now hangs in the hall at The River House. Beetle records on a card attached to the back of Susanna's portrait that Samuel was Chief

Ordnance Officer during the siege of Gibraltar between 1779 and 1783. An epitaph written by some anonymous hand in Gibraltar on his death in February 1793 certainly refers to him in humorous terms as a storekeeper:

> Here ought to have lain but alas welladay
> The bones of old Cockraft one distant away;
> A storekeeper honest and true to his trust,
> Who never knew a fear, but of bearing August;
> For thirty long years would they yet more to come
> In the path of bright honor, his course he held on.
> On friends or on foe never once turned his back
> As astraddle he sat on the top of his sack.
> But peace to his ashes wherever they lie
> For worthy old Cockraft no friends need to sigh
> Since all who true courage and honesty love
> Trust his stores are laid up in mansions above.

I am not sure when the RAOC came into existence, nowadays I think called unimaginatively the Logistics Corps, but perhaps Samuel was a founder member!

He may have been posted to some appointment in the Tower of London after leaving Gibraltar. The *Gentleman's Magazine* of 1791 records that he died at his residence at High Holborn that year by drinking poison in mistake for his gout lotion. His wife, Susanna, was buried in the Tower at the chapel of St Peter Ad Vincula. We have a slip of paper dated November 27th 1898 signed by W.J. Kendall, Chaplain to the Forces, Tower of London to the effect that Susanna Cockcroft (sic) was listed in the register of burials AD 1770. But this date poses a real problem because if it is correct she could not have been alive in Gibraltar in the siege and if she did die in 1770 why was she buried in the Tower before her husband left Gibraltar? Anyway Beetle has written that her portrait was painted about 1790. It appears to be of a woman in her late fifties or early sixties, which would make sense as her two sons were born in 1760 and 1763. We will come to them later on.

Her younger sister was certainly in Gibraltar at a later date for we have a copy of her fascinating and harrowing account describing her experiences during the cholera epidemic of 1804. This is known as Mrs Baynes' Journal. She also had a brother, Lt.-Gen. Sir John MacLeod, Royal Artillery, who married Lady Emily Kerr, daughter of the 4th Marquis of Lothian. We have an account of the death of their son,

Lt.-Col. Charles Macleod, copied out in the same exercise book as the journal and drawn from extracts from Leach's *Rough Sketches* and Napier's *History of the Peninsular War*. This is so stirring that it is worth recording here even though he was only related to the Cockraft family by marriage through his aunt Susanna.

At the river Coa:

> On 21st March 1800 he was a Lieutenant in the 62nd Regt [The Wiltshire Regiment, later the Duke of Edinburgh's Royal Regiment, now Royal Gloucester, Berkshire and Wiltshire Regiment, RGBW]. He served with the 43rd The Royal Greenjackets on an expedition to Copenhagen in 1807. In the Peninsula at the Coa he succeeded to the command of the regiment at Cuidad Rodrigo. The citation reads 'As the regiment approached the Coa, we perceived a part only of our cavalry, infantry and artillery had yet crossed the bridge. It became therefore indispensibly requisite for us to keep possession of a small hill looking down on and perfectly commanding the bridge, until everything had passed over, cost what it might. I trust I shall be pardoned for saying that the soldiers of the old and gallant 43rd, and that part of our own battalion whose lot it was to defend this important hill, proved themselves worthy of the trust. If any are now living who defended the little hill above the bridge, they cannot fail to remember the gallantry displayed by Major Macleod of the 43rd who was the senior officer on the spot – how he or his horse escaped being blown to atoms, when in the most daring manner, he charged on horseback at the head of a hundred or two skirmishers of the 43rd and of our regiment mixed together, and led them in making a dash at a wall lined with French Infantry, which were soon dislodged, I am at a loss to imagine. This gallant officer was killed afterwards whilst heading his regiment at the storming of Badajos and was sincerely regretted by all who knew him.'
>
> (Leach's *Rough Sketches*)

And another account of the same action:

> Major Macleod of the 43rd rallied 4 coy on a hill just in front of the passage, and was immediately joined by a party of the 95th [The Derbyshire Regiment, later with the Nottinghamshire Regiment became The Sherwood Foresters, now The Worcester and Sherwood Foresters] and at the same time two other companies were posted by Brevet Major Rowan on another hill flanking the road – these posts were maintained until the enemy, gathering in great numbers, made a second burst when the companies fell back. At this moment the right wing of the 52nd was seen marching towards the bridge, which was still crowded with the passing troops. Macleod, a very young man, but with a natural genius for

war, immediately turned his horse round, called to the troops to follow and
taking off his cap, rode with a shout towards the enemy. The suddenness
of the thing and the distinguished action of the man produced the effect
he designed: a mob of soldiers rushed after him, cheering and charging as
if a whole army had been at their backs, and the enemy skirmishers,
astonished at this unsuspected movement stopped short. Before they could
recover from their surprise the 52nd [also Rifle Brigade, now RGJ] crossed
the river, and Macleod following at full speed gained the other side also
without a disaster.

(Napier's *History of the Peninsular War*)

At Badajos:

Before the 43rd joined the division Col Macleod long and earnestly
addressed his men expressing entire confidence in the result of the attack,
and concluded by impressing that he trusted to the honour of all listening
to preserve discipline and to refrain from any species of cruelty on the
defenceless inhabitants.

   . . . In one of these attempts, Col Macleod, of the 43rd, A young man
whose feeble body would have been quite unfit for war (he had been
previously wounded), if it had not been sustained by an unquenchable
spirit, was killed. Wherever his voice was heard there his soldiers gathered,
and with such a strong resolution did he lead them up the fatal ruins, that
when one behind in falling, plunged a bayonet into his back, he
complained not and continuing his course was shot dead within a yard of
the sword blades . . .

   Yet who shall do justice to the bravery of the soldiers, the noble
emulation of the officers? Who shall measure out the glory of Ridge, of
Macleod. Of Nicholas or of O'Hare of the 95th who perished on the
breach at the head of the stormers, and with him nearly all the volunteers
for that desperate service.

   Lt.-Col Macleod had early given proofs of ardent military attachment.
His services commenced under his father's friend, Scott Cornwallis, upon
whose death in India he was the bearer of despatches to England
announcing that event. He was next employed at Copenhagen and
frequently in the Peninsula, and succeeded to the command of the
regiment at the affair on the Coa, when Hull was killed. His character
and services are best epitomised in the words of the illustrious
Commander, who with the glory of his own deeds has transmitted to
posterity the name of Macleod. The following is an extract from Lord
Wellington's despatch announcing the fall of Badajos:

In Lt.-Col Macleod of the 43rd Regt, who was killed in the breach, His Majesty has sustained the loss of an officer who was an ornament to his profession and was capable of rendering the most important services to his country.

Macleod, who had only attained his 27th year, was buried among springing corn on the slope of a hill opposite to the Regimental camp; six sorrowing hearts, the only officers of the 43rd able to stand, laid him to his grave. His brother officers desirous of recording their affection and respect, erected a monument to his memory in Westminster Abbey, in which is engraven the above extract.

Napier on Macleod

Such a man was Susanna's nephew. Her brother must have been a distinguished soldier too, to have risen to the rank of Lt.-General. But it is her sister who has left the most indelible record in the form of 'Mrs Baynes' Journal'. This document was written in July 1824. It records in horrifying detail her experiences in Gibraltar during the cholera outbreak of 1804. The copy left to us is written in a clear hand in a plain school exercise book dated 1887 and entitled Plymouth College – C.M. Cockcraft – Mathematics! It was copied from a previous copy by another relation made in 1880.

Margaret Baynes was married to Alexander Baynes, a clergyman. He was in his 65th year and had some form of palsy. They had been married for forty years and had had fifteen children, of which four had been born dead and another three appear to have died in infancy. On the assumption that she was about sixty in 1804 she would have been born in 1744 (this would fit well with the dates we have for Susanna). She was living in Gibraltar as part of the military garrison with her husband, her daughter and son-in-law, who was a clergyman serving the forces, and their three young children, the eldest aged four and a half. To cut a long story short, which should be read in full to grasp the horror, her daughter gave birth to a fourth child; within a week cholera broke out in the local population and soon reached the garrison; she herself survived, but she lost her husband, her son-in-law, her daughter and all the servants in the course of three weeks. Her description of the illness, the deaths and trying to protect the corpses for a Christian burial against soldiers armed with bayonets who were charged with supervising the immediate disposal of all who had died the previous night, while looking after three small children and an infant with no mother's milk, is graphic in the extreme. It gives one a fair idea of what conditions must have been like during the plague or indeed any virulent and fatal epidemic before the miracles of modern medicine. Eventually, after an appalling voyage home in a quarantine ship, she made it back to England with her four grand-children.

The story goes that all five of her sons were killed on the same day at the Battle of Waterloo ten years later. But I find this a little hard to believe because a Baynes/Macleod family tree drawn by a relation (O'Hara Steward? Maybe the same person who copied out Mrs Baynes' Journal in 1880) shows clearly that of the five sons one was a General, two were Colonels, one was a Major and one a Captain. All were in the Royal Artillery. It seems so unlikely that all were killed without any reference to this event in a record made in 1898, or in their mother's journal of 1824. Perhaps the truth may be that they all fought, rather than were killed, at Waterloo. I am reluctant to cast doubt on such a good story but can find no real evidence to support it! Margaret Baynes lived to the great age for those days of eighty-eight. She must have been some lady.

Her sister Susanna, whose portrait we have, had two sons, Samuel Charlton Cockcraft and William. There is a rather charming much smaller portrait of Samuel in uniform in the drawing room at the River House. I do not think it too fanciful to detect a resemblance to his mother. He was born in 1763, was a gentleman cadet at Woolwich by 1773 and was commissioned into the Royal Artillery in 1779. He too is recorded as having served in the siege of Gibraltar, but after that we lose him. He may have gone to Canada. His name does not appear in the Army List after 1794.

William, Beetle's great-grandfather, went into the Navy in September 1780 as a servant to Lt.-Fortescue, the 1st Lieutenant of HMS *Victory*. There is a detailed list of his progress from ship to ship and from rank to rank until his first command as a Lieutenant of HMS *Winchelsea* at the Nore in 1805. On The Glorious First of June 1784 he was a Midshipman on HMS *Brilliant* so must have taken part in Howe's famous victory in the Atlantic. Family tradition has it that the small picture in the drawing room is of the *Brilliant* and the slim young naval officer in the oval frame is William. Later on he returned to the Brilliant as First Lieutenant in 1795. He was in command of HMS *Sussex* at Sheerness from 1807 to 1816 and three of his six children were born aboard her, not presumably a particularly comfortable or hygenic labour ward by modern standards! Finally he became Warden of Deptford dockyard, retiring from the Navy in 1831. His date of birth is listed in one document as 1760 making him an elder brother to Samuel Charlton, but in another he is shown as a younger brother. This seems much more likely as he probably joined the

Navy as a boy of twelve or thirteen. He married a Miss Wylde, a cousin, so Beetle records, of the Earl of Mar and Kellie. But it is through his letters that we know William best. He was clearly a devoted but a strict father. Most of these letters are written to his third son, Macleod Baynes Cockcraft, born in 1819, who in turn became a naval cadet and whose claim to fame so far as we are concerned came on the SS *Albert* where he held the rank of Mate in the Naloo War off the coast of West Africa in 1844. There is a little sketch of the *Albert* and a magnificent ceremonial naval sword in the drawing room. This sword carries the following inscription:

> Presented to Macleod B. Cockcraft, Esquire, R.N. by the merchants and other residents in Rio Nunez, Africa in grateful acknowledgement of his services while commanding H.M. steam-ship Albert, in protecting their lives and property during the Naloo War, Feb 1844.

Under the heading SPLENDID GOLD MOUNTED SWORD the newspaper report goes on:

> Lieutenant Cockcraft, when in command with the rank of mate of the Albert steamer, in February 1844 performed very essential service to the merchants and residents on the Rio Nunez coast of Africa. By his active exertions many lives and a great deal of property were saved during the Naloo War, and the persons on whom the benefit was conferred have subscribed to present him with a sword worth a hundred guineas. We have been favoured with a sight of it and it certainly is extremely gorgeous. It is of naval pattern and the summit of the hilt is an African lion encircled with oak and laurel leaves, with a dolphin on the guard in high relief, all of gold. The scabbard is encompassed in navy blue velvet, with elaborately chased gold mounting, composed of naval trophies, and having the arms of Lieut Cockcraft enamelled. The blade is highly decorated with characteristic emblems relating to the event. Mr Cockcraft was made lieutenant on the 23rd September 1844. We believe he is about twenty five years of age and is a very promising officer.

This sword traditionally hung over the family fireplace for over sixty years, first at 8 Lower Ward, Windsor Castle and then at Renagour. Unfortunately we could not find room for it that position at the River House so it is on the wall.

Sadly we have no record of Macleod's subsequent career to know if the expectations of the newspaper at the time of the Naloo war were fulfilled. But I think if he had become an Admiral we would have heard about it! His father's letters to him as a midshipman could be pretty tough. We have a number of them. They are very difficult to decipher because of his habit, due to the high cost of postage, of writing across and at right angles to the previous text. One of them starts like this:

My dear Macleod

Your welcome and satisfactory letter of 27th of last month I duly received, and arrived by the first mail that leaves for Malta. I should have been pleased to have seen it better written as I know you can do. It appeared like the hand of an illiterate person unused to write. My dear boy, it is a disgrace to the education you have received. You do not spell Gibraltar right and the names of persons was spelt with small letters instead of capitals . . .

This must have done wonders for the morale of a young midshipman under tough naval discipline far from home!

Other letters appear to be to his eldest son, William Wylde Joseph Cockcraft, Beetle's grandfather, at school at a much younger age. They deal with mundane matters like laundry and pocket money. Their tone is far more indulgent; and three of William's incredibly neat beautiful copperplate handwritten replies are still in existence. Written at the age of eight perhaps they explain why the eldest son was treated more leniently in his father's letters than his much younger brother; or perhaps William senior just became more cantankerous as time went on!

W.W.J. Cockcraft, Beetle's grandfather, born in 1804, was commissioned in 1825 into the 58th of Foot (the Rutlandshire Regiment, later the Northamptonshire). He served until 1855 when he retired on full pay as a Captain having held the brevet rank of Lieutenant Colonel. He served in Nova Scotia and in New Zealand where he took part in the expeditions against the Maoris. He married Anne La Trobe Wright in 1829. The La Trobes were an old family of French origin from Montaubon in the Lanquedoc in the sixteenth century. There was clearly much pride in this connection hence the fact that Beetle's second name, like that of his father William, was La Trobe.

William, Beetle's father, was born in 1842, the eldest of four children. His three younger sisters married in due course into the Blackett, Bulkely and Tyler families and bred prolifically, hence Beetle's confusingly numerous cousins. He rose to the rank of Lieutenant Colonel in the Royal Marine Artillery and like his father before him saw action in New Zealand against the Maoris in 1863/4 for which he was awarded a medal. His friend and shipmate in his early days was Prince Louis Mountbatten, later the Marquis of Milford Haven (father of Earl Mountbatten of

Burma). He was Beetle's godfather and to him Beetle owed his Christian name; and in due course his own daughter was christened Louise! Three letters exist from Prince Louis: two to Beetle's father dated 1889 and starting 'Dear Old Cockcraft' and 'My dear old Cocky', and one to Beetle dated 1918, just after the first war, when Beetle was clearly seeking help with employment, starting 'My dear Louis'.

Beetle's mother was a Forbes Calland from South Wales who died in 1998 when he was only eighteen. His father married again and had one daughter, Frances, by this second marriage, who later emigrated to South Africa. He died in 1908 leaving effects totalling £2,298.3s.4d.

Five generations of Cockcrafts had thus given a century and a half of loyal and devoted service to King and Country without having been given much opportunity by a grateful nation to acquire any wealth! And Beetle himself followed this tradition.

My mother-in-law's family came from a very different background to Beetle's, one of land ownership, land management and the Church. We still have three silver entrée dishes and one gold snuffbox to remind us of her Percy ancestors. These only appear on very special occasions. They belonged to Charles Manners Sutton, Archbishop of Canterbury in the early years of the nineteenth century. The snuffbox was a gift from George III on his appointment as Archbishop. The story goes that an official went to see Charles Manners Sutton, who was Dean of Windsor, the day afterwards to offer him the post; to which he replied, 'You are too late, His Majesty has already appointed me.'

The entrée dishes bear the Archbishop's mitre and are hallmarked 1805. His eldest daughter, Mary, inherited them on his death. In 1806 she had married Hugh Percy, who was born in 1784. He became Bishop of Carlisle in 1827 and died at Rose Castle in 1856. We have a cutting of his lengthy and effusive obituary from the local paper, the *Carlisle Patriot*, and a print of a portrait of a distinguished looking man in his Episcopal robes. A note in Granny Jane's hand says: 'He was described as a great farmer and reputed to be the best judge of a horse in all the district, frequently driving his own four horses all the way to London' – strange qualifications for an eminent Churchman we might think nowadays! Until one remembers that of course he would have been an exact contemporary of Bishop Proudie and those other great Church of England clerics celebrated by Trollope in *Barchester Towers*.

After his death his elder brother, Lord Lovaine, became the fifth Duke of Northumberland, inheriting the title from his cousin at the ripe old age of eighty-seven. So Louise's Percy connections are fairly remote.

The Bishop and his wife produced three sons and eight daughters before she died in 1831. The third of these sons, Hugh Josceline, had three children of whom the youngest daughter was Agnes Ellen Percy, Louise's grandmother. Somehow three of the set of four entrée dishes found their way to her and in due course one to each of her three daughters, Margery, Phyl and Jane. The fourth went to Hugh Josceline's second daughter, Mary, whose own granddaughter Josceline Browne kindly sold it to Louise. By then Louise had also inherited number two from her Aunt Phyl and number three from Granny Jane; but we lost number one, which had belonged to Aunt Margie, by a whisker when we learnt that it had been sold in a Bonham's auction just weeks before we discovered its whereabouts. The gold snuffbox followed a similar tortuous route down the generations. Doubtless the three entrée dishes will split conveniently once again between three daughters next time round, but who gets the present from George III to his Archbishop of Canterbury is less easy to divine! The only other mementos of Bishop Percy are an episcopal purple sovereign purse and an admission pass No. 214 to the Coronation of King William IV and Queen Adelaide.

Agnes Percy married Frederick George Mather, a land agent, who lived at Huntley Hall near Cheadle in Staffordshire. His father, Louise's great grandfather, had married Caroline Penelope Sneyd, who had inherited the house from her own father Admiral Clement Sneyd. We have the sale particulars of Huntley in 1816 and a watercolour of a charming red brick Georgian hunting box. It must have been a significant house for it had twelve bedrooms and stabling for eight horses. It was demolished between the wars. Caroline Penelope came to a sad end for she was burnt to death at Huntley when her nightgown caught fire. Apart from her son she had three daughters. One married a Philips, one a Child and the third was a spinster. From the Philips and Child connections came Louise's numerous distant cousins including the Lloyd and Grant families.

Fred and Agnes Mather had five daughters, two of whom died in infancy. Margie, Phyl and Sylvia (always called Jane, except as a child when she had the nickname Tab) had a happy childhood in Staffordshire before the 1914–18 war. Phyl was married first in 1921 to Clive Campion, a land agency student with her father at Huntley, who subsequently became a somewhat mercurial but quite delightful stock-broker. He flew his own aeroplane, enjoyed shooting and had an old black Labrador called Meg. They lived in Surrey and are buried in a lovely graveyard on top of a hill above the church at Peaslake. They were devoted to Louise and treated her as the child they themselves never had. Phyl and Jane were both widowed in their sixties and were inseparable right into their nineties, but resolutely and probably sensibly refused to live together, for, gentle and kind hearted as they were, they shared a determined independence of mind. Margie the eldest married last. I remember her as a widow living at Leatherhead also in Surrey. She had one daughter, Nell Percy-Smith, who sadly died fairly young. This account of Louise's family thus brings us round full circle to her parents, Beetle and Jane, and her own girlhood decribed in Chapter 1.

Appendix II

My Family

Nicksons, Wigleys, Scholefields and Dobies

IN 1971 George MacDonald Fraser, author of the 'Flashman' books and *The General Danced at Dawn*, wrote the definitive work on the Anglo-Scottish Border Reivers entitled *The Steel Bonnets*. To quote from the blurb on the dustcover of the edition reprinted by Collins in 1986:

> Four hundred years ago, when Queen Elizabeth reigned in a comparatively peaceful England, the people of the English-Scottish frontier country were living in the grip of systematic raiding, feud and organised gansterism. This was the work of the Border Reivers – the rustlers and marauders who raided night after night in the hills and farmlands from Berwick to the Solway, shaking loose the border, in spite of all that two governments could do to stop them.
>
> Theirs is an almost forgotten chapter of British history, preserved largely in folk tales and ballads. It is the story of the great raiding families – the Armstrongs, Elliots, Grahams, Johnstones, Charltons, Scotts, Kerrs, Nixons and others, of the outlaw bands and broken men, of such folk heroes as Kinmont Willie, Jock of the Side and Fingerless Will Nixon, of feuds like the terrible Maxwell-Johnstone vendetta, of the hot-trod pursuits and the great battles of the English and Scottish armies across the Marches.

The graveyard of the bleak little church at Bewcastle is full of Nixon graves. MacDonald Fraser tells us that there was an alternative spelling of Nicksoun. It seems probable that, in the way of differing versions of surnames centuries ago, Nickson also became another alternative. The Nixons or Nicksouns were both Scottish and English coming from Upper Liddesdale as well as from around Bewcastle. They were often described as having many 'loose men'. (There is no comment on the morals of their women!)

> The sons of Nick were a troublesome breed, and an important part of the Armstrong- Elliot- Nixon-Crosier confederacy. Although a smaller and less compact family than the Armstrongs, they were important enough to have Thomsons, Glendinnings and Hunters living 'under them'. Their notable characters included the aforementioned Fingerless Will, Archie of the Steile and Ill-drowned Geordie.

There is no direct link known to me between these Border Nixons and the earliest Nickson ancestors that we can trace in Lancashire and Shropshire in the latter half of the eighteenth century. But I like to think, and it seems most likely, that some Nicksons drifted south in pursuit of employment, love or both, and gradually became more law-abiding and in consequence a good deal duller. I also like to think that my mother's family, the Dobies, who certainly came from around Lockerbie in the seventeenth and eighteenth centuries, shared some of the same Scottish Borders background for they lived not many miles away across the bleak Eskdale Muir from those earlier Nixons. They were probably descendents of French or Hugenot exiles called Dubois. They too were connected by marriage to Johnstones, Armstrongs and Kerrs. In Dumfriesshire they varied their spelling to Dobbie.

I have a letter dated 1922, written to my grandfather Richard Wigley Nickson from his Uncle George, then an old man, referring to walks in the Staffordshire countryside with his own father (my great-great-grandfather William), which by virtue of its recollections from some 150 years ago, perhaps adds a little more authenticity to my own wishful thinking. It reads as follows:

My Dear Richard,

I send you the letters, which you read over, having an apparent relation to a number of our ancestors who apparently lived by their strong arms, and some of whom 'died in the air'. [Presumably this must mean death by hanging?!]

Strangely enough, on thinking this matter over, I recollect many long walks I used to have, as a boy, with my father all over the lovely district surrounding the neighbourhood of Stafford-Ingestre, Rickescote, Shirley-wych, Baswych etc. He could repeat with an excellent Scotch accent practically the whole of Burns poems, and for hours on those walks he used to do so.

It came to my recollection on Sunday night, after thinking the matter over, that he many times referred to his ancestors who intermarried with the Elliots, and Grahams in Scotland, and, strangely enough, your father does not seem to have been aware of this, though certainly your Uncle William had some inkling of it.

Your affectionate uncle
George Nickson

Four hundred years have elapsed since the Borders finally saw some peace and stability, the Crowns of England and Scotland were united and we have moved from one Elizabethan age to another. We know not how our Nickson ancestors fared in the seventeenth and the first half of the eighteenth centuries. The first clue comes from three silver coins, one of them a Charles II crown, the other two William III; they give the dates of birth of Elizabeth 1774, George 1780 and Sarah 1782. This particular George, must, I think, have been the father of the William who recited Burns in the letter quoted above, and thus was my great-great-great-grandfather. We also have a note of baptism of a Sarah Cheadle born to Mary Cheadle (née Nickson) in 1754, which would take Mary Cheadle back to the 1730s, but have no record of her brother if indeed she had one. George had three sons, John born in 1805, George born in 1819 and William, of whom we know remarkably little, except that from the letter quoted above. His occupation was described on his marriage certificate as 'Gentleman'. He had thirteen children. My father records 'that as far as we know this was his only occupation'! Certainly he seemed unable to finance his second son John, born in 1837, for he apparently had to turn to his older Uncle John to assist him to join the younger Uncle, George, in business in Liverpool about 1860. George died in 1864 and was buried in Shrewsbury. 'Old Uncle John' was a partner in Samuel Fletcher and Sons of Manchester, and apparently lived in considerable state at a house called Woodlands Park near Altringham. He had two daughters, Fanny and Sarah, and my father could just remember being taken to visit Aunt Fanny at Woodlands when she was an old lady and he was a small child.

The Uncle William referred to in the letter to my grandfather was the eldest of 'Father William's' thirteen children and the writer was a very much younger son, who eventually succeeded my great-grandfather as Chairman of the family business when he died in 1912. This was the business of 'George and John Nickson' founded in 1837, on which our family fortune (such as it was) was based for over a hundred years. They were Provision Merchants and Importers, i.e. Wholesale Grocers, until in 1912 the Kirkdale Mill was acquired, on which the company's manufacturing operations were centralised and where a range of canned goods was produced including in particular the 'Gold Dish' brand of choice ox tongues. The company was incorporated in 1896 and became the largest canner of tongues in the country, which were sold to good quality grocers including Harrods and Fortnum and Mason. I remember that ox tongue was a frequent and much coveted item on our family lunch table on high days and holidays. The large empty tins also made remarkably good dog bowls.

My great-grandfather, John Nickson (1837–1912), seems an austere, strait-laced, Victorian figure from his portrait and from various

photographs, bearded, serious and severe. None of my father's somewhat
irreverent recollections did anything to dispel this image. (I can hardly
believe that any of my own grandchildren will regard me in this light. I
think that I must seem to them to be a convenient and usually rather
badly behaved playmate.) He had married Isabella Wigley, daughter of
Richard Wigley of Welshpool, in 1863. He was twenty-six and she was
six years older; nevertheless they produced six children, which must
provide an encouraging example for those career girls of the twenty-first
century who decide to postpone their families until their thirties. Judging
from her portrait it does seem possible, though rather unkind, to suggest
that Isabella may not have had many earlier opportunities to marry. She
had been a girlhood friend of Elizabeth, one of John's six sisters, and from
some correspondence at the time it seems clear that the Nicksons felt that
John was marrying above his station, and that the Wigleys were socially
rather upmarket. Hence, perhaps, the reason that my grandfather,
Richard, my father, Geoffrey, and I all have Wigley as our second name.
I have, as one of my most prized fishing books, a copy of *The Compleat
Angler* inscribed 'Richard Wigley 1824'. So our family passion for fishing
certainly goes back two hundred years from skills learnt on the trout
streams of the Welsh Marches on this side of the family, and I suspect at
least as far from my mother's family, the Dobies, on the burns and rivers
of Dumfriesshire. We have a small portrait of Richard Wigley, grey
haired, thin lipped and somewhat disapproving, in a blue coat, as a result
of which my father always called him 'the little blue man'.

John and Isabella lived at Frodsham and Birkdale and later built a
retirement house in the Conwy valley in the early 1900s. My grandfather
like my father was a second son. It was fortunate for me that neither of
their elder brothers had sons! The eldest boy, yet another George (how
did my parents resist the pressure to christen me George, William or
John?) went into the Church. He had a distinguished career. He went to
Corpus Christi, Cambridge where he got a First in the Theological
Tripos in 1887. He was a broadminded Evangelist. After various teaching
posts and livings he was appointed Suffragan Bishop of Durham in 1906
and went on to become Bishop of Bristol from 1914 to 1932. He retired
to Church Stretton, near Shrewsbury, where there had been a Nickson
house at some time called The Mount, on St John's Hill, where the
original founder of the family business was buried, and where my father
and his two brothers were educated. He was a talented amateur
silversmith, who made his own Bishop's crook, and a keen trout
fisherman. He used to fish the River Test at Leckford in company with

his chauffeur called Hitchcock. My father recalled that he always liked to cast too long a line, cracking off his fly in the process, to the accompanying shout from Hitchcock: 'Look out, ours has gone again, M'Lord'; to which the Bishop was wont to respond with his favourite swearword: 'Perdition, Hitchcock, Perdition.' I remember him as a very kind, twinkly, old man, who left me all his fishing rods when he died in 1949, though my sister Mary describes him as 'rather scary'. She writes:

> His younger daughter Marjorie was my Godmother, though I hardly knew her in childhood – except that she mysteriously painted her face white-only later in her brave, arthritic and lonely old age. She never failed to remember birthdays and Christmas, the presents never quite what one wanted, but so wonderfully wrapped in layers of pristine tissue paper and satin ribbon that they were a privilege to open. I knew his eldest daughter, Cousin Dorothy, who was always sweet to me, much better as she so often stayed with my grandparents when life became too hot for her with her Bishop father after she had 'turned' and become a Roman Catholic. I had no real idea then what 'turning' meant, but being a rebel at heart myself, thought it sounded immensely romantic and dashing. I fear the reality must have been far from either – misery for all. It was clearly monstrous of her to allow her father to read of her conversion in the newspapers – BISHOP'S DAUGHTER TURNS TO ROME – without telling him first, equally his Christian forgiveness doesn't sound as if it passed the test with flying colours!

Elsewhere in this book there are accounts of visits to Windsor Castle and Balmoral by Louise and myself. My sister has a letter on Windsor Castle writing paper written by Uncle George Bristol in June 1914 when he was summoned as the new Bishop to preach in the Chapel Royal and stay the night. He stayed the night before with the Dean of Windsor.

> The ceremony of Homage was rather a stiff affair [he wrote]. A Royal carriage came at twenty minutes to eleven with flunkeys and I, dressed in scarlet and purple, got in and was driven to the side of the castle where the King lives, shown up into a most beautiful corridor with pictures, gold decorations and tapestries.
>
> There the Master of the Household met me and talked for a time. Then Lord Crewe, the Minister in Attendance, came, and one or two others. In a few minutes a footman announced that His Majesty was ready. We filed into a rather small room, one of the Gentlemen in waiting preceded and announced 'The Bishop of Bristol, Your Majesty'. The King sat on a chair with a scarlet hassock before him, I bowed, advanced and bowed again and then knelt in front of him placing my hands together in a sort of praying

attitude. The King placed his outside mine while Lord Crewe read out the oath sentence by sentence, which I repeated after him. Then I rose, the King held out his hand, which I shook, made another bow, picked up my cap, backed out and at the door made another bow and disappeared. Oh! I forgot to say that as soon as the oath was made I kissed a purple Bible held out by the Deputy Clerk to the Closet on a scarlet cushion.

The King never said a single word. He is very small, growing bald and looked the most anxious and tired man I have seen for a very long time. I am told he will probably talk to me tonight after dinner . . .

The letter continued later that evening:

The King and Queen came in. He was in black evening dress with scarlet reveres, wearing various medals, the blue ribbon of the Garter with the garter on his left leg. She was dressed in white satin closely embroidered with silver all over and glittering in the light. The King came to me first, shook hands, said a few words and passed down the line. The Queen did the same on the other side. Then we filed into dinner. I took in Lady Bertha Dawkins, the Lady in Waiting and sat between her and the Queen. Never in my life have I seen such magnificence.

He goes on at some length to describe the table decorations and the menu. Then continues:

. . . I was kept busy nearly all the time talking to the Queen. She wanted to know a lot about the miners, whether I was married and had children [he had two daughters] what Jarrow was like and so forth. Then she started on the suffragettes and said pretty strong things about them. I assured her that the annoyance they were causing herself and the King was arousing great indignation, and she said she hoped it was so.

There was a break in the conversation then and I talked to Lady B D She got onto Lloyd George and I told her stories about him. To my horror she leaned over and said to the Queen, 'the Bishop of Bristol Knows a good story about L G' I said to Her Majesty 'I am afraid it will horrify you'. 'Not at all' she replied. So I told it and she shook with laughter and said 'You must tell the King that afterwards!' From that time onwards she kept me talking.

Later after dinner and some more descriptive passages Uncle George at last got to talk to George V.

The King was in quite a jolly mood. He asked me all about my work and where I had been and so forth. Then he began to talk about the Insurance Act and Lloyd George. I told him the story about Lloyd George and he went off into fits of laughter. [The tragedy is that Uncle George never recorded the story so we shall never know if it was printable or not.] Then the King got onto the suffragettes. I should think he kept me talking to him on politics and all sorts of topics for nearly three quarters of an hour. He was the easiest man in the world to talk to and I never felt nervous all the time. He talked quite freely about his work. I said to him 'I fear, Your Majesty, must frequently wish you could get away into solitude and quiet for a time'. 'Yes' he said 'it's the most difficult of things to get'. I said 'I like nothing better than a trout stream away from letters etc'. He said 'Ah yes, I like that, but they follow me everywhere'.

The next day Uncle George preached his sermon to the Household. He says he had no idea how it was received. Finally he had a long conversation with the Private Secretary Lord Stamfordham. He concludes, 'Evidently the anxiety in the King's circle about the Home Rule Bill is very great. It has all been the most interesting experience.'

Uncle George was undoubtedly the outstanding member of his generation of our family. He was held in great affection and respect by my father and my uncle and was always referred to as 'The Pope'. He tried to persuade my father to go into the Church when he in his turn achieved a First in classics at Cambridge, reportedly saying with a shameless degree of nepotism, 'With my contacts you could be the youngest Bishop in the Church of England.' To my father's credit he resisted that pressure and followed his own vocation, becoming a brilliant and much loved schoolmaster. Finally and significantly, as already described in Appendix I, Uncle George was the first catalyst between the Nickson and Cockcraft families. So I have reason to be grateful to him for much more than his fishing rods!

I think, too, that my great-grandfather took out our Armorial Bearings through the College of Arms when Uncle George became a Bishop. Perhaps this was part of the protocol in those days. This was the Coat of Arms which I arranged to have 'matriculated' to Scotland in 1994 when I became a Baron together with the family motto '*Pedem prolatum referro nunquam*', which, being freely translated, means that having put our foot down we don't change our minds, a mixed metaphor of which my father would not approve!

So, to return to my grandfather, Richard Wigley Nickson; he was born in 1868. He had three sisters and in addition to his elder brother, George, two other brothers, William, who died in 1921 and Arthur, who accompanied him into the family business. The latter lived at Treaddur Bay in Anglesey and had a yacht. Mary recalls that 'He pressed half-crown coins in a secret goodbye handshake into one's expectant little palm and was extremely genial, but brought telephone calls to an abrupt halt, saying, "Well, Goodbye," in mid-sentence, when he, or more probably we, had said enough.' He left us some furniture including a very useful enamelled top kitchen table, known as 'Uncle Arthur', on which at Renagour, countless fish were gutted, dogs washed and laundry dumped. I think Lucy now has it. There were also miscellaneous underclothes including thick long Viyella pants. All longjohns in our family now go by the generic name of 'Uncle Arthurs'. Such is his claim to fame; great uncles, like prophets in their own country, clearly have no honour among their own descendants.

Richard became Chairman of G and J Nickson Ltd until his death in 1945. He was essentially a Liverpool businessman, commuting every day by chauffeur driven car, first from Hoylake and then from the family home, a charming house called Hinderton Lodge at Neston. My memories of him are curiously grey. His sons called him 'the Governor' but I don't recall any good stories about him from any of them. They certainly respected him but I have the impression that it was the Bishop who had the greater influence.

Elizabeth Jane Howard's four volume saga about the fictional Cazalet family and particularly her first volume, *The Light Years*, provide to my mind a good flavour of what family life must have been like for the Nicksons in the 1930s: a family business to provide employment and security, a comfortable but not an affluent home, servants of course in those days, cook, parlour maid, kitchen maid, chauffeur and gardener, family house parties, tennis, croquet, a spacious garden, tea in the summer house with raspberries from the kitchen garden, and a haven for the school holidays for an impecunious Eton assistant master, his wife and their two children. But in *The Light Years* everything revolved around 'the Duchess', the grandmother in Elizabeth Jane Howard's story. I suspect it was the same at Hinderton Lodge for my grandfather had married Mary Scholefield at Bootle in 1898; according to my sister on the rebound, for she told him she could only give him second best. She was always in love with Bishop Uncle George. She was a much more powerful character than my grandfather, two years older, and something of a blue-stocking. She had helped to found the Parents' National Education Union, or PNEU for short, a collection of private schools for children. James Scholefield, her great uncle, born in 1789, had been Regius Professor of Greek at Cambridge from 1825 until his death in 1853. I suspect that any charm, wit and scholarship that may be in our genes comes from the Scholefields, while the duller quality of cautious practicality may be more typical of the Nicksons and Wigleys; not for nothing is my sister Mary's second name Scholefield!

My grandmother was indeed a great influence on my sister, who remembers everything so much better than I, and can recall it all so much more entertainingly and vividly. Neine, as we called her, the Welsh for Granny, was a powerful matriarch. Two of her sons never married and perhaps in the case of the youngest, my Uncle Dick, this was a case of cause and effect, for she dressed and brought him up as a girl until he was seven, with unsurprising results. Nowadays he would certainly have 'come out' at a much earlier age and perhaps, who can tell, have had a happier life. 'Poor, delightful Uncle Dick!' to quote Mary again. 'He tossed up between being a concert pianist and an architect, had huge talent but succeeded at neither, played tennis at Wimbledon, kept interesting if disreputable company and cost the family a fortune. Blackmail letters were sent to his eldest brother, who controlled the family purse strings. Money trickled through his fingers like sand but he had huge charm.'

He was always wonderful company when he came to stay with us in Scotland, and always liked to keep in touch. He was notoriously unreliable and unpunctual to the frequent annoyance of my mother on his visits to Eton. His main architectural project was the design of Lagos Cathedral and he spent much time in Africa. He used occasionally to return home via Tripoli when I was stationed there in 1951. I was blissfully unaware in those days of his sexual proclivities. Only later did it occur to me why he was always so keen to bathe with young Guards Officers and to suggest that swimming in the nude was so much more fun! My father who was very tucked up about any matters to do with sex never acknowledged in any way that his brother was a homosexual. I think I only learned about it from my sister. Uncle Dick died in Oxford, a sad and rather crippled old man. Mary and I attended his funeral amidst a pretty queer congregation in every sense of the word. The Priest said he could imagine his two brothers welcoming him to Heaven with the words: 'My dear Dick, how wonderful to see you.' I could not help thinking irreverently that they would be far more likely to say, 'Hello, you've turned up at last. You're late again'!

Neine must have been a formidable mother-in law and doubtless my own mother, a fairly strong character herself, must have had some difficult times early in her marriage. My grandmother always put my parents in separate bedrooms when they came to stay. She was a collector of ornaments and furniture. Most of the better pieces that were not sold by Uncle Dick to pay his debts are now scattered round the family and came from her. I remember weeping copiously at Sunningdale, my preparatory school, aged ten, when some assistant master broke the news to me that she had died suddenly at Cefn in 1940. I have a letter written by her to my father the very day before she died.

Her father, David Scholefield, had married twice. Her mother Mary Bridge died when she was quite young, so Neine, as the eldest daughter, had to play a big part in bringing up her small brother and sister as well as her three half brothers. Much later at the start of the 1939–45 war one of these half brothers, Uncle Jos, who lived in Malibu Beach in California, offered to have my sister and me for the duration of the war. With a German invasion thought to be imminent this must have been a tempting offer for our parents. Many families with similar opportunities did send their children to North America. Yet there is no evidence that our parents ever gave it serious consideration. It would be hard to imagine any circumstances under which my fiercely possessive mother would ever willingly have been parted from her children.

The Bridge family came from North Wales and William Bridge, my great great grandfather, is buried in Conwy. This is undoubtedly the reason that my grandparents started to holiday in the Conwy Valley and eventually bought a small farmhouse, which they progressively enlarged, in the early 1900s. My great grandfather, John Nickson, then bought a small farm next door and built a new house in one of the fields for his retirement. For the next seventy years these two houses, Cefn and Cefn Isaf, and the Caerhun estate which my uncle Jack bought from the Aberconway family in 1953 became the main home of the Nickson family. Hinderton Lodge was sold when my grandfather died in 1945. My uncle made his home at Cefn after the war and my parents moved to Cefn Isaf when my father retired from Eton in 1955. We spent all our summer holidays as children at Cefn before the war and during the war it became our holiday sanctuary from the bombs and later the flying bombs of the South East. All my boyhood memories were centred at Cefn. Here I learnt to fish and shoot. For eighty years the family worshipped in the isolated little thirteenth century church of St Mary's Caerhun, overlooking the marshes where the wigeon flighted, and built on the site of the Roman fortress of Canovium where the ford crossed the River Conway on the main route between London and Holyhead. The church was arcticly cold in the wartime winter. I can remember nursing my chilblains as I listened to the whistling of the wigeon outside during the interminable Welsh sermons. Here all the Nicksons are buried from our great grandparents to our parents plus assorted uncles and aunts. Here my sister was christened as was our own second daughter Lucy. There is a brass plaque on the north wall in memory of three generations, each of which provided churchwardens at various times.

My Uncle Jack served in the Royal Welsh Fusiliers in both the 1914–18 and 1939–45 wars and on his retirement created a beautiful garden at Cefn, later joining this up to my parents' garden at Cefn Isaf, so that by the 1960s there was the unusual arrangement of two substantial family houses, out of sight of each other but in the same large garden. These houses were on the opposite side of the River Conway to the world famous Aberconway garden of Bodnant in a wonderful gardening climate. I can well remember camellias in full flower and unfrosted in an early January snowfall. My father increasingly thought of himself as Welsh, just as I now like to think of myself as a Scot, and of course he did have Welsh blood in his veins through his Wigley grandmother. He taught himself to speak the language sufficiently well to carry on simple conversations with farmers, in the village and with the beaters on shooting days.

I had always assumed through my boyhood and as a soldier that one day I would make my own home at Cefn. My uncle died in 1969 at a time when I was heavily involved in my job in Scotland, our young family were growing up there, our own home and all our friends were there. When I inherited from him it became immediately clear that if any of the family money was to be saved the family business in Liverpool should be sold. This was no easy matter for my father, who with all his many virtues was no businessman, but stepped into the breach as Chairman. A sale was achieved not without considerable difficulty in 1972. But it took me another five years to realise that the small estate with its three tiny tenanted farms and some woods and the two houses, in one of which my parents were still living, would be a perpetual financial liability and that our future lay irrevocably in Scotland. It was the right decision and one that has proved absolutely correct for me and my family in every way. But I agonised over it; first of all in 1972 over selling Cefn, the house in which we had spent all our happiest holidays as children, and then later, when my parents finally moved to live with my sister and brother-in-law, Cefn Isaf and the remaining land in 1979. Pulling up one's family roots particularly from a place with so many nostalgic and happy memories can never be an easy process. Our own children had become fond of North Wales, and felt deeply about the two houses and the Church at Caerhun. It was sad for them but much more so for my parents. They were wonderfully understanding and helpful, and remarkably positive about it considering that they must have long cherished the hope that we would live in the home they had kept warm for us over so many years. However they were both approaching eighty and realistic enough to know that they could no longer cope there on their own. So they accepted with gratitude the generous offer from my brother-in-law, Charlie Sheepshanks, and my sister to go to live in the wing of their home at Arthington Hall in West Yorkshire.

I have written a lot about my uncle Jack. There have been endless television programmes in recent years on the 1914–18 war and how of course it is approaching ninety years since that dreadful time. The same interval, I reflect, as separated my parents' births from the Battle of Waterloo. So perhaps it is worth recording some of my uncle's own recollections of those last desperate weeks of the war in September and October 1918 taken from *The War the Infantry knew*, the history of the 2nd Battalion The Royal Welsh Fusiliers. This was the unit in which Siegfried Sassoon, the poet who wrote *Memoirs of an Infantry Officer*, served at an earlier stage in the conflict. Jack Nickson went out to France aged eighteen and joined B Company, 2nd Battalion. His company commander was a huge man, a character of great valour and experience, Wynn Kirkby, universally known as 'Uncle'. For 7 September the history reads:

> Since we went into the Aveluy Wood sector early in August there had been a practically continuous performance of trench warfare, followed by more or less open fighting. None of us had taken off our clothing during that time, and we had been wet many times since we waded the Ancre. Our casualties had been nearly 360, and we had come out of action as one company. Baths, change of clothing and haircuts were badly needed . . . Some of our reinforcement officers were slow to absorb existing conditions, so Greaves, never the most patient was inclined to be irritable, but 'Uncle' was loud in his praises of two very young subalterns he had been lucky – his usual luck – in getting to his company. One of these was J.E.N.

By 11 September they were sent to take over the front line just south of the village of Gouzeaucourt, (near Cambrai and Arras). B Company was in front. The area was a network of old trenches from 1917, much broken down and quite shallow in places, the wire was very sketchy and there were no dugouts. B Company's only shelter was a cubby-hole on the left with a tin roof, that Kirkby and Nickson shared. My uncle continues:

In B Company several sentries, men of the latest draft, were found with unloaded rifles, Two of them on being questioned said they did not know how to load. The morning was that of a perfect early autumn day with bright sunshine. It was very quiet and still, not a shot was being fired along the whole front. Perhaps the quiet was rather ominous. We had finished breakfast in B Company HQ, and Thomas, our cook, an old soldier, was in his shirtsleeves washing up. Suddenly at 9.20, we heard in the distance what sounded like a long ripple spreading in a wide arc along our front, and almost immediately a hurricane of shells descended on us. Uncle and I lay down in our shelter, biting the dust. We realised at once that this was something quite different from yesterday's shelling, and was almost certainly the prelude to an attack. Where we were the shells, as yesterday, were falling about twenty yards behind the trench. This intense bombardment lasted 40 minutes, then it lifted as suddenly as it had started. No one in our post had been hit. We scrambled up and heard shouts from the trench – 'Here they come'. Someone fired the rifle holding the SOS rocket; it popped out of the muzzle about a couple of feet and burned out on the ground. The Germans were coming over the skyline in extended order, in sections, on each side of the communications trench which entered our line at this point. Two men were carrying a light machine-gun, one firing the gun from his hip as he walked, the other holding the box with the cartridge belt. In front of us the first lot were quite close. Thomas jumped up from among his pots and pans, where he had been crouching, and shot the nearest man in the hindquarters as he was about to get down into the trench. The Hun jumped high into the air, turned round and ran as fast as he could. The nearest post of the unit on our left had disappeared along the trench, leaving a long stretch empty, and our flank in the air. A section or so of the attackers got in there, but Sergeant Lee picked up a Lewis gun, jumped out on top, and getting a position for the gun, shot eight of them. Lee was a very stout hearted fellow: he was acting C.S.M. since the previous day's reshuffle consequent on casualties.

'Uncle' told me to go quickly to the far end of our line and see what was happening there, so I ran off down the trench: it had been almost completely blown in. I picked my way over masses of broken earth, and could not find a man alive. Three of our posts had been wiped out. At the far end one small post had survived, and in spite of the men who could not load their rifles, was firing away merrily. The Germans on their front were just beginning to appear in an extended line on the crest. Our artillery was now putting over a very effective shrapnel barrage. These raiders began to waver, some lay down, then they got up and all ran back. I could hear firing and bombs bursting at the end I had come from, but after a time that ceased and all was quiet there. I had left the fight in a very open state, with the Germans coming along strongly against our isolated post of about a dozen men. I listened intently but could hear no sound. It was impossible to know what had happened. The post at my end numbered eight or ten sound men. A few wounded men, who were able to move had joined them from the next post. All the rest had been wiped out, I knew. As far as I had been able to see no German had come over in the middle part of our sector, but only against the two end posts. The question was, who was at the other end.

I started to go back along what was left of the trench, stopping frequently to listen. When I had gone about halfway I heard stealthy steps approaching. Whoever it was had evidently heard me and was playing the same game; he too stopped frequently, then came on a few steps when I was not moving. We were stalking each other. At last the point came when we were bound to meet round the next bend. I felt that the tactical move was to be round the corner first so as to have the 'drop' on the other man: so, getting ready to shoot at sight, I stepped round the traverse. Simultaneously a large figure leapt round the other end. We both made a sort of half lunge with our revolvers, then shouted 'don't shoot', in the same breath. It was 'Uncle'. The whole thing was quite dramatic, it would have looked really good on the films.

The main part of the raid had been repulsed, thanks chiefly to Sergeant Lee and a few others of the Old Army in the post. When I got back to them they were sitting in a group calmly cleaning their rifles and discussing the morning's shooting. B Company's losses had been heavy; we were reduced to about twenty men all told . . .

That night B company were relieved by D company and my uncle goes on:

> Hughes, commanding D, was very upset that we had failed to remove all our dead; he said it was bad for the morale of his own men, which was no doubt true, but we had all we could do to get away our wounded, for to add to our difficulties, two of our stretcher bearers had disappeared.

The official narrative continues with the comment that during this action British losses were probably greater than the Germans because of the bombardment. '. . . but the honours were with us. Nickson, a newly joined subaltern fresh from school, carried on like a veteran, showing any amount of resource and pluck.' This is where he won his first Military Cross.

Five days later on 19 September they were in the front line again in some trenches crossing the main road into Gouzeaucourt village. They were heavily shelled.

... and our artillery retaliated which made matters worse. Both sides worked up to such a pitch that Fritz, evidently expecting an attack, put down a regular SOS barrage on us. A message came that a fighting patrol of one officer and fourteen men with two Lewis guns was to go at midnight to the enemy line, find out if it was still occupied, and, if the enemy had left, take possession and send back word. The order ended with the usual exhortation to kill and capture large numbers of the enemy, which nobody in his senses ever took any notice of. The first difficulty was to get out of the trench and through the barrage. We lumbered along getting more and more strung out as we went. Even with the shelling going on the noise of the patrol sounded to me like the whole British Army on the move. The men with the Lewis guns kept falling into shell holes with tremendous crashes, and crawling out cursing. Progress was very slow. After a time I decided to park my cumbersome command and go forward with the sergeant and one man. Having gone what seemed several miles, actually I expect about a hundred yards, we came to the wire and lay down to have a look at it. It seemed more than adequate – a thick black mass. A Verey light which went up fell almost on top of us, and burned on the ground beside us for an incredible time, lighting up every thing as clear as daylight. It seemed impossible we were not seen. We saw a number of heads in coal-scuttle helmets just beyond the wire, looking over the top and moving up and down. When the light went out it was so dark I couldn't see the sergeant lying by my side. We discussed the situation in whispers. The question was, should we go back and get the patrol and start a fight. My sergeant was very much opposed to this, and the more I thought about it the more I was inclined to agree with him. Finally I decided that honour would be satisfied if we went in and reported what we had seen. We found the rest of the patrol with some difficulty; most of them were fast asleep. On the way back we came across several wounded men from our 14th Battalion lying out in no-man's-land, and took them in. It was beginning to get light when we reached the trench. Apparently we had been away a very long time, because 'Uncle' was having a tremendous row over the phone with Battalion HQ; they wanted a report on his patrol in the worst way; no doubt Brigade was worrying them. As soon as the news went back that we were in everyone seemed satisfied, and what we had to report didn't seem of any consequence.

That night we were relieved. The company marched, organised as two platoons with 100 yards between them. The men went at a tremendous pace down the slope to Dessart wood, particularly those behind, and the hundred yards dwindled to about ten. We were in fact in one tight bunch when a 5.9 shell landed in the middle of us. We all fell flat – then got up feeling ourselves. Not a single man was touched. On Fins ridge the cookers were waiting for us with a meal of porridge. I never remember tasting anything so good. We marched on most of the night to good huts at Lechelle. 'Uncle' and I took it in turns to ride our fat pony. The men were in tremendous form, singing hymns all the way. The G.O.C. passed us on the road. He offered congratulations on the Gouzeaucourt show, and shouted to the men 'Well done B company; did you get the bayonet to work?'

A fortnight later the final narrative takes place.

On the evening of October 7th 'Uncle' was summoned to a Company Commander's conference. He brought back word that we were for it early next morning.

There was to be a night attack on the village of Villers-Outreaux by the 115th Brigade. This proved a failure and a deadlock was reached with 'everyone seeking cover from the hail of machine-gun bullets which poured over the top'.

But B and C Companies of the R.W.F were still moving up as reinforcements. 'The night was dark and wet. Colonel Norman met us at the end of the sunken road. He told us the attack had failed, that our supporting tank had not turned up, but B Company was to go ahead and do its best to try to get into the village. There was no time to make any elaborate plan of advance and no object in doing so; we did not know what to expect and we were not fired on. Leading to the village was a long straight piece of pave road alongside which was a light railway. The ground along the railway was very broken so we marched in fours straight up the road fixing bayonets as we went. Suddenly German SOS rockets went up all round and we were fired on heavily from a trench just ahead. Almost at the same moment our belated tank came lumbering up behind spitting fire into our backs. We scattered in all directions taking cover as best we could. The tank came right into the middle of us and circled round, shooting at anything moving it could see against the lights of the Show. A lot of our men were hit. 'Uncle' was lying on the ground riddled from the trench in front and the tank behind, but he kept on shouting to the men to 'get on with it', and to the tank to get elsewhere. (He is so large that he could harbour a good many missiles without an important part being touched.) By this time Fritz was barraging the road heavily with howitzers and trench mortars. The shells burst with tremendous crashes on the hard pave; one of them hit the tank and, most happily, put it out of action. Just before that, one of our men had attempted to lead it against the wire by putting his tin hat on the butt of his rifle and walking ahead with his rifle held up in front of him. He was killed at once. It was impossible to see in the half light who he was, but it was a most gallant act.

Uncle Jack was one of those hit from behind by the tank with a bullet in the back of the knee. He was out of action for some minutes but then got going again. The action continued for along time. The account describes more fierce fighting before eventually C Company and the remnants of B Company took a number of prisoners, captured the village and saw the enemy in full retreat . . . 'In the late afternoon when Nickson was sitting in H.Q. reporting his Company's doings his leg became stiff; he suffered later from a very bad attack of tetanus.' His going from the Battalion was dramatic, like the deeds in which he was so active a part, and about which he has written such vivid passages.

Uncle Jack's last words in the history read: 'General Cubitt came up in his car and, on his way back, picked me up and took me to the Field Ambulance in Aubencheul. The road was blocked with a mass of odd transport, and we were held up by what appeared to be a hopeless deadlock; but the General stood up on the back seat and withered them with such a magnificent gush of language that they scattered hastily, leaving a way through.' As dramatic was the chance identification in hospital by his Company Commander 'Uncle' of the commander of the first tank. The manuscript account of what Kirkby said to him is milk and water; anyhow the original is quite unprintable.

Uncle Jack was invalided home, perilously ill with tetanus. The story goes that my grandmother was by his bedside in hospital and was told he was bound to die. She persuaded the nurse to give him a double dose of morphine. Miraculously he survived. His war had only lasted four weeks. In that time he had won two MCs. I owe him a great deal.

This then brings my account of the Nicksons up to my father's generation, leaving my sister and myself as the last of our line to carry the name. But we have six children and seventeen grandchildren between us to take the ship forward, albeit voyaging under different flags.

I have made only passing mention of my mother's family, the Dobies. It is her father's book and his record of that family that is largely responsible for motivating me to attempt these reminiscences. He too in his seventies set out to chronicle his family origins, and very well he did it. I have only one copy of the 'Dobie Book', which belonged to my mother and was dedicated to her, to me and my first cousin, David Dobie. It would be presumptuous to attempt to recycle it here. Suffice it to say that the Dobies came from Dumfriesshire. They were farmers in the seventeenth and eighteenth centuries and our branch seems to have been based round Lockerbie. Two farms in particular feature, Kirkton, and Tundergarth, which owes its claim to fame to the fact that the nose cone of the Jumbo jet, that was blown so tragically out of the sky in 1982, landed here. Curiously enough some of the same names that feature in connection with the Nixon Border Reivers at the start of this chapter occur as relations by marriage or in my grandfather's account of Dobie kinsmen: Armstrongs, Jardines, Maxwells, Johnstones, Kennedys and Kerrs. There is a detailed family tree in the book going back to about 1625.

My great-great-grandfather, William Johnstone Dobie, started the Dobie medical tradition, which has been continued for six generations. He was born on 13 January 1795, an intensely cold day after which occurred a snowstorm from Crawford Muir, and at the subsequent thaw there was found on the estuary of the Esk a collection of bodies: viz, 1840 sheep, 9 cattle, 3 horses, 2 men, 1 woman, 45 dogs and 180 hares! He went to Edinburgh to study medicine but must have had the nineteenth century equivalent of a 'gap' year, having been introduced to a Captain Nixon(!) of the *Nightingale* with whom he sailed to Orkney, Davis Straits and Cape Farewell. After various vicissitudes he became House Surgeon at Dumfries Infirmary, married Jane Kerr and took up General Practice near Gresford in Denbighshire.

My great-grandfather, William Murray Dobie, was born in 1828. He too studied medicine at Edinburgh University and graduated with first class honours and a number of prizes for surgery in 1848. He was a contemporary and friend of Lord Lister, studied under Professor Syme and became a house surgeon at Edinburgh Infirmary. He moved to Chester where he practised for the rest of his life becoming Honorary Physician to the Chester Infirmary in 1876. He was a keen amateur astrologist, discovering a small crater on the Moon and a Nova star 'cygni'. He was a passionate naturalist and a great friend of Charles Kingsley, Canon of Chester Cathedral and author of *The Water Babies*. He was a man of distinguished appearance as his handsome portrait shows. Our love of birds probably comes from the Dobie family, rather than the Nicksons, though in Victorian times the passion for collections of birds eggs and specimens makes curious reading today. His diary records that on 29 June 1856 he shot two redwings and on 25 December a bullfinch!

He became doctor and friend to the Gladstones of Hawarden. Two days before the Prime Minister W.E. Gladstone died in 1898 he issued the following bulletin: 'Mr Gladstone's condition remains unchanged since the report issued at 8 o'clock. The slight rally is for the present maintained and he is now sleeping quite peacefully.' There must have been some old phonograph records made of Gladstone's voice at some stage and some correspondence in the press about them much later. To which my grandfather replied as follows: 'I count myself indeed fortunate to have conversed with Mr Gladstone and to have heard his voice. At the time my father attended him during his last illness at Hawarden in 1898. I was consulted about a minor point and remarked to him, "Sir, your voice is clear," to which he replied simply, "I used to like the sound of my voice very much but it is different now." I do not think he would have wished the old phonograph records to be preserved.'

Another cordial friendship existed between William Murray Dobie and the first Duke of Westminster, whose family he attended. He used to fish Loch Stack and the Laxford. He developed a passion for fishing, which he handed on to four of his sons, his grandson and his great grandson, and as I can trace this addiction back to Richard Wigley through the other side of my family, it is scarcely surprising that it has played such a part in my own life. My grandfather records a story that on tipping a ghillie at Lochmore his father received the reply: 'Maybe it will be as well for you if you come back here again'! There was another story told of this ghillie that he went out fishing with the first Duchess (Constance, daughter of the Duke of Sutherland) and her friend. All morning the Duchess was far the most successful, but after lunch the luck was reversed and her friend caught all the fish. Donald, on being asked by the much-puzzled Duchess to explain the reason, dourly replied, 'Ye've got the wrong rod.' The best flies had of course been prepared for the Duchess, and a change of rods had accidently been effected by the ladies during their lunch hour. On another occasion the Duke had a bad cough and sent word that he needed some medicine. Having no drugs with him Dr Dobie was at first nonplussed, till he remembered a packet of Chlorodyne lozenges, so dissolving twelve of them in a six ounce bottle of water he sent it to the lodge with instructions to take a tablespoonful three times a day. The Duke was much pleased with the effect. My grandfather's account of his father continues:

> He dressed in the old fashioned professional style: top hat, frock coat, stand up collar and black bow tie. He was anything but tidy and often had his handkerchief three parts out of his coat tail pocket.
>
> Amongst other little foibles was his habit of carrying at least two watches, but his special chronometer disappointed him if it varied by two seconds a week. He now and again would leave the gas turned full on and unlit, and so frequently did this happen, flooding his consulting room, that the maid at last declared to his wife 'that the doctor is not fit to have a tap at all'.

The tradition of fishing holidays at Loch Stack for the Dobies as guests of the Grosvenor family continued for the next sixty years. My mother's brother caught his first salmon there as a boy just before the first war. The Duke walked over the hill to congratulate him. He continued to fish there until his death in the 1970s. In 1992 my second daughter, Lucy, and I were asked over to fish the Laxford by Janie Grosvenor (previously Duchess of Roxburgh, now Janie Dawnay). We had a tremendous day and afterwards took photographs of the head stalker and another ghillie, which I was able to stick in the Conon photograph book alongside identical views of the river, my great-grandfather, my grand-father and the two ghillies referred to in the stories above, smoking their clay pipes below massive beards, taken exactly 100 years earlier.

William Murray Dobie died in 1915. By then my grandfather had followed in his footsteps, with a First in medicine from Edinburgh University, sent for by his father's friend Lord Lister, to become his 'dresser' in London, joining his father in practice in Chester, becoming in his turn Resident physician and surgeon at Chester Infirmary, much honoured and much loved by his patients. One medical episode is worth recording in connection with the Westminster family.

The Duke's only son, the Westminster heir, developed acute perito-nitis in about 1907. My grandfather diagnosed this and urged an immediate operation, which as a surgeon to Chester Infirmary he was well qualified to perform. But Bendor wanted a second opinion from London. When the eminent surgeon eventually arrived by train he confirmed the diagnosis; but insisted on sending for his own instruments by another train. It was too late. Thus, the story has been handed down that my grandfather could have saved the little boy's life, and so the eventual succession to the Westminster dynasty would have been very different. I have on my desk, in front of me as I write, a foot long silver ruler presented to Henry Dobie by the then Duchess, presumably having delivered her of this son in 1899. It is inscribed 'H.D. from S.G.' with her coronet. It is also inscribed 'D.N. from J.N. Nov 10th 1981' – a gift to me from my mother when she accompanied Louise to Buckingham Palace for my Investiture as a Commander of the Order of the British Empire.

I remember my grandfather, Harry Dobie, as a delightful, small, gentle, kind old man with a wonderful head of snow white hair. I inherited many of his bird books including a set of Lilfords inscribed by the author. He was a great amateur naturalist, writing a very specialised treatise on the colour of raptor's palates! Hen harriers had a deeper shade of blue than any other hawks. He kept a large aviary and was able to observe in precise detail the method by which crossbills extracted larch seeds from the cones, which was described in *British Birds*. He had a big collection of stuffed birds and birds eggs, now I think in Chester Natural History Museum. I can remember getting into a real row as a small boy because I took them out from their cabinet into the garden of their house in Chester on a rainy day to make them perch in the bushes. They were none the better for their wetting. He too was a passionate fisherman in Wales and Scotland. In 1929, aged seventy-three, he caught the then record sea-trout for Loch Stack, weighing 13 lbs. My grandmother was a less sympathetic character to a child. She seemed pretty disapproving and acidic. I suspect I led my sister on to join me in behaving rather badly.

This account brings the reader full circle back to Chapter 1, and to my recollections of my parents and parents-in-law.

Index